DATE DUE		
MAR 17 '7		
APR 15 '7		
FEB 2 4 1983		
GAYLORD 234		PRINTED IN U.S.A.

Memoirs of My Services
in the World War

1917–1918

Memoirs of My Services in the World War

1917–1918

George C. Marshall

With a Foreword and Notes by
Brigadier General James.L. Collins, Jr.

ILLUSTRATED WITH
PHOTOGRAPHS AND MAPS

HOUGHTON MIFFLIN COMPANY BOSTON
1976

Maps by Samuel H. Bryant

Library of Congress Cataloging in Publication Data

Marshall, George Catlett, 1880–1959.
  Memoirs of my services in the World War, 1917–1918.

  Includes bibliographical references and index.
    1. European War, 1914–1918 — Personal narratives, American. 2. Marshall, George Catlett, 1880–1959.
  3. European War, 1914–1918 — Regimental histories — United States — 1st Division. 4. United States. Army.
  A.E.F., 1917–1920. 1st Division. I. Title.
  D570.9.M37 1976   940.4′81′73 [B]   76-10834
  ISBN 0-395-20725-8

Printed in the United States of America

C 10 9 8 7 6 5 4 3 2 1

76-848

Foreword

Tʜɪs ʙook, written between 1919 and 1923, is George Catlett Marshall's record of World War I as he shaped and experienced events. His account begins as the United States entered the war that had already been going on for two years and nine months. The Triple Alliance of Germany and Austria-Hungary (Italy, the third power, at first remained on the sidelines) waged war against the Triple Entente of Russia, France, and Great Britain. By the end of 1914, the protagonists had fought to an uneasy stalemate on the plains of northern France in the west and on the flatlands of Russian Poland and the Ukraine in the east. In late 1914, Turkey entered the war on the side of the Central Powers, thus severing the main Entente supply route to Russia, but to offset this partially, Italy, in May of 1915, declared war on Austria-Hungary, thereby opening a new front on the southern border of Austria.

Serbia — the site of the assassination of the heir to the Austro-Hungarian throne, the initial *casus belli* — had been knocked out of the war when Bulgaria entered the conflict on the Austrian side. But in August 1916, encouraged by the success of a Russian offensive against the Austro-Hungarians, Rumania joined the Entente, now called the Allied Powers.

At sea, the great battle of Jutland in 1916 resulted in a stand-off between the surface fleets of Germany and Great Britain, although the undersea battle continued apace. On January 31, 1917, Germany proclaimed unrestricted submarine warfare and on February 3 the United States severed relations with Germany, as did many Latin

American nations and China. The sinking of numerous American ships, the revelations in the "Zimmermann Telegram" (in which the Germans proposed returning Texas, New Mexico, and Arizona to Mexico on condition that the latter join Germany if America entered the war) were the proximate causes of the U.S. declaration of war against Germany. Eight months later, the U.S. also declared war against Austria-Hungary.

It was not an especially auspicious time for the U.S. to jump into the fight, because the fortunes of the Allies were at low ebb. The submarine campaign appeared ready to starve out the Europeans; the Russian Revolution had erupted, forcing the abdication of the Czar and making continued Russian participation in the war problematical; the great Anglo-French offensive designed to end the war was breaking on the barbed wire of the Hindenburg Line at the cost of more than a quarter-million casualties; the British renewal of the assault resulted in the long battle of Passchendaele, costing an equal number of casualties; the French were unable to help the British because half a hundred divisions were exhausted, and General Pétain had just relieved General Nivelle to try to restore the morale and discipline of the French Army; the Italians were soon to be in rapid retreat from the Austrian successes at Caporetto. All in all, 1917 — except for the entry into the war of the U.S. — was disastrous for the Allies. But there were glimmers of hope on the horizon. The U.S. with its great human and industrial resources promised reinforcements the Central Powers could not match. The war at sea was slowly improving for the Allies as the convoy system was introduced in mid 1917, and, with the help of American destroyers, reduced shipping losses and increased German submarine sinkings.

Although the Navy was relatively well prepared for combat, the Army was not. The call-up of most of the National Guard for duty on the Mexican border in conjunction with the Punitive Expedition into Mexico in pursuit of the bandit Pancho Villa had served mainly to show how unprepared we were for modern warfare. Our arsenals contained less than a million rifles and little else. We didn't even have an organization to fight in the European style — the regiment and the provisional brigade were our largest combat formations. Including the 100,000 National Guardsmen still in state service, the total strength of the Army was less than 310,000 on April 6, 1917.

One of the first tasks of the Army was to form a "Combat Division" and send it to Europe to reassure our sorely tried Allies that we really meant business and intended to fight the land war as well as the sea war — we had entered the conflict primarily over the issue of unrestricted submarine warfare.

Major General John J. Pershing, the commander of the Punitive Expedition and junior Major General in the Regular Army, was chosen as the commander of the American Expeditionary Forces. He hastily selected four Regular Army infantry regiments from the Mexican border, and when he combined them with the necessary supporting units, the "Combat Division," later to be redesignated the First Infantry Division, came into being. Initially all units were under strength and short of officers. To make up a full-strength division it was necessary to transfer men from other regiments and rely on many untrained recruits. Officers to fill out the staffs were provided from stateside commands and from the reserves. General Pershing, who could not wait for the division to be assembled, sailed for Europe. He and the embryo staff of General Headquarters American Expeditionary Forces left New York harbor aboard the S.S. *Baltic* on May 28, 1917, a scant seven weeks after our declaration of war. Pershing hand-picked the staff from combat veterans of the Indian Wars, the Spanish-American War, the Boxer Rebellion in China, the Philippine Insurrection, and, most recently, the Mexican border expedition. The First Division was similarly selected from the cream of the Army and it was with this division that Captain Marshall sailed.

Appended to the Memoirs are three accounts of trips taken with General Pershing after the Armistice. These appear to be extracts of letters from Marshall to his first wife, Elizabeth (Lily) Coles Marshall. Lily Marshall died of a heart attack in 1927. About two years later Lieutenant Colonel George Marshall met Mrs. Katherine Boyce Tupper Brown, a widow with three small children. In October of 1930, Marshall and Mrs. Brown were married, with General Pershing acting as best man. The three stepchildren were brought up in the Marshall home and, childless himself, George Marshall was the perfect father to them all. One of the great tragedies of his life was the death of Allen, who was killed at the head of his armored platoon at Anzio in May of 1943.

George Catlett Marshall was noted more for his diplomatic and military skill than for his literary talent. Although he always encouraged professional military writing, his personal contributions were extremely limited. Except for a brief period early in the century when he was an instructor at the Army's Staff College and prepared portions of Army manuals on *Map Making and Topography* and *Cordage and Tackle,* practically all his writing was in the form of Army Operational Orders, letters, or editorial changes to staff papers. In fact, no substantial body of his writing was known to survive until recently, when his stepdaughter, Molly Brown Winn, discovered the manuscript of the present book in the attic of General Marshall's house in Leesburg, Virginia. The existence of the work *had* been known. Mrs. Winn in late 1940 was preparing a scrapbook of pictures and news clippings for her stepfather's birthday and in searching through an old footlocker came across the manuscript. General Marshall explained that he had written it while stationed in Washington just after the First World War. He had wanted to put his impressions of that war down on paper while they were still fresh in his mind. Later, he had been in contact with Houghton Mifflin with a view toward publication. The publisher felt that more work needed to be done on the book, but before it could be accomplished, then Lieutenant Colonel Marshall in the summer of 1924 went to China for duty with the Fifteenth Infantry.

After General Marshall's death his widow told his biographer, Dr. Forrest Pogue, that the General had asked that the manuscript be destroyed and she was under the impression that his wish had been carried out. It is probable that one copy had been burned and the paper discovered by Mrs. Winn had been overlooked. Indeed it is fortunate that it survived for it sheds new light on the formation of the attitudes, beliefs, and values of one of the greatest men of the twentieth century. The seventy-nine years of General Marshall's life included fifty years of remarkable contributions to his country both in war and in peace. As Chief of Staff of the United States Army from September 1, 1939, until November 1945, he was America's first soldier during all of World War II. His experiences during Work War I unquestionably affected his decisions during the later war. For example, his direct observation of trench warfare foreshadowed his insistence on youth and physical fitness as prerequisites for command positions and his strong advocacy of strategic maneuver rather than frontal attack. After leaving his post as Chief of Staff he answered President Truman's call to head a mission to China, although he privately considered it to be a lost cause from the start. He next undertook the arduous duties of Secretary of State, although at the age of sixty-seven he had long since earned an honored retirement. Was it from the compassion gained first hand for the suffering of the French people in 1917 and 1918 that sprang the "Marshall Plan" for the economic recovery of Europe? Certainly, Europe was prostrate and devastated when he proposed the program during a speech at Harvard University on June 5, 1947. But Secretary Marshall did not stop there; he pressed hard to win Congressional support and public acceptance of his concept. His actions were recognized in 1953 by the award of the Nobel Prize for Peace; the first occasion on which a military man had been so honored.

In 1949, after having overseen the first faltering steps of the North Atlantic Treaty Organization he again retired, but again not for long. Despite ill health he accepted the call of a humanitarian organization and became President of the American Red Cross. Once again he showed his compassion for mankind at the expense of his own health. And this was not to be all, for President Truman called on him when a strong hand was needed at the helm of the young Department of Defense during the Korean War. For a year, beginning in September of 1950, General Marshall bore the heavy burdens of preparing and equipping our Armed Forces for combat in the Far East as well as the general supervision of their employment. He finally achieved a quiet life of retirement when he left the post of Secretary of Defense on

September 11, 1951. Looking back on his life of public service one can conclude that President Truman was close to the mark when he told Marshall that ". . . no man has ever given his country more distinguished and patriotic service than you."

Contents

Illustrations

following page 128

Major George C. Marshall

Captain Marshall; Colonel Voris; Lieutenant Hugo; Major Drain; Madame Jouatte; French refugees, 1917

Colonel Marshall and Major General Henry T. Allen. *Photo by Signal Corps, U.S.A.*

First Division officers waiting to hear General Pershing before Montdidier; Colonel Marshall addressing assembly. *Photo by Signal Corps, U.S.A.*

Colonel Campbell King, General Hines, Colonel Marshall at Beauvais, June 1918

Cartoon history of the First Division: Officers

Troops in a chapel at Vaux, November 5, 1918. *Photo by Signal Corps, U.S.A.*

Recommendation concerning promotion of Colonel Marshall to General Officer

Staff Officers, Eighth Army Corps, January 11, 1919

Marshal Pétain and General Pershing at Metz, April 29, 1919

Photograph presented to Colonel Marshall by Marshal Foch

Invitation to Buckingham Palace garden party

Photograph taken at garden party and inscribed by Colonel Marshall

General Pershing in London Victory Parade, July 19, 1919

General Pershing and Colonel Marshall inspecting battlefields, August 1919

Inspecting Montfaucon, August 1919. *Photo by Signal Corps, U.S.A.*

Inspecting St. Mihiel Field, August 1919. *Photo by Signal Corps, U.S.A.*

En route home after World War, September 1919

Leviathan docking at Hoboken, September 8, 1919. *Photo by Signal Corps, U.S.A.*

(These photographs are from George C. Marshall's personal collection.)

Maps

November 5, 1920

General John S. Mallory
15 University Place
Lexington, Virginia

My Dear General Mallory,

Last summer during one of our delightful rides I commented on the advice I would give a young officer going to war, based on my observation of what had constituted the success of the outstanding figures in the American Expeditionary Forces, and you asked me to write out what I had said. A discussion with Fox Conner this morning reminded me of my promise to do this, so here it is.

To be a highly successful leader in war four things are essential, assuming that you possess good common sense, have studied your profession and are physically strong.

When conditions are difficult, the command is depressed and everyone seems critical and pessimistic, you must be especially cheerful and optimistic.

When evening comes and all are exhausted, hungry and possibly dispirited, particularly in unfavorable weather at the end of a march or in battle, you must put aside any thought of personal fatigue and display marked energy in looking after the comfort of your organization, inspecting your lines and preparing for tomorrow.

Make a point of extreme loyalty, in thought and deed, to your chiefs personally; and in your efforts to carry out their plans or policies, the less you approve the more energy you must direct to their accomplishment.

The more alarming and disquieting the reports received or the conditions viewed in battle, the more determined must be your attitude. Never ask for the relief of your unit and never hesitate to attack.

I am certain in the belief that the average man who scrupulously follows this course of action is bound to win great success. Few seemed equal to it in this war, but I believe this was due to their failure to realize the importance of so governing their course.

Faithfully yours,

G. C. Marshall, Jr.
Major, General Staff
Aide-de-Camp

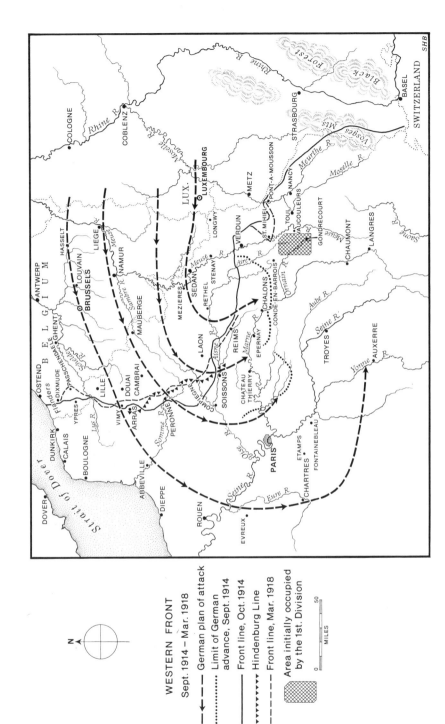

WESTERN FRONT
Sept. 1914 – Mar. 1918

German plan of attack

Limit of German
advance, Sept. 1914

Front line, Oct.1914

Hindenburg Line

Front line, Mar. 1918

Area initially occupied
by the 1st. Division

N

0   50
MILES

SHB

SWITZERLAND

BASEL

Black FOREST

Rhine R.

Rhine R.

COLOGNE

COBLENZ

Moselle R.

Vosges Mts.

STRASBOURG

Meurthe R.

Moselle R.

NANCY

METZ

PONT-A-MOUSSON

LUXEMBOURG

LUX.

TOUL

VAUCOULEURS

GONDRECOURT

CHAUMONT

LANGRES

Saône R.

LONGWY

VERDUN

ST. MIHIEL

Meuse R.

Aire R.

Aire R.

STENAY

SEDAN

RETHEL

MEZIERES

Meuse R.

Sambre R.

Meuse R.

NAMUR

LIEGE

HASSELT

LOUVAIN

BRUSSELS

B E L G I U M

ANTWERP

GHENT

Scheldt R.

OSTEND

DIXMUDE

PASSCHENDAELE

Flanders

YPRES

Lys R.

LILLE

DOUAI

CAMBRAI

VIMY

ARRAS

PERONNE

Somme R.

COMPIEGNE

SOISSONS

LAON

Aisne R.

REIMS

CHALONS

CONDE-EN-BARROIS

Ornain R.

Marne R.

EPERNAY

CHATEAU THIERRY

Ourcq R.

Oise R.

Aube R.

Seine R.

TROYES

AUXERRE

Yonne R.

Yonne R.

PARIS

ETAMPS

FONTAINEBLEAU

CHARTRES

Eure R.

Seine R.

EVREUX

ROUEN

Seine R.

DIEPPE

ABBEVILLE

Oise R.

MAUBERGE

CALAIS

BOULOGNE

DUNKIRK

DOVER

Strait of Dover

CHAPTER I

The First Months

THE DECLARATION OF WAR on April 6, 1917, found me on duty in San Francisco, as Aide-de-Camp to Major General J. Franklin Bell.[1] Since December 1916, I had also been filling the position of Department Adjutant in the absence of Colonel Benjamin Alvord, who was on a long leave of absence.[2] The work was heavy and pressing following the termination of diplomatic relations with Germany. The entire National Guard of the west coast had been called into the federal service and was attempting to guard the important bridges, tunnels, and railroad key points scattered over that extensive area. A large majority of the clerical force had been loaned to the Southern Department for the period of the border trouble, which left us very shorthanded.

Almost simultaneously with the declaration of war a code telegram was received by General Bell informing him that the President had subdivided the Eastern Department into three departments, and that he, General Bell, would relieve General Wood in command of the Department of the East.[3] Formal orders came a few days later directing the change of command to take effect the 28th of April. We started east about the 26th. Mrs. Marshall and her mother remained at Fort Mason to complete the hurried packing of our household effects.[4]

I arrived at Governors Island, our new Headquarters, about half a day in advance of General Bell, who had made a detour to visit relatives in Kentucky.[5] On his desk were about four hundred and fifty letters and telegrams addressed to him personally. Realizing that a continuous flood of these communications was inevitable, I established myself within the first half hour and undertook to clear the desk by utilizing the services of four stenographers. General Bell's daily increment of semipersonal telegrams and mail amounted to about one hundred and fifty communications, and of course there were visitors without number. By working continuously throughout the day and most of the night, I managed to keep abreast of the flood.

Our immediate problem at Governors Island was the selection of the candidates for the Officers' Training Camps, and the organization of these camps. Also the determination of the numerous cantonment sites which were destined to be located within the Eastern Department. General Bell developed Grippe on the train, and retired to the Rockefeller Institute, keeping this a careful secret from everybody except Mrs. Bell and me. I visited him every other evening, in the meantime having authority to act in all matters in his name. The General's former Aides-de-Camp hurried to his assistance. Major Ewing Booth relieved Halstead Dorey in charge of the training camps.[6,7] "Duke" Bridges soon reported as Department Inspector.[8] Jack Murphy arrived about a week later and made a tour of the training camps to determine if they were adequately equipped.[9]

The next few weeks were the most strenuous, hectic, and laborious in my experience. I worked day and night; dictated letters and interviewed callers at the same time, frequently carrying on simultaneously two telephone conversations. Tremendous pressure was being brought to bear to secure the designation of favored sons to attend the training camps. By following a fixed policy of noninterference with the regularly prescribed method of selection we managed to survive this period.

Great difficulty was experienced in securing any adequate supply of suitable mattresses, blankets, and pillows, for the training camps along the northern border of New York. The market had been completely gutted by the Allies and it was next to impossible to secure anything on the eastern seaboard. Mattresses, for example, were unobtainable east of Chicago, and the short time available prior to the opening of the camps on May 15th necessitated all shipments being made by express. As a matter of fact the pathetic difficulties we encountered in equipping the training camps to accommodate a total of forty thousand men were an impressive demonstration of our complete state of unpreparedness. It is now almost impossible to realize that the resources of the entire United States were apparently taxed to the limit to prepare for this comparatively small number of prospective officers.

The selection of cantonment sites in the northeast proved a complicated and exacting duty. There were few places in that thickly populated region with adequate railroad facilities, good water, and sufficient acreage which could be adapted to the purpose. Unfortunately, little had apparently been done to locate possible sites prior to the time the situation demanded them. On the west coast we had already arranged for two sites, one at American Lake and one near San Diego. General Bell, through his personal endeavors, had succeeded in prevailing upon the citizens of the vicinity of American Lake to acquire the property and present it to the Government. The declaration of war prevented the culmination of a similar arrangement at San Diego.

During the latter part of May, several hospital units passed through New York and embarked for service abroad, and on the 28th of May, General Pershing arrived with his staff.[10] The latter rendezvoused in my office and from there proceeded to the boat. A heavy rain was falling. General Pershing and General Bell, with the former's Aide, Captain Collins, and myself, followed them to the tug which carried them to the *Baltic*.[11] I was in a most depressed frame of mind over being left behind.

Returning from the dock I stopped at my quarters for a moment. Mrs. Marshall had observed the officers of General Pershing's staff as they walked past the house. Dressed in antiquated civilian clothes, coat collars turned up in the absence of umbrellas or raincoats, they were not an imposing group. She remarked, "They were such a dreadful-looking lot of men, I cannot believe they will be able to do any good in France." So little did anyone realize of the vast task awaiting these men and of the remarkable vision and broad judgment they were to display.

The departure of these small groups from New York quickly exhausted Governors Island of all supplies of the character required on such occasions. Becoming worried over the fact that no arrangements were being made for a properly organized port of embarkation, General Bell went to Washington about June 5th, taking me with him. On our arrival there he took up with the Chief of Staff the question of arrangements for the organization of a port of embarkation at Hoboken. He was informed that the Depot Quartermaster in New York would have charge of the matter, and was at the time making preliminary arrangements for the embarkation of a division within the next week or ten days.

General Bell talked this over with me and we agreed that such an arrangement would never work and that he, as commander of the Eastern Department, would bear the brunt of the inevitable criticism. As I recall, he then had another talk with General Bliss, the Chief of Staff, but without apparent success.[12] We discussed this at the Shoreham Hotel, where we were staying, and in order to make it a matter of record, he sent me down to the public stenographer to prepare a memorandum to the Chief of Staff for his signature. In this memorandum I quoted the paragraph of the Field Service Regulations which governed the organization and control of ports of embarkation. General Bell submitted the paper, and this was, I am inclined to believe, one of the first occasions where the Field Service Regulations, instead of the Army Regulations, were considered by the War Department in the conduct of the war. A few days later the War Department directed General Bell to carry out the provisions of the Field Service Regulations just referred to, and appoint a commander for the Port of Embarkation. He at once designated an officer for this duty, but the latter only arrived abreast of the leading elements of the infantry of the First Division, which detrained in the Jersey City meadows and immediately marched on board the transports.

My detail on the General Staff had already been determined upon but General Bell had requested a delay in its announcement in order to afford him an opportunity to secure a desirable assignment for me. On our way to Washington he told me to inquire around and decide where I wished to go. He would then use his influence to secure me that assignment. When I arrived at the War Department, a brief survey of the situation convinced me that no one knew what the best assignment was other than one in France. I was told that the General Staff officers for the division then being assembled for immediate embarkation would be selected from the officers who sailed with General Pershing. I particularly desired the job as Operations Officer with this division, but as this seemed out of the question, I told General Bell I would let fate determine my assignment.

Returning to New York a day in advance of the General, I reached Governors Island about 9 P.M. Mrs. Marshall met me at our door with a telegram, which had been sent from Washington by General Sibert about half an hour prior to my leaving that city, asking General Bell if he would be willing to release me for field service with General Sibert abroad.[13] Unaware of General Sibert's exact assignment, I did know that this meant France, and joyfully dispatched a wire to General Bell, repeating the message. On trying to telephone him at the Shoreham I found he had left Washington, and it was not until the next evening, when General Bell reached Governors Island, that I was able to get in touch with him. He graciously permitted me to write his reply to General Sibert, and the following morning a telegram from The Adjutant General announced my detail on the General Staff and directed me to report to General Sibert at the Pennsylvania Station in New York at a certain train arriving the next morning. I failed to locate General Sibert on the train specified, and did not find him until an hour or two later at the Army Building near Bowling Green. There I learned for the first time that he was the commander of the combat division and that I was to be the Operations Officer.

The next day and a half was a confusion of preparation for my departure for France and for Mrs. Marshall's departure for her home.

On the afternoon of June 10th General Sibert inspected the transports at Hoboken docks of the former North German Lloyd Line. These boats were largely fruit liners of the South and Central American trade, and were in process of being converted into transports. The guns had not yet been mounted and all the bunks had not then been installed. Nevertheless that night most of the infantry of the First Division detrained in the Hoboken meadows and marched aboard the boats. The night was dismal, with a drizzling rain. Most of the laborers about the docks and all of the onlookers beyond the iron fence bordering the street were German. The average stevedore looked as though he were a member of the crew of some German submarine. It was not a very encouraging prospect.

About 3 A.M., I was standing at the window of the shipping office with the newly appointed commander of the Port of Embarkation, watching the endless column of infantry pouring slowly through the courtyard into the covered docks. Except for the shuffle of their feet there was little noise. It was an impressive and forbidding scene. After a long silence I remarked, "The men seem very solemn." In a rather dramatic fashion he replied, "Of course, they are. We are watching the harvest of death." I hurriedly left the window and hunted up a more cheerful companion from the staff.

Secretary Baker and General Bliss had inspected the boats that afternoon, but did not remain overnight.[14] We were assigned our staterooms and thereafter never left the ship until we landed in France. All of the 11th we lay alongside the dock, but on the 12th our vessel, the *Tenadores,* pulled up the Hudson opposite Grant's Tomb and anchored there in great "secrecy" — cheered by all passing excursion boats — until the morning of the 14th. The installation of the antisubmarine guns was the cause of this delay.

At four o'clock on the morning of the 14th we weighed anchor and steamed slowly down the river. A dense fog made navigation so difficult that we anchored off Governors Island. About 7 A.M., the fog lifted and we steamed out of the harbor and through the gap in the submarine chain off Fort Hamilton.

The *Tenadores* led the first division of the fleet, escorted by the cruiser *Seattle.* Off our port bow was the *DeKalb,* carrying the Fifth Marine Regiment. I had last seen her years before as the *Prince Eitel Frederic* in the harbor of Yokohama. Three other transports made up the first division, and another converted cruiser on our starboard bow, with one or two destroyers, completed the convoy. A fuel ship accompanied the destroyers.

Shortly after losing sight of the coast we began the monotonous lifeboat drills. Everyone was new to everything; the men to their organizations, the sailors to the ship, and the officers of the Headquarters to each other. All were enthusiastic over their selection for the first "Great Adventure," but each seemed to realize that this was no jovial party and that few of this first company would return unscathed.

The first exhibition of target practice by our sailor gun-crews for the hastily mounted 6-inch guns was rather disastrous to morale. The only thing they succeeded in hitting was the horizon and the foreground — which was too extensive a bracket to encourage a feeling of security from submarines. However, the usual soldier wit made a bon mot which produced much laughter, re-establishing cheerfulness.

The staff of the First Division included Colonel Frank Coe, Chief of Staff, Colonel Cruikshank, Adjutant — with Campbell King as an Assistant — Colonel Cheatham, Quartermaster, Major James A. Drain, Ordnance Officer, Lesley McNair and myself, as Assistant Chiefs of Staff, G. K. Wilson, W. C. Sherman, and Franklin Sibert as Aides, Alvin C. Voris, Chief Signal Officer, Colonel Bailey K. Ashford, Chief Surgeon, with Maybee as an Assistant, Colonel H. A. Smith, Inspector, and Beverly Read, Judge Advocate.[15] Major Frank McCoy sailed as a passenger to join General Pershing's staff in France.[16] One battalion of the Twenty-eighth Infantry was on the boat, and several casual officers, including a Colonel Heron of the English Supply Department. Altogether we had a very congenial company and succeeded in diverting ourselves and each other throughout the voyage.

One example of our unpreparedness for war was the fact that the staff of the division met for the first time aboard the boat. A few members had attended a short meeting at the Army Building in New York prior to sailing, but this was merely for the purpose of giving directions as to baggage, stateroom assignments, etc. It was not until we were aboard the *Tenadores* that most of us were informed of the organization prescribed for the division of which we formed a part. We found the infantry regiments had been increased about threefold in strength and contained organizations previously unheard of, which were to be armed with implements entirely new to us. Considering that we were starting on an expedition with an objective 3000 miles across the sea, it seemed rather remarkable that we should have embarked without knowledge of the character of the organization we were to fight.

Most of the men were recruits and many were issued their arms after boarding the train in Texas en route to Hoboken. The personnel of the division was not impressive. Many of the men were undersized and a number spoke English with difficulty. In the matter of Lieutenants, however, we were especially fortunate. Each of the training camps had been called upon to select the best 15 or 20 candidates for immediate overseas service. This meant that out of the 2500 in each camp the First Division received the twenty best. I have never seen more splendid looking men and it makes me very sad to realize that most of them were left in France. These officers from the training camps first reported to me in my office as Aide-de-Camp to General Bell. I recall crossing over to New York on the government ferry with nine of them, each with a bride. I never learned of the career of two of these officers, but I do know that each of the other seven was killed fighting in the First Division.

On the voyage we busied ourselves studying the organization of the British and French armies and a mass of papers that had been turned over to the War College by the English and French Missions. No one of us had a definite conception of the character of the war, and certainly none of us understood the method in which the staffs of the Allied armies functioned. In the light of later experience, some of the questions asked and ideas proposed now seem ludicrous. Today it is inconceivable that we should have found ourselves committed to a war while yet in such a complete state of unpreparedness.

Our minds were frequently concerned with the question of German submarines. The Navy personnel running our ship and controlling the remainder of the convoy appeared very capable and businesslike, but I accidentally learned that a large number of the sailors were recruits and as ignorant of their duties as our First Division men were of a soldier's duties. We suffered some discomfort at night from poor ventilation, as only hasty arrangements had been made for closing all the ports and other apertures to prevent the showing of lights. It was very uncomfortable except on deck. General Sibert, his son Franklin, Campbell King, and I decided to sleep on deck and had our cots and bedding rolls brought up. We found this quite comfortable, though it would not have been practicable in rough weather.

On a certain morning we expected to meet the flotilla of American destroyers from an English or French base, which were to safeguard our passage through the danger zone. They did not appear and we were not informed of the reason. That night after the four of us just mentioned had retired on deck, we were startled by a shot fired from the *DeKalb* more or less across our bow. At the same time, the cruiser *Seattle*, which had been steaming in the lead, turned and headed back through the convoy. One or two more shots were fired, I believe, and the deck lights on one of the ships in our rear suddenly flashed on as though she had been struck and they were lighting her up to aid in the launching of lifeboats. Immediately all the ships changed their course, increased speed, and began to zigzag off in different directions.

King and I sat up on our cots and watched the show. We were particularly concerned over the display of lights on the boat in rear of us. A few minutes later an officer passed by and whispered that one of our transports had been sunk, which rather confirmed the impression we had already gained. It gave one a very peculiar feeling to realize that we were heading off in the dark and leaving behind us somewhere a shipload of companions adrift on the ocean. Fortunately, the report was incorrect, and, while we were given no definite information that night, we rather favored the idea that some amateur lookout had received a too vivid impression from the trail of a porpoise or shark. At any rate, I recorded the day as uneventful in the Division Diary. Later this entry had to be changed, as I will explain in due time.

At daybreak the morning following our submarine excitement, a column of American destroyers broke out of the mist and bore down on us at top speed. The sea was rough and they made a very dramatic appearance cutting through the waves, pitching and tossing with every motion of the water. There were about six destroyers in this squadron, and they distributed themselves on the flanks of the transports, with much cheering back and forth between the sailors and soldiers. All felt more secure in entering the danger zone with these additional guards.

Either the same night or the following, a few of us were confidentially tipped off that two German submarines were operating dead ahead. There followed a refitting of life preservers and much discussion as to the best course of action if our ship was torpedoed. I remember the perturbation of those assigned to the lifeboat in which I was to be a passenger, over the fact that in being launched it must pass directly by that section of a lower deck where several hundred stevedores were under orders to assemble for assignment to such life rafts as might be found in the water. Cruikshank, as Adjutant, had picked out this particular boat for Campbell King and himself, and, as an unsolicited favor, had assigned me to it. The basis for the selection was a gasoline engine, but a brief survey disclosed the fact that the engine merely added weight, and there would never be enough gas to go more than a few miles.

The stevedores were much exercised over the submarines. Everyone assumed the last thing they would do in an emergency would be to remain passive on their assigned portion of the deck while the officer in charge selected for them a salubrious location on a raft. A false alarm about this time proved the correctness of the assumption, for many of the men hastened to the top deck and were getting into the boats before anyone had time to intervene.

CHAPTER II

Early Days in France

O N THE EVENING of June 25th we sighted Belle Isle in the mouth of the Loire River. A vessel looking much like an old Ohio River tug came out to meet us and proved to be a French gunboat. We passed Belle Isle and about sunset anchored in the mouth of the river. Everyone relaxed from the strain of the submarine menace and had a good night's rest — only to learn the following morning that we had been in greater danger that night than at any time during the voyage, as two German subs made quite an effort to get into the convoy. Early on the morning of the 26th, a French launch came down the river and pulled alongside. A number of French officials including the Captain of the Port, the naval commander of the District, Bertie de Chambrun [1] — later to be a French Aide-de-Camp to General Pershing — an American naval officer and Colonel Rockenbach, the American Quartermaster just assigned to St. Nazaire, boarded the boat.

We weighed anchor and steamed up the river, which had the aspect of an extensive bay. It was a beautiful sunny morning and the green hill slopes and little cottages along the northern shore gave us all an agreeable impression of what France was to be. The stream gradually narrowed, until at St. Nazaire we entered the basin at the foot of the principal street of the town. Our vessel, the *Tenadores,* led the way and was first to dock. A small crowd of the French inhabitants collected along the edge of the basin and at the end of the street to watch our arrival. Most of the women were in mourning. Very few men were in evidence. There was not a cheer, and the general aspect was that of a funeral. Once we had tied up to the dock, General Sibert went down the gangway and I followed him to secure the distinction of being the second man ashore at an American base port in France.

We found that a cantonment was in course of preparation for us on the high ground outside of the town. General Rockenbach and a few other American officers from General Pershing's staff had arrived about two days ahead of us and naturally there had been no time to make much preparation.[2] The fact of the matter was, General Pershing did not receive notification of the destination of our convoy until about four days before our arrival.

General Sibert and several of his staff motored out to the camp before lunch. Riding with a French officer, I decided to initiate a policy of familiarizing myself with the French language by speaking French on every suitable occasion. Intending to comment on the wonderful morning, I remarked, "Je suis très beau aujourd'hui." He gave me an odd look and I mentally translated my remark. During the ensuing twenty-six months I never spoke French again except when forced to.

We found a partially completed camp or cantonment awaiting us, with the novel Adrian or Simon portable barracks for shelter. All of us immediately wondered why we in the Regular Army had spent so many years under canvas on the Mexican border and in other hot localities, when this much more economical, comfortable, and practicable method of sheltering troops existed.

About the middle of the day the first troops disembarked, a company of the Second Battalion of the Twenty-eighth Infantry leading the way. We were very anxious that the men should make a good appearance in passing through the town, but most of them were ignorant of the first rudiments of march discipline and were busy looking in the shop windows and observing the French crowd. Some slight applause greeted the march through, but it was apparent that all of St. Nazaire suffered from a deep depression due to the collapse of the much advertised French offensive of April 17th. We were to learn later that numerous elements of the French Army were practically in a state of mutiny during the latter part of April and the first part of May, and Marshal Joffre's principal mission in coming to the

United States had been to secure at the earliest possible moment a detachment of American troops on French soil.[3] The First Division was the detachment and it was hoped that our mere presence would serve to build up the morale of both the army and civilian population of France.

The troops of the division marched into camp during the next few days as rapidly as the vessels could be unloaded, as fast as the several divisions of the convoy arrived. Docking facilities were very limited and it was exceedingly hard to make rapid progress. On the ways of the local shipyard stood the skeleton of the French liner *Paris*, whose construction had been started just before the outbreak of the war. It was rather an odd coincidence that General Pershing sailed on the *Paris* three weeks ago (September 15, 1921) on his mission to confer the American Medal of Honor on the French and British Unknown Dead.

As an example of the state of discipline of the First Division, the following incident occurred on our second day ashore. A tall, rangy-looking soldier was on duty as sentinel in front of General Sibert's office. His blouse was unbuttoned and a watch chain extended across the front, between the pockets. A French General, commanding the local region, approached the sentinel and exhibited an interest in his gun. The sentry obligingly handed the General his weapon and retired to the door of the office and sat down on the sill. I personally got him up, got his blouse buttoned and his rifle back. This man was probably one of those remarkably gallant fellows who fought so hard and died so cheerfully not many months later.

We were all much disturbed, the second and third days in St. Nazaire, by the report of an attempted assault on a French peasant girl by one of our men. She accused him of having grabbed her and pushed her down, she making her escape, very much frightened. He claimed she was bringing in the cows and made eyes at him, and he merely was trying to kiss her. A court was convened within 24 hours and the man sentenced to thirty years' confinement, and the sentence immediately approved. The French people were thunderstruck at such a procedure, and, while it was very drastic so far as the particular individual was concerned, there can be no doubt but that it made a lasting impression, not only on the men of the First Division, but on most of those who followed.

I doubt if any soldiers in the history of the world were ever so considerate and so respectful of the rights and interests of inhabitants in a war-ridden country, as were ours. A man of the First Division would no more think of picking up an apple from the ground under a peasant's tree than he would of committing some serious offense. The men really were so good that the French early adopted the practice of complaining if they even scratched the soil. I am inclined to think the remarkable behavior of the personnel of the First Division, while making such an unmilitary appearance in their slouchy uniforms and exhibiting so few traces of formal discipline, created the impression in the minds of the French officials that our soldiers were kindly, timorous oafs. Certainly they gathered the impression that we understood nothing of the military business, since this division was supposed to be the pick of the Regular Army, and yet it looked like the rawest of territorial units.

General Pershing visited St. Nazaire a few days after the arrival of the division and made a very strenuous inspection of the camp and the port facilities in the harbor. He directed our division commander to send a battalion to parade in Paris on July 4th. The Second Battalion of the Sixteenth Infantry was designated for this historic duty. We were all much depressed over the prospect of sending a battalion largely made up of recruits to make the first appearance of American troops in the French capital. There was no time for rehearsing and the units were shipped to Paris where they were received with tumultuous enthusiasm by the French populace. I rather imagine, however, that the higher French military officials were further strengthened in their erroneous conception of the American soldier by the unmilitary appearance of this battalion.

During these first days at St. Nazaire we learned something of the famous submarine battle in which we had participated. After hearing Admiral Gleaves of the cruiser *Seattle* recount the Navy version of the affair, General Sibert asked me what note I had made of it in the Divisional War Diary. When I told him that I had recorded that day as uneventful, he directed me to revise the Diary so as to show that we had participated in a naval engagement. Unfortunately, the completed sheets of the Diary had already been forwarded to the War Department and, in accordance with orders, a copy had not been retained. I, therefore, forwarded a substitute page to the War Department, but made a mistake of one day as to the date. The naval records of the war will therefore show the first submarine engagement as having occurred on June 21st, while the First Division Diary records the same event on June 22nd. All were entertained in reading the thrilling account of this affair released to the American press on July 4th by George Creel.[4]

Many difficulties were encountered in our efforts to conduct training for the recruits during our short stay at St. Nazaire. The nearest open ground, free from crops, was on the coast some nine miles distant. It was necessary to march the troops a total of 18 miles in order to reach the drill ground and return to camp. The division at this time possessed two automobiles. One was a Cadillac which came with the Fifth Marine Regiment, and the other was a three-passenger French sedan for General Sibert. As a consequence of this dearth of transportation — the animals not having yet landed from the last division of the convoy — Generals Bullard and Bundy, the two brigade commanders, had to walk at least 18 miles per day in order to observe their units.[5,6] The best that we could do at St. Nazaire was to teach the men how to march with a minimum of fatigue and road expansion.

About this time began the first of a series of detachments of officers from the First Division. Men were ordered away almost daily to new assignments and we never saw them with the division again. This continued throughout the summer and fall of 1917. During that period the division had to supply the officer personnel for most of the jobs developing in the Service of Supply and at General Headquarters. I recall that in November 1917, just after we had come out of the line from our first trench warfare training, orders were received which detached from the division in one day every remaining field officer of infantry, except two newly assigned regimental commanders.

While at St. Nazaire we were called upon to send an advanced

detachment of officers to the area surrounding Gondrecourt, about
fifty kilometers south of St. Mihiel, which was designated as the training area for the division. In preparing instructions for the officers
selected for this duty I made my first acquaintance with the job of
Town Major. We had to send an officer to fill this position in each
village and it was necessary to give them a complete dissertation regarding their obligations and responsibilities.

Much excitement followed the announcement of our destination,
and my next problem was the preparation of orders for the entrainment of the division. "40 Hommes — 8 Chevaux" were still a mystery
to the American soldier and I am sure that none of those who were
present at the first loading of American troops on a French train will
forget the scene, the comments and the misunderstandings. Each
officer had valuable suggestions as to how the thing could better be
managed. Our battalion organization did not fit the French unit train.
Therefore, the officers damned the stupid French for making up such
a train, overlooking the fact that virtually all of this type of rolling stock
in France was arranged in these standard units to facilitate the rapid
transportation of large masses of troops. The train consisted of fifty
cars, principally flats and boxes, with usually two small passenger cars
(second class) on the end.

During loading operations we were surrounded by French officials
assisting and observing — largely the latter. We soon learned that a
formal report, covering all of our failings, would be submitted as the
natural consequence of every embarkation. The trouble was our
GHQ took these very seriously until they learned to accept them
somewhat like observations regarding the weather. Unfortunately,
for us, the First Division, as the only child, caught the devil throughout this formative period.

With the departure of the troops from St. Nazaire, General Sibert
and certain members of his staff motored to Paris. The division Chief
of Staff, Colonel Coe, and I went up by rail and found that a special
compartment had been placed at our disposal on the assumption that
it was for General Sibert. We reached Paris the evening of July 13th,
and were met at the Gare Quai d'Orsay by George Patton, who commanded General Pershing's Headquarters Troop.[7] We put up at the

Hotel Vernet, just off the Champs Elysées, where Palmer, Drum, General Ireland, and a number of the other members of the GHQ Staff were staying.[8,9]

General Pershing's office at this time was located on the Rue Constantine and we called there early on the morning of July 14th. On this visit I learned that General Pershing had that day adopted the Sam Browne belt, and I had Frank McCoy order one for me. McCoy, Logan, Colonel Coe, and I went out that morning to watch the Bastille Day parade.[10] This was our initial glimpse of first-class fighting troops of the French and we saw selected men with the colors from most of the regiments in the Army.

While we were in Paris, Colonel Coe received notification of his promotion to a permanent colonelcy in the Regular Army and he treated me to a dinner at the Café de la Paix to celebrate the event. I little thought on that occasion that two years later I would dine there with the manager of the café, by reason of my acquaintance with him while he was Mess Officer for the First Division Headquarters, and an acting Aide-de-Camp to General Bullard.

General Sibert left Paris by motor on the 15th, en route for Gondrecourt, and Colonel Coe and I accompanied him. Our road lay along a portion of the battlefield of the Marne, and near Bar-le-Duc we saw the first evidences of devastation. We reached Gondrecourt that night and found that the Headquarters Troop and officers had already arrived by rail. Young Theodore Roosevelt had shortly before landed in France and was assigned to the division, and he was among those awaiting us.[11] American officers at this time were not allowed orderlies and, therefore, had either to look out for their own baggage and possessions or trust to luck. It failed us on this occasion, as we found that our trunks and bedding rolls had been left out in a heavy rain all of the previous night. The mess established was similar to the usual impromptu affair for a short-maneuver camp in the United States — soldier chow slung at you and on themselves by casual soldier waiters, plenty of grease in the food, on the table, and frequently on the guests — quantity and not quality being the standard of the cook.

Locating my first French billet, I found a little room on the second

floor at the back of an equally little house. Its one window overlooked
a minute courtyard with a high retaining wall, beyond which was a
small garden on a level with my window. There was a lilac tree on one
side of the courtyard below. The family consisted of Madame Jouatte,
a rather homely, vigorous French woman, of forty-five years, with
dark eyes and hair, and of medium height and weight. Her husband
was a little, weazened fellow, who looked like a scoundrel — and later
proved to be one. Living with them was a rather handsome woman of
thirty years, a refugee, whose home was north of Chalôns, within the
area occupied by the enemy. She had lived within the German lines
for several years and had finally succeeded in being repatriated via
Switzerland. Her husband was in the French Army and she had a very
cunning little girl of eight years, named Nannette. Madame Jouatte's
only son was a prisoner in Germany, having been captured during the
fighting around Verdun in 1916. My room contained a little bed of
the Napoleonic type, a washstand, two chairs, and a fireplace. At first
it seemed very small, but later with the cold, dreary weather, it proved
to be an ideal billet.

I have given rather a detailed description of this house and household, because my next six months were spent here, the most depressing, gloomy period of the war. We often referred to it as the Winter of
Valley Forge, and Madame Jouatte was in no small measure responsible for my being able to keep a stiff upper lip and wear an optimistic
smile those days.

We found the Headquarters of the Forty-seventh French Chasseur
Division, commanded by General de Poudrygain, located at Gondrecourt, and the elements of the division scattered throughout the
area assigned to the First Division. These men, who were to assist in
our training, made a wonderful impression on our men. The Chasseurs were picked fellows of an unusually vigorous type; they wore a
dark blue tunic and an Alpine hat of the same shade. They had a
magnificent fighting record and in their first review gave us one of the
finest martial displays we had ever witnessed. De Poudrygain was a
little, wiry man, with one eye, which shot sparks every time he talked.
His instructions from the French authorities evidently required him
to force our training at the most rapid possible pace, and we had the

devil's own time trying to convince him that we first had the problem of training raw recruits in the elementary duties of a soldier. As a matter of fact, we never did make an impression on him, and he continued with an elaborate training program, while we struggled to teach our recruits one half of the day the first principles of the business and then, to keep the peace, to put them through the French advanced program the remainder of the day.

At this time we labored under a very grave disadvantage without realizing its cause. The French were determined to commit us to the trenches at the earliest possible moment, since the morale of their soldiers was seriously depressed and it was felt that nothing but the actual presence of American soldiers fighting in the line would satisfy the "poilus." All subordinate French officials in any way connected with us undoubtedly had their instructions to push our training to a rapid completion. They could not understand that this Regular unit was an entirely new organization filled with recruits. Regiments with a strength of 700 men in May had, during the ensuing weeks, lost about one half of this small trained personnel, and by the assignment of recruits had then been raised to a strength of 2000. All the old non-commissioned officers had been promoted to a commissioned grade and the best of the privates made noncommissioned officers. It was vitally essential that our men be disciplined and the organization reasonably well trained before entering the line, since a reverse, however small, suffered by the first American unit committed to the battle would have had a most depressing effect on all of our Allies, would have encouraged the enemy, and would certainly have given the politicians in the United States an opportunity to play hob with the Army. We were assumed to be highly trained Regulars — the pick of the American Army — and explanations would not have done any good in the event of trouble.

General Pershing naturally must avoid any suspicion of disagreement with the French authorities during this formative period. He, along with all the rest of us, was assumed by the Allies to know little of major warfare. Any failure on his part to follow their advice would naturally be utilized to his disadvantage. As a final complication, though a very natural one, we had to contend with the French ignorance of the characteristics of the American as an individual, of his ways, and of his methods of getting results. A Frenchman does not readily adapt himself to new ways — in fact, he feels the French method is the only method. We are adaptable, and it was this trait alone that made it possible for us to survive the difficulties of this period. American General Headquarters did not approve of the French methods of instruction, but did not order us to discontinue them. At the same time, however, they did give us very drastic orders to conduct certain training along American lines. We were in the position of one who would "be damned if he did, and be damned if he didn't," and the humble soldier was the principal sufferer. He worked overtime and all the time. He sang French songs and was virtually a Frenchman during the forenoon, and spent the afternoon being "cussed out" as an American "rookie."

The men accommodated themselves to their strange surroundings with remarkable celerity. They were soon on intimate terms with the families of the peasantry with whom they were billeted. They took a great fancy to the vigorous, snappy-looking French Chasseurs. When the Paymaster arrived and made the first payment in France, a number of the soldiers had two months' or more pay due. Deductions, for Liberty Bonds, insurance, etc., were unheard of at this time, and the men received the large amounts due them in the flimsy French paper money. I saw soldiers throw franc notes into the air and let them blow down the street. They bought everything in sight and completely demoralized trade conditions in the small towns of that region. On Sunday the roads and lanes were dotted with quartets consisting of an American soldier, a French Chasseur, and two girls, with large paper bags filled with provender, bound for an outing at the expense of the prodigal American. This first payment fully confirmed the French in their belief that we were rotten with money and ripe fruit for the French shopkeepers. The situation was so bad that General Sibert called a meeting of the regimental commanders to consider means and methods of curtailing future repetitions of this financial orgy. Fortunately, subscriptions to the Liberty Loans soon tied up most of the pay.

Despite the ready money available, the men were practically without tobacco during the first month in the Gondrecourt area. They craved cigarettes above everything. Chocolate could be purchased at a price in most of the French shops at this time, but good American tobacco was unobtainable. This situation, I have always felt, was instrumental in producing one of the most positive reactions in the AEF. At the time the YMCA was in its infancy, had no transportation and only sufficient personnel to do a little work in Paris for the hundred-odd men of the Headquarters Troop. The Censor would not permit the newspapers to print anything regarding the American troops except the bare fact that some had arrived and had paraded in Paris. Unfortunately, the Censor did permit the papers to comment on what the YMCA was doing for the men in Paris, and the New York *Herald* and the London *Daily Mail,* in their Paris editions, had daily references to the entertainments, suppers, etc., that were being arranged by the YMCA for the petted darlings of GHQ. These papers reached the fighting men of the First Division, who were without tobacco and whose ration at this time was a very restricted one. The fact that they were ignored in the news of the day as well as in the matter of special food and smokes, and the fact that the more favored ones in Paris, living under comfortable conditions, were receiving all the attention, enraged practically every soldier. I have seen them throw the papers into the streets and stamp on them. They did not reason out the true explanation of the situation, and there was born in them at this time a hatred of the "Y" which rapidly spread through each newly arrived unit and has continued until this day. When the first YMCA hut was erected — in Gondrecourt — the men shunned it for a time. The YMCA officials were helpless in the situation. They had done the best that was possible, but they suffered from one of those peculiar twists which so quickly mold public opinion in an army.

With the first week of our arrival in the Gondrecourt area there began a series of visits from more or less prominent people and officials of the Allied governments and from the United States. It was next to impossible to attend to the daily work because of the number of guests, newspaper correspondents, and inspecting officers from GHQ, etc., who were continually at one's elbow. We were "Exhibit A" of the AEF, and there was no "B," "C," and "D." Review followed review in rapid succession; first for General Pershing, and then for Marshal Joffre, President Poincaré, General Pétain, and many others.[12,13] A day never passed without at least one visitor, and sometimes a dozen. We had practically no transportation in the division at this time. As I recall, we possessed three automobiles, three motorcycles, and two trucks. Orders would come late in the evening for a review at eight-thirty the following morning. Officers at GHQ did not always realize that the troops were scattered through a region some 25 miles long and that considerable time was required to transmit the orders and to make the necessary marches, not to mention the thousand and one other details. Following the Armistice, divisions were assembled for review with ease and dispatch, because of the hundreds of trucks placed at their disposal for transporting the foot troops. "Walker's Hack" was the only certain transportation that we had, but no one else seemed to realize this.

An amusing incident occurred in connection with the review for Marshal Joffre. On the way out to the field selected for the ceremony our automobile passed a loose mule curiously watching the traffic along the road. Someone remarked that he'd bet that mule would attend the review. Sure enough, when we lined up behind the Marshal, who faced the division, "the scenery lover from Missouri" showed up and seemed fascinated by the guest of honor. The mule evaded all efforts at capture and continued to return to the reviewing party, where he was an interested and restless spectator.

The last week in July I had the good fortune to be designated to accompany four Colonels from the division, Coe, Duncan, Allaire and Doyen of the Marines, for a visit to the front at Verdun.[14,15,16] We stopped at Souilly (the Headquarters of the Second French Army) on our way up the "Sacred Way," the famous road which was so widened and trafficked as to supply all the French troops in the fighting around Verdun. General Guillaumat was in command and received us with every courtesy, and his officers explained the workings of the staff. The General's office was the same one occupied by Pétain during the famous defense. To me it was a very historic and interesting spot. The large and complicated staff organization was beyond my grasp. If anyone had told me then that fourteen months later I would be Assistant Chief of Staff, and Chief of the Operations Section of the General Staff, of an army more than five times the size of Guillaumat's and would do business every morning in that some room — the prediction would have evoked derisive laughter.

We dined and slept several hundred feet underground in the Citadel of Verdun, as guests of the commandant of the Fortress. During the day we visited a number of the most interesting points in the line, notably Fort Douamont, where we had our first "close shave." Our Marine Corps chauffeur had such a very, very close shave that he dropped all of his souvenirs and disappeared with the car into a nearby ravine.

On my return to Gondrecourt I found an order from GHQ, directing me, in addition to my duties with the First Division, to arrange cantonment areas for three divisions. The first one, centering around Neufchâteau, was to be occupied by the Twenty-sixth Division. Borrowing the Marine Cadillac — thus nearly immobilizing the division — I started out the following morning. I stopped in Neufchâteau to get in touch with the French Commandant d'Etat. Seemingly, the entire population turned out to meet me. A formal luncheon was hastily arranged, at which the Marine Sergeant and I were the guests of honor. I recall particularly a delicious dessert of "Fromage de la Crème, artistically arranged on a huge platter, a welcome change from the hash and canned tomatoes of the First Division mess. Inspired by the champagne and the necessities of the occasion, I essayed my first French speech, which was no more verbless than all succeeding ones, but which, with one exception, was my most successful.

During the ensuing few weeks I traveled more than a hundred miles a day, inspecting villages for their billeting accommodations, arranging for the construction of Adrian barracks and bathhouses, and explaining to the French officials the American organization and its requirements.

I was most fortunate in having to do business with an unusually efficient Frenchman who knew how to say "yes" or "no" without polite adornment. After completing the Twenty-sixth Division area, I started the preparation of two more — one for the Second Division and one for the Forty-second Division. The matter had now grown so large that the French sent in a selected, high-ranking General Staff officer to relieve the Commandant d'Etat of the growing responsibility. This proved unfortunate, because the new arrival had every quality irritating to an American, and I, seemingly, had all those distasteful to a Frenchman. I finally told him that if he would leave a free hand to his subordinate, everything should be arranged satisfactorily, as had been the case before his arrival.

He was quite furious and apparently made a report of the occurrence to his General, because the latter appeared the following day. I explained the situation to him — that excellent progress was being made, due to the complete understanding between the original Commandant d'Etat and myself, until the recent arrival of the former's successor. I told the General that I had been quite frank in the matter because not only time would be lost but we would never get anywhere so long as unfortunate selections of this sort were allowed to continue.

He evidently considered me a young, inexperienced American, and at first was inclined suavely to make light of the matter, and wished to consult my immediate superior. When I explained that my orders came to me direct from GHQ, and that nobody else was concerned in it, and that I had been given no instructions except to make such arrangements as seemed suitable to me, he was dumfounded. The idea that an officer of my years should be turned loose in a foreign country without detailed instructions and with the briefest of orders to carry out a complicated mission — the first of its kind for us — was totally contrary to all French practice. However, he immediately condescended to do business with me and assured me that the troublemaker would be withdrawn. I thanked him very earnestly and had the temerity to suggest that this incident might be utilized by him to explain to the higher French authorities the necessity of using great care in selecting officers for assignment to duty with the American forces. I remarked that the ability to speak English was not the principal qualification, that it was more a question of picking out men who could be impersonally direct in their dealings, concise in their speech, and, if necessary, brutally frank in expressing their opinion. Later developments convinced me that I had cast my bread upon the waters to little purpose.

French line officers were fond of calling the war "La Guerre du papier," because of the frequent and voluminous orders received; the Staff officers termed it "La Guerre de petit changement," because it seemed to them as fast as a plan was made or an order issued, instructions were received from higher up requiring a change. My first series of changes came at this time. Just as I had completed all arrangements for the billeting area of the Twenty-sixth Division, and had construction under way in most of the villages, of Adrian barracks, mess shacks, kitchens, bathhouses, and recreation huts, I received a letter from GHQ, informing me that the strength of the infantry companies had been increased from 200 to 250 men, and the machine-gun units heretofore assigned to battalions were regrouped into brigade battalions, leaving but one company with each regiment. This upset our calculations for every village assigned to infantry. It became necessary to extend the limits of the area, to arrange for additional construction, and to reassign units. The French officers concerned were well accustomed to changes in orders, but they were shocked that we so unexpectedly changed our basic organization.

After readjusting the "Yankee Division" district, I started to stake out the area for the Second Division, centering around Bourmont, about midway between Neufchâteau and Chaumont, but I was quickly forced to return to Neufchâteau following the receipt of further information from GHQ, then in Paris, indicating another change in organization, which would require further adjustments of billeting assignments. The layman would be inclined to place the blame for these changes on the vacillating policies of Regular Army officers. The truth of the matter was that it was an inevitable result of our condition of unpreparedness. The organization given the First Division had been hashed together during the few weeks following the arrival in the United States of the English and French Missions, and it was only natural that further investigation and some experiments with the new organization should demonstrate the advisability of minor changes. General Pershing's initial problem in France was the preparation of Tables of Organization for the first million men.

Before completing my work in the Neufchâteau district I made a radical change in personal living arrangements. To avoid the hurly-burly of the poorly run division mess, I arranged with my landlady, Madame Jouatte, to install a mess in her home, using the dining room. She would do the cooking and run the mess. Sugar, white flour, canned milk, etc., not obtainable in the French market, would be supplied by me from the Army commissary. I had noticed that her household ate in the little courtyard in fair weather, and in the kitchen in bad, and this suggested to me the use of her dining room. Colonel Hamilton A. Smith, who was later killed at Soissons, Major Lesley McNair, Captain Paul H. Clark and Lieutenant Jean Hugo, great-grandson of Victor Hugo, were invited to join this mess.[17]

The arrangement proved a unique success; the meals were delicious, Madame Jouatte was "très gentille" and eccentrically amusing, and the atmosphere was very cozy and homelike — in decided contrast to everything else in Gondrecourt. We started off with straight French cooking, and the desire of Smith to have a cracker with his lettuce upset Madame Jouatte so seriously that it was weeks before we dared to propose any further innovations. In time, however, due apparently to a decided affection for us, she reached the point where American biscuits and hot cakes were almost a daily event. I remember the delicious dish she prepared of lye hominy, and that she consistently refused to taste it.

The personnel of the mess changed from time to time due to the frequent detachment of officers from the division for duty elsewhere in France. Smith, McNair, and Clark were early ordered to Chaumont, and I invited Major James A. Drain and Voris to replace them. The last-named officer taught Madame Jouatte the art of making biscuits, and we were delighted when we found the "footprint" of a large white hand on the back of her waist following his demonstration in the kitchen. She became quite cheerful under our daily banter and we found her a ready target for assumed flirtatious advances. Once when she displayed great consternation over a daring remark addressed to her by a member of the mess, we inquired of Hugo whether she was offended or if she understood us. He replied, "I think Madame is alarmed, but pleased"!

Lieutenant Hugo was an interested observer of passing events in Gondrecourt. Through "inside information" he followed the course of many sentimental affairs between our doughboys and the fair peasant girls of that community. The French soldiers, according to Hugo, were out of luck, because each American was, by comparison, a millionaire. But these incidents were not confined to Inter-Allied relations. Hugo called our attention to the fact that Monsieur Jouatte, a shriveled-up little man, frequently went forth with a pair of field glasses hung on his shoulder, and he explained how this Lothario from a position on a nearby bridge scanned the windows of a certain house on the bluff. If a black petticoat was displayed, M. Jouatte hastened to see his inamorata; otherwise, he put up his field glasses and returned moodily home. By personal observation, we confirmed this tale and were moved by a violent desire to administer a thrashing to our worthy Madame's faithless spouse.

CHAPTER III

The Fall of 1917

O NE OF OUR SOLDIERS engaged in an argument regarding the seasons of the year in France, and closed his discussion with the statement that there were but two seasons — August and winter. The events of the latter part of August are included in this chapter, principally for the reason that the weather turned cold and the last chapter seemed a little long.

On the 19th of August I left Gondrecourt to witness the offensive planned by the Second French Army for the front north of Verdun, immediately to the east and west of the Meuse River. General Sibert, Colonels Coe, Duncan, Alexander, and Buck, and Captain Sherman and myself were given this opportunity, but I was particularly fortunate in being the only one assigned to the celebrated Moroccan Division.[1,2] We motored through Bar-le-Duc to Souilly and there had the plan of battle explained to us by General Guillaumat and his staff. We then separated and were conducted by French officers to our several divisions. The horizon was dotted with observation balloons and the air was filled with the roar of the guns. The artillery preparation had commenced two days previous.

We passed within thirty yards of a beautifully camouflaged railroad train consisting of a naval 14-inch gun, with its ammunition cars, and living quarters for the crew. Our American chauffeur had never heard gunfire except in hunting, and he did not spot the gun, which fired just as we were abreast of it. The car went into the ditch, out of it and over the hill, seemingly in one jump. He did not take his foot off of the accelerator until we virtually pulled it off. The following day while he was washing his car, a Boche shell demolished the adjacent building and threw bricks and mortar dust over the machine. Naturally, he returned to the First Division with all the airs and tales of a veteran.

On our way to the front we called on the local corps commander, General Corvisart, at Fromerville. He entertained us at dinner and was very nice to me when he learned that I had been over most of the battlefields of the Russo-Japanese War, where he had been with the Japanese Army in the capacity of a Military Attaché. Incidentally, he had been closely associated with General Pershing in Tokyo, and recounted how Mrs. Pershing had stepped into his home one morning and told his wife that her husband had just been promoted from a Captain to a Brigadier General.

I did not reach the Headquarters of the Moroccan Division until long after dark. Here I found General Degoutte, later to command an army at Château-Thierry, established with his staff in a newly constructed dugout, hewn out of the rock in the forward edge of the Bois Bourrus. His Headquarters overlooked Chattaincourt, le Mort d'Homme, and Hill 304, the last two being celebrated key points of the Verdun battlefield. To reach the dugout, my French guide conducted me about half a mile through the forest. It was very dark and the roads and trails were jammed with traffic. Guns were firing, apparently from every portion of the woods and a number of heavy ones were located close to our trail and always seemed to fire just as we were abreast of them. From the edge of the forest, just beyond the Headquarters dugout, a marvelous panorama of war was unfolded. No-man's-land followed more or less closely the valley immediately below the woods and its course could be traced for ten kilometers to the west and as far as Douamont on the east. The entire zone was illuminated by the ghostly glare from hundreds of star-shell parachute lights. Beyond, within the Boche lines, tremendous flashes from the explosion of the French shells flared here and there in the dark. The entire artillery of our ally was in action, methodically breaking down the enemy's trenches, demolishing his dugouts, and clearing gaps in the wire. This fusillade was continued for a total of five days — day and night — before the infantry advanced.

General Degoutte was most considerate and hospitable, and his staff officers were the finest-looking body of Frenchmen encountered by me during the war. It appears that the French were very careful in their selection of officers for duty with Colonial troops, and assigned only the most vigorous, positive types to this special duty. The division Chief of Staff, Colonel Kastler, took me under his wing as it were, and afforded me assistance in seeing everything possible. I was a Captain at this time, with no experience whatever in major warfare, and he was a Lieutenant Colonel with medals for exceptional service in Africa, and numerous decorations for splendid gallantry during three years of European war. We were to meet a year later in the same region, this time he functioning as Chief of Staff of an army corps at Verdun, while I was to be a Colonel and Chief of Operations of the First American Army, in which his army corps was serving. The front of his corps was then to include Chattaincourt, and we were to have numerous arguments over the orders formulated for his corps by the Operations Section of the American Army Staff.

There was no room in the crowded divisional headquarters for me to sleep, as the staff was at full strength in preparation for the battle, so I was assigned a place in the dugout of the Chief Engineer of the division, located in rear of the forest. About eleven o'clock that night my French guide conducted me over the same trail, back past the same traffic, to this dugout. In company with a French Staff Officer, who was also visiting the Moroccan Division, I was assigned a compartment forty feet underground.

At three the following morning I dressed and started forward to Division Headquarters. In my dugout, forty feet below the surface, all was quiet, but as I climbed the steps the first faint roar of the bombardment became audible and increased until, as I emerged from the door of the dugout, it had assumed deafening proportions. In the dark, the flare of the guns all along both sides of the valley in which the Engineer Headquarters were located gave me the impression of the Connellsville coke region at night, except that the latter would have seemed as quiet as a country churchyard by comparison. I had some difficulty in finding my way forward to Division Headquarters, as I had not yet observed the trail by daylight, and there were numer-

ous offshoots. Pitting my French against the roar of the guns, I succeeded in obtaining the necessary directions to keep me on the right
road.

The 20th [of August] was occupied in studying the plans for the
battle and in going to various points to observe the bombardment,
once under the guidance of General Degoutte. He told me that this
was the greatest artillery concentration up to that time in the history
of warfare — there were 22 artillerymen for every 20 infantrymen —
but he did not tell me that the reason for this was the necessity for
launching an offensive so as to guarantee success to the infantry with
a minimum of loss. The fiasco and hideous losses of the previous
April had destroyed the aggressive spirit of the French infantry. The
Verdun offensive of the following August was a carefully staged affair, primarily for the purpose of restoring morale by demonstrating
to the infantry the possibility of carrying out offensive operations
without suffering heavy losses. Of course such an unusual concentration of artillery would not be practicable on an extensive front, and
therefore, could not be expected in a large battle; but it was essential
in this particular instance for psychological reasons.

A portion of le Mort d'Homme, the Bois de Cumières, and the Côte
de l'Oie were the objectives of the Moroccan Division. Its right thus
rested on the Meuse River. General Degoutte explained to me that he
was placing one company of Zouaves east of the river within the zone
of the flanking division, in order to insure the capture of the little
village of Champ, to prevent the possibility of German machine-gunners raking his infantry west of the river, in the event the adjacent
French division failed to take the village. These Moroccan fellows
considered themselves the great assault division of the French Army,
and believed their infantry to be much superior to the average French
infantry. Their prior record and their services during the remainder
of the war fully justified this belief. They took no chances on the
possibility of failures by the ordinary French infantry adversely affect-
ing them. The arrangement for the capture of Champ was an example of this.

Forty-five minutes past four on the morning of the 21st was H-
hour, and Kastler and I went out on the forward slope of the hill to

witness the advance. A low fog covered No-man's-land and all of the forward Boche positions, but the crest of le Mort d'Homme and the Bois de Cumières projected themselves above the mist. As the moment arrived, the thunder of the guns changed to the unmistakable drum-fire, but what was occurring below the screen of fog remained a mystery for some time.

With the rising of the sun the fog lifted, revealing a cloudless sky literally filled with aeroplanes. On this morning I saw five planes crash. The first one apparently received an accidental hit from a shell coursing through the air on its way from the French artillery to some German position. The plane fell in a vrille, spinning around, tail up. The rays of the sun were reflected on the highly varnished yellow wings with their red, white, and blue markings and gave it the appearance of a falling mallard duck, as it dove into the fog. The trace of the barrage, marked by clouds of dust and smoke, was visible as far as the eye could see to the right and left. The panorama appealed to me as a picture battle — never again was I to witness anything approaching it in dramatic effect. Later it always seemed that battles were inextricably connected with cold and rain, and mud and gloom.

Kastler soon returned to the Headquarters dugout to receive reports from the front. There being no one who could be spared to look after me — a very fortunate state of affairs — I struck off downhill toward the front, avoiding the trenches and moving across the fields. The German artillery was doing very little firing. Without experiencing any particular difficulty or danger, I reached the jumping-off positions of the French troops and there found some of the reserve battalions of the first-line regiments preparing to move forward. I also encountered the first increment of German prisoners. They were covered with dirt and dust, and all were sick from the effects of the continuous gassing they had experienced during the previous five nights. I called out to the first column, "Do any of you men speak English?" and a bare-headed little fellow near the rear replied, "I do, I am from Detroit." Another one called to me, "I am from Brooklyn, and I will be glad to get back there." The little one said something in German to the other prisoners, who thereupon stared at me. He explained to me, "I have just told these fellows that you are an American officer, and that this proves our officers have lied to us about the United States not sending over troops."

I worked my way forward through Chattaincourt toward the ruins of Cumières, which lay at the base of the Côte de l'Oie, a ridge branching off to the right into a neck of the river. Much embarrassed in my progress by the inability to speak French, I fumbled about a great deal, but saw so much of interest that I did not mind the difficulties.

At this time a reserve battalion on the right of the division was organizing on the crest of the ridge to attack eastward, at right angles to the main operation, down the Côte de l'Oie. I had not been told of this feature of the plan. It was not included in the initial operation, and apparently was not to be undertaken unless the preceding maneuvers had been carried out successfully.

By this time the Germans had succeeded in directing heavy artillery fire on the area occupied by this battalion and the officers appeared to experience some difficulty in holding their men in place. The latter were endeavoring to collect in a sunken road which gave some shelter from the German fire. The attack which followed was wonderfully spectacular, as every man was in view, from the leading skirmisher to the last reserve. Grenade fighting could be clearly witnessed and the explosion of every Boche shell spotted. Just about this time I learned that I was accompanying and watching the attack of a portion of the famous "Foreign Legion." It had been referred to as "Le Légion des Etrangers," which conveyed nothing in particular to my mind until the afternoon of the attack. I was naturally thrilled to realize that in my first battle I should be with the regiment so picturesquely described by Ouida in her book, *Under Two Flags*.

In returning to Division Headquarters late in the afternoon of the 21st, I suffered a most humiliating experience. The German artillery fire had increased during the day but could hardly be called violent. Avoiding the trenches and walking over the top, I encountered a wide strip of barbwire entanglement with no gap in the immediate vicinity. To save time I picked my way through the wire, which was about three feet high. Just as I reached the middle of the network the enemy opened up with a fusillade of shells on that particular locality.

I could not lie down because of the wire and to stand up was to invite a casualty from the flying fragments, so I hurried through, leaving a large piece of my trousers behind me.

Speaking of artillery fire reminds me of an illustration that morning of the thousands of shells that may fall without doing any damage, and the heavy casualties which may result from a lone shot. Through my glasses I was watching a column of about one hundred and fifty Boche prisoners being brought back over the crest of le Mort d'Homme. They were laboriously picking their way through the maze of great shell craters, when a single German shell of heavy caliber dropped squarely in the column. I don't know how many casualties it caused, but it seemed to me I could see figures of men flying in every direction.

The afternoon of the following day telephone instructions were received from Gondrecourt directing me to return to the First Division. Motoring back through Bar-le-Duc, I reached my destination after dark and found that Colonel Coe, who had just been promoted to the grade of Brigadier General, was leaving the division, and that I had become Acting Chief of Staff. As I was only a Captain, General Sibert could not arrange to have me given the permanent appointment, but he submitted a recommendation for me to be promoted to the grade of Lieutenant Colonel in order that I might continue as Chief of Staff. As General Pershing was without authority to make promotions by selection, no result was heard from this until my name appeared in the first list of selective promotions, published shortly after Christmas.

At this time General Sibert was charged with organizing a corps school in Gondrecourt. It was necessary for the division to furnish most of the officer and enlisted personnel to construct and operate the school, and then to furnish the students to take the courses. This nearly exhausted the supply, and most of the companies only had one officer for duty. Our training was progressing rapidly so far as the schedule was concerned, but the officer personnel was changing even more rapidly, and each newcomer had to pick up the training schedule where he found it. This proved particularly embarrassing when a newly assigned regimental commander arrived without experience in

trench warfare methods and unfamiliar with the new regimental organization.

Our friends in the Forty-seventh French Chasseur Division had
come to understand the peculiar situation which existed in the First
Division, and we were moving along very smoothly in our work with
them when, unfortunately, they were ordered into the line and the
Eighteenth French Division was sent to replace them. A warm and
sincere friendship had sprung up between the Chasseurs and ourselves, and on their departure we had beautiful silk fanions, or flags,
made for each of their battalions. These were presented after the
Chasseurs had entered the line, by a committee from the First Division, and were received with deep expressions of appreciation.

Before leaving Gondrecourt the Chasseur Chief of Staff and his
two assistants called me in and formally presented me with a Boche
machine gun captured by the division at Moronvillers in the April
offensive. About the same time, Colonel Kastler, Chief of Staff of the
Moroccan Division, presented me with a Boche rifle which had been
captured by the Foreign Legion in the Bois de Cumières the day I had
been with them. Through this incident I learned that Madame
Jouatte's son had been taken prisoner by the Germans in the Bois de
Cumières in 1916. It was an odd coincidence that I had witnessed the
recapture of the same woods.

General Bordeaux, the commander of the newly arrived French
division, was a Frenchman of the stiff, punctilious type, and it quickly
became apparent that we would be involved in a long repetition of the
training we had already received. He also planned for a number of
demonstrations by French troops. We had found that these demonstrations did not do us much good. They were rather cut-and-dried
affairs and it was very hard for our men to take in the important
points. We wished to be given problems by the experienced French
officers and then left to work them out for ourselves, as best we could.
After this we wished to have the French officers criticize our solu-
tions, impersonally and impartially.

I explained our situation and wishes to the Assistant Chief of Staff
of the Eighteenth Division. He said he thoroughly understood our
point of view, but that he doubted whether he could prevail upon

General Bordeaux to change his plans. The following day he informed me that General Bordeaux would not consider any alteration in his program and would proceed according to his arranged schedule, which he did the following day, completely throwing out our own arrangements.

Some drastic action was necessary. We could not afford to lose the time which would inevitably be lost if we followed General Bordeaux's scheme. General Sibert explained this to the French commander as best he could, but without result. I then prepared a letter which set forth our position and stated clearly just what assistance we desired from the French, and in conclusion it informed General Bordeaux that if he could not accommodate himself to the proposed arrangement General Sibert regretted very much that we would have to go our own way.

To insure accuracy of understanding I had Lieutenant Hugo translate the letter into French, and then had Captain Seligman, another of our Liaison Officers, who had not seen my English draft, retranslate Hugo's translation back into English. I feared Hugo's native politeness might cause him to smooth down the embarrassingly frank portions of the letter so that the meaning and emphasis would be lost. It was necessary to repeat this procedure three times before I succeeded in obtaining a French translation which conveyed the exact meaning intended. This letter General Sibert signed, with the result that General Bordeaux met the specific requests in every particular, but I learned later from members of his staff that he was much hurt and incensed, and probably would never forget the incident.

Under the new arrangement our progress in training was very satisfactory and much more rapid than in any previous period, but the division was still a long way from being sufficiently trained and disciplined to justify its entry into the line. One Sunday morning at this time, M. Clemenceau appeared at our Headquarters, and said that he had been to Chaumont to see General Pershing, but had found him absent and so had come to see General Sibert. Clemenceau was not then Premier, but I imagine he was preparing for his approaching responsibilities.[3] One of the battalions of the Twenty-sixth Infantry was having a Field Day, and we took him there to get a look at our men under the most favorable circumstances. He was much pleased over the various competitions, particularly those between the machine-gun crews, but it was not until he was literally spattered with blood in his ringside seat during a particularly vicious boxing match that he registered enthusiastic appreciation of the American soldier. His great object at this time was to brace up the French morale and regenerate the offensive spirit, so the rugged fighting qualities displayed by our men were to him pleasing indications of our prospective power on the battlefield.

M. Clemenceau left that evening for another visit to Chaumont, but, as we learned later, he failed again to find General Pershing, who was absent on some inspection trip. The following day, about September 2nd, as I recall, he returned to Gondrecourt, this time accompanied by General de Castelnau, and the latter's Chief of Staff.[4]

General Sibert received the party in his small office and I was the only other person present. M. Clemenceau made a short talk about the importance of the early entry into the line of American troops, and said that General de Castelnau would outline the arrangements he proposed to accomplish this. The latter then described a sector of the line northeast of Lunéville, a very quiet front, where he considered the opportunities for first experience in the trenches were unusually good. He explained how our troops would be brigaded with French troops and given every opportunity to secure actual front-line experience under the careful guidance of veterans and with a minimum of risk. He asked General Sibert if the manner proposed for obtaining this first experience seemed satisfactory to him, and the latter replied that it appeared satisfactory. Then General de Castelnau remarked that he would return to the Headquarters of the Group of Armies of the East, at Mirecourt, and give the necessary instructions to arrange for our entry into the line about September 12th. This was "a facer." General Sibert immediately explained that he was not empowered to make any such arrangement; that such decisions rested entirely with General Pershing.

Up to this moment everything had gone smoothly, though I thought I had noticed a very strained expression on General de Castelnau's face. Now, however, Clemenceau rose from his chair and walking back and forth in the little room, made an impassioned statement in English regarding the seriousness of the situation and the absolute necessity of the immediate appearance of American troops in the trenches. General Sibert had explained the status of the division as regards recruits and officers, and to this subject M. Clemenceau now addressed himself. He said it was not a question of our getting the division in perfect shape before committing it to the line. He said it was a question of losing the war; that the strength of the French soldier was exhausted; that his morale had reached its lowest point; that he had begun to doubt the good faith of the United States, because months had passed and no American troops had ever been seen in the line. He said he had tried to see General Pershing and had not found him and the matter was so vital that he had come to General Sibert direct, because the Americans must enter the battle and make some sacrifice to prove to the French soldiers that they meant business and were there to fight to a finish.

The situation was very embarrassing to General Sibert, and he tactfully replied that he thoroughly understood the feelings of M. Clemenceau, but that he was without power to take any action. Furthermore, however critical the existing condition of affairs, he thought M. Clemenceau and General de Castelnau would understand that for the Americans to commit their first organization to the line before it had had sufficient training to meet the enemy on equal terms would be taking a very grave risk, the unfortunate results of which would react as heavily against the French and English as against ourselves. He called attention to the fact that the world assumed that the First Division represented the pick of the Regular Army, when, as a matter of truth, it was an entirely new organization and its ranks were filled with recruits. For the reputed pick of our Regular Army, on its first appearance in the line, to suffer a serious or possibly an ignominious reverse would have a calamitous effect on the morale of the American soldier and on the Allies as well.

M. Clemenceau and General de Castelnau left immediately after the interview and General Sibert remarked to me that, while the plans of GHQ for our entry into the line set the date several months ahead, he felt sure that M. Clemenceau would bring sufficient pressure to bear to send us to the front in a very short time. We did not move on September 12th, but we did enter the sector northeast of Lunéville on October 20th.

I have given a rather lengthy description of the foregoing interview because it illustrates the great difficulties under which General Pershing was then operating, and the tremendous pressure which was being exerted to force premature action on his part.

This is the first mention I have made of General de Castelnau, a little, heavy-set man, and a splendid type of the old Royalist. He commanded the Group of Armies of the East, and Gondrecourt lay within the zone under his control. When we first arrived, he called to greet the division and was entertained at lunch. General Sibert had organized a new mess and General de Poudrygain had furnished him a French cook, as the First Division seemed devoid of any talent of this nature. The waiters, however, were American. One of them apparently sampled the champagne to a considerable extent during the luncheon to General de Castelnau, with the result that the waiter spilled a large dish of creamed fish sauce on the General's shoulder and down the front of his blouse, more or less completely obliterating his decorations. We were all appalled, but de Castelnau never faltered in his conversation and completely ignored the catastrophe. I believe General Sibert wiped him off, while one of the Aides pursued the waiter into the street via the kitchen.

Training was now conducted with increased zeal, if that was possible, and we exerted every effort to obtain the full complement of horses, trucks, rolling kitchens, etc., that we then lacked. The overseas cap had not yet been adopted, and our men were alternating between a campaign hat and a steel helmet. This was not a practicable combination for the trenches since neither one could be folded up, so General Sibert had some model kepis made of olive drab material and from these selected one which our Division Quartermaster had manufactured near Nancy. This was the first appearance of the overseas cap in the American Army, and while not exactly of the type finally adopted, it was sufficiently like it to be worn.

The cold raw days of the French fall now descended upon us and made the training in trench warfare particularly difficult, as the practice trenches filled with water, and few of our men had more than one pair of shoes. We were suffering at this time from a lack of many necessary articles of clothing. The serious deficiency in socks was finally met by a large purchase near Nancy, but the shortage in shoes could not be overcome in this way. The damp French climate and the continuous exposure caused the men's feet to swell, which necessitated their wearing a larger-sized shoe than would have been required in the United States. The sizes of the shoes shipped to France were based on the Quartermaster tables determined from long experience in the United States, with the result that the larger sizes were quickly exhausted and we had an excess of the small. I saw men with their feet wrapped in gunnysacks making long marches and going through maneuvers, in the mud and snow.

In September I was called to GHQ at Chaumont, and my opinion asked regarding the schedule of training which had just been prepared. On this trip Colonel Alvord invited me to lunch at General Pershing's château, though the Commander-in-Chief was absent at the time. I visited Chaumont on one or two other occasions, in company with General Sibert, and usually stayed with Frank McCoy, who had a delightful mess with Colonel de Chambrun, some other French officer, Colonel Logan, and Captain Eustis.

During the early part of October we suddenly received an intimation that we would go into the line northeast of Lunéville about the 20th, and I was ordered to proceed, with two officers from Chaumont, to General de Castelnau's Headquarters at Mirecourt, to make the preliminary arrangements. Colonel Malone and Colonel Drum were the representatives from GHQ, and we motored east from Neufchâteau to Mirecourt, which lies in the plain just west of the Vosges Mountains.[5] De Castelnau received us in his red breeches and blue blouse, and the resulting conference was very interesting. I was intent on securing arrangements most convenient to the division, while the two officers from GHQ were intent on establishing a precedent with the French for the training of American troops in French sectors. It much resembled a game of poker, and my own position was a very difficult one because some of the ideas of GHQ seemed undesirable to us in the division.

It was finally arranged that one infantry battalion and one artillery battalion of each regiment would enter the line at a time, each serving a tour of ten days. The other battalions would be carried to the front in the same trucks which were to return the battalions completing their tour. Our battalions were to be directly under the control of the several French regimental commanders, and all under the direction of General Bordeaux, commanding the Eighteenth French Division, which was to precede us into the line. Our regimental commanders were not to be permitted any part, other than that of observers, for a period of ten days. Division Headquarters would remain at Gondrecourt, and would only send a representative to the sector.

Upon the completion of this interview we returned to our respective stations to await the decision of General Pershing. In due time orders were received for Colonel Hanson Ely, the then Chief of Staff of the First Division, and myself, to make a preliminary reconnaissance of the sector in company with Colonel Malone and Colonel Drum from GHQ.[6] We met them on a cold, frosty morning at Colombey-les-Belles and motored on through Port St. Vincent and Dombasle to Sommervillers, the Headquarters of the Eighteenth French Division. After a conference with General Bordeaux, we motored out to the front, dividing in two parties, Colonel Malone and myself taking the left of the line. The sky was clear and there was not the sound of a gun. We walked through miles of trenches and saw few soldiers.

Two little hills, connected by a low saddle, lay just within No-man's-land near Aricourt, and were called Les Jumelles. In a tunnel under the saddle we had lunch with the French commander, and afterwards walked down the rear slope of the saddle, where Malone became interested in something on the ground nearby. I walked on a few steps and looking back saw he was still tarrying. Noticing that he was standing in a group of two or three fresh shell holes, almost the only ones we had seen that morning, I called his attention to this and remarked that he was located at about the only point of the front at which the Boche appeared to fire. He then for the first time observed the shell holes, and at once moved on, but we had hardly progressed seventy-five yards before the first enemy shell we had heard that day — and I believe Malone's first hostile shot in the World War —

sailed over Les Jumelles and landed with a crash in the spot just vacated by him.

The infantry battalions selected for the initial entry into the line embussed in the Gondrecourt area on October 20th, and were transported straight through to the sector. The artillery had been in training at Valdahon, about two hundred miles south of us, and the batteries had to be transported to Sommervillers by rail.

The enthusiasm of the infantrymen reached its highest point when the automobile buses moved off at the commencement of the final stage of their long journey from America to the front. The men presented a curious spectacle. The overseas caps had not yet been received and the stiff-brimmed campaign hat was out of the question; consequently, each soldier had met the situation as best suited his fancy. Many had purchased olive drab kepis of the Belgian type, with a gold tassel hanging from the front tip; a large number had cut off the brim of the campaign hat and wore the close-fitting skull piece; a few had fashioned for themselves headgear from bath towels; and some wore the dark blue Alpine caps, evidently procured from their Chasseur friends. Aware of the reason for this array, we were all much amused, but the staff officers from GHQ were scandalized and registered a very poor opinion of the division.

The Einville sector, as it was called, extended southeast through Aricourt to the Rhine-Marne Canal. It had been the scene of heavy fighting in August 1914, when de Castelnau successfully stopped the advance of Prince Ruprecht's army across the Grande Couronne de Nancy. Many of the villages were destroyed at that time but it was not the scene of any activity thereafter. As a matter of fact, it was so quiet a front that at one point where a small village lay partly within the German's lines on the edge of No-man's -land, the inhabitants, including little children, could be observed going to church on Sunday mornings.

Our battalions were distributed among the French regiments and during the first forty-eight hours in the line remained under the control of the French Major whose battalion they had relieved. General Bordeaux issued a number of special instructions governing the control of the American troops, and among these was a prohibition against any American patrol going beyond their own wire. This meant that the German patrols would have the freedom of No-man's-land at night, while our men must confine their activities to their own lines.

One officer from First Division Headquarters was on duty at the front and General Bordeaux was concerned to see that this officer gave no instructions to our troops. I was sent from Division Headquarters with the second lot of battalions going in, and was received by General Bordeaux in his mess and given a billet in Sommervillers. The wide front over which the troops were distributed and the distance one was compelled to travel on foot to reach the front made my task of keeping in touch with the battalions a very onerous one. Starting at daylight I would generally be occupied until late in the afternoon tramping from one center of resistance to another.

My first inspection revealed an unfortunate mix-up which had a rather interesting explanation. I found that insufficient trucks had been provided for the infantry to carry machine guns, certain other equipment, and the full ration prescribed. These had, therefore, been left in the Gondrecourt area to be sent forward by other transportation. When the infantry which had just completed its tour in the line came to embuss, the same shortage was found, and equipment and rations, with details to guard them, were left at a number of points in the sector.

The first movement of our troops into the line had been carried through with such smoothness that no difficulty was anticipated when arrangements were made for sending forward the relieving battalions. The order for this relief had been prepared by a staff officer of General Bordeaux's and then had been revamped by him to meet the changes I proposed. This occurred in Gondrecourt, two days before the relief. After the French officer had returned to the front he telephoned me that Colonel Frank Wilcox, of the Sixteenth Infantry, then on his tour of observation in the trenches, had requested that a baggage truck be furnished his Regimental Headquarters detachment for the return trip.[7] I reminded this staff officer that we had just arranged for an additional truck for this purpose in the instructions for the relief and that no change in the instructions was necessary. As my French was rather doubtful, I called on Captain

Seligman, tour Liaison Officer, to confirm, my statement. Seligman chattered into the telephone for a few minutes and then turned to me and said, "It is understood then that 'en principe' no truck for baggage will be furnished." This was my first meeting with that mysterious expression "en principe," whose dark and devious meanings stood revealed only to a native-born Frenchman. Fearlessly I replied, "Yes," and, all unknowingly, eliminated not one truck "en Wilcox," but thirty-two trucks "en principe" from the train the French were furnishing us.

The lesson learned was invaluable to me in my later dealings with our Allies. From that time on I undertook to learn the delicate shades of meaning in French military terminology. Many times thereafter a French staff officer would employ the phrase "en principe," and I always brought him to a prompt halt and requested that he commit to writing whatever he had to say.

CHAPTER IV

The First Raid and
the Final Training

THE FIRST THRILL of service in the trenches soon passed with a realization of the mud and other discomforts and the dearth of excitement. The Einville sector was not a cheerful or a busy front. Serious operations in this section of France were not contemplated by either side. The garrison was small and the companies were scattered in widely separated points called "centers of resistance," connected only by deep bands of barbwire. The artillery on both sides contented itself with a few ranging shots each day and these were so directed as to avoid causing casualties. The enthusiastic activity of the newly arrived American artillery tended to break the calm and stirred the enemy to retaliatory measures.

At dawn on the morning of November 3rd, I left my billet to visit a particular center of resistance occupied by the Second Battalion of the Sixteenth Infantry. My automobile was waiting in front of the French Division Headquarters and as I entered the car General Bordeaux hurried out of his office and called to me, "Les premiers Américains ont été tués." (The first Americans have been killed.) He inquired as to my destination and told me that there was where the casualties had occurred.

The General then asked me to wait a moment in order that he might accompany me. Securing his overcoat he got in my car, and at his request we drove first to the Infantry Brigade Headquarters. There we learned that at about four o'clock in the morning an intense German artillery fire had been directed on the center of resistance previously referred to, which had caused the death of three Americans and had wounded twelve or more others. No one then knew the object of this heavy fire and no report had been received indicating a raid. While we were learning these details the wireless operator at the Infantry Brigade Headquarters intercepted the daily wireless communiqué sent out by the German government. In this was the statement that fourteen North Americans had been captured in a well-executed raid north of the Rhine-Marne Canal.

General Bordeaux was much excited, as this was the first direct intimation of a raid, and we hurried on to Regimental Headquarters. The Colonel commanding told us that several Americans were reported missing, but that it had been thought they had merely lost their way during the relief, as they had first entered the trenches that night, and might easily have become confused.

We pushed on from Regimental Headquarters and soon had to leave our automobile and walk forward across country and through the communicating trenches. On our arrival at the Headquarters of the American Battalion Commander, we found that fourteen men were unaccounted for, but that it was still believed these men might have lost themselves during the relief, as the night had been dark and rainy. General Bordeaux and myself, accompanied by Lieutenant Jean Hugo, pushed on forward to ascertain for ourselves the real facts in the case. Most of the communicating trenches had been caved in by the heavy and accurate artillery fire, and we were frequently forced to expose ourselves. When we reached the position of Company F, Sixteenth Infantry, in which the casualties had occurred, we located the company commander. He believed that a raid had taken place, but had not himself seen any Germans. A few minutes later we encountered a French Liaison Lieutenant who had found a German helmet in one of our trenches. This seemed proof positive that the enemy had penetrated the position and that the missing men were probably prisoners.

As we worked our way forward we encountered more and more difficulty in getting through the trenches, as they had been pretty well demolished during the brief bombardment. In crawling over a blocked portion of the front-line trench we were fully exposed to view from the German lines, and at the same time had an unobstructed view of the ground in our front. There, in our wire entanglements, we saw a gap about three feet wide, which had evidently been blown by a long torpedo charge, as a shallow furrow extended through the gap. Close by lay an unexploded Bangalore torpedo, and leading away from the gap across No-man's-land to the German lines was a white tape staked out about a foot above the ground.

Here was conclusive evidence of a German raid, and, in a dugout a short distance beyond, we found the bloody traces of a fight. The missing men had all been stationed in this particular section of trench.

Another breach was located on the other side of the angle made by this first-line trench, and there were other traces of fighting. The bodies of the first three Americans who fell in the war — Corporal Gresham, Private Enright, and Private Hay — were just being removed from the ground where they had fallen. One of the three had had his throat cut, and this was seized upon by some as an evidence of German brutality.

During our walk forward General Bordeaux had asked me many questions concerning the reasons for our entry into the war, and the feelings of our men on the subject. In our various contacts with those connected with the raid, he had asked a great deal regarding the fighting that took place. It was very hard to get at the real facts, as the men who — as it afterwards developed — had seen most of the affair, had been evacuated with wounds, or were sleeping, exhausted, in their dugouts. For some time I could not understand exactly what was in the General's mind, until finally I became convinced that he feared our men had not made a sufficiently determined resistance. All the while I had been deeply concerned over the events of the night because of the prohibition against American patrols going beyond their own wire. This made the men feel that they could not protect themselves, and our officers especially were out of sympathy with this order.

I told General Bordeaux that he need entertain no fears with regard to the fighting of our men; that we might worry over their lack of technical skill, but that there could be no question regarding their individual bravery. Seizing the opportunity, I dwelt on the order which restricted our patrolling, and I hazarded the opinion that General Pershing would be much concerned when he learned of this phase of the matter.

I was not able to ascertain whether or not General Bordeaux took me very seriously, but it was apparent he did not like the trend of the conversation, and was distinctly worried over my intimation regarding General Pershing. When he started back I expressed a desire to remain and examine more carefully into the situation. The General thought I had better go back with him, but I succeeded in remaining without giving offense.

On the following afternoon the three American dead were buried near the little village of Bathelemont. As I was the only American officer present, excepting a Lieutenant in command of one of our companies, I made a written report on November 5th, 1917, to the Commanding General of the First Division describing the ceremony. I have recently located the original copy of this report in the archives of the War Department, and deem it of sufficient interest to quote it at this time:

> By command of General Bordeaux, 18th French Division, the bodies of Corporal Gresham, Private Enright and Private Hay, Company "F", 16th Infantry, were interred with religious and military ceremony at Bathelemont on the afternoon of November 4th.
>
> An altar was improvised and elaborately decorated in the village, and the chaplain of a French regiment conducted the church services in the presence of the following detachments of troops:
> One company of French Infantry,
> One section of French Artillery,
> One section of French Engineers,
> One detachment of French sailors,
> One company of the 16th Infantry,
> One section of the 1st Battalion, 5th Field Artillery,
> One squad of Company "D", 1st Regiment of Engineers.
> A Major of French Artillery commanded the troops.
>
> Following the church ceremony the cortege proceeded to a field adjacent to the village and formed on three sides of a square, the bodies being placed in front of the graves on the fourth side. An American flag, provided by the French, had been placed over the caskets.
>
> At two o'clock General Bordeaux, accompanied by his full staff, his

Infantry, Artillery and Engineer Chiefs and a representative of the French Corps Commander, arrived and took position with the troops.

The troops presented arms and the French field music and band played a funeral march. The chaplain performed the religious ceremony at the graves. Then General Bordeaux advanced to the center of the square and addressed the troops and then the dead. A copy of his address is attached hereto.

The Company of the 16th Infantry fired three volleys and its trumpeter sounded taps. All the troops were then marched by the graves, saluting as they passed. General Bordeaux and his staff advanced to the graves, saluted and departed.

Throughout the ceremony at the graves French batteries, from their positions, fired minute guns over the village at the German trenches.

The entire ceremony was one of the most impressive I have ever witnessed and made a profound impression on all who were present.

Later in the day I called formally on General Bordeaux and told him that if you had been present I knew you would have expressed to him your appreciation of the honor he had paid to our first dead, and that your Division, the entire American Army, and the American people would always feel grateful for his action.

General Bordeaux's remarks at the graves of these three Americans were an eloquent tribute to their services. Immediately after the ceremony I requested him to write what he had said, which he did in a nearby shelter. Lieutenant Hugo assisted me in its translation, and I have always been glad that it occurred to me at the time to make of record this historic address. I will not quote the entire speech, but it seems appropriate to repeat here the last paragraphs:

"Men! These graves, the first to be dug in our national soil, at but a short distance from the enemy, are as a mark of the mighty hand of our Allies, firmly clinging to the common task, confirming the will of the people and Army of the United States to fight with us to a finish; ready to sacrifice as long as it will be necessary, until final victory for the noblest of causes; that of the liberty of nations, of the weak as well as the mighty.

Thus the death of this humble Corporal and of these two Private soldiers appears to us with extraordinary grandeur.

We will, therefore, ask that the mortal remains of these young men be left here, be left to us forever. We will inscribe on their tombs: "Here lie the first soldiers of the famous Republic of the United States to fall on the soil of France, for justice and liberty." The passerby will stop and uncover his head. The travelers of France, of the Allied countries, of America, the men of heart, who will come to visit our battlefield of Lorraine, will go out of the way to come here, to bring to these graves the tribute of their respect and of their gratefulness.

Corporal Gresham, Private Enright, Private Hay, in the name of France, I thank you. God receive your souls. Farewell!

During the next twenty-four hours I was actively engaged in informing the other American units scattered over our extended front, of what had occurred and what lessons might be drawn from it. I reported the known details of the raid to General Sibert, and thereafter occupied myself with the duties of the day and plans for the future. But the incident was not to be so quickly dropped. A Board of Officers from General Headquarters was convened to examine into all the circumstances connected with this raid, and to make recommendations which would tend to avoid future losses of prisoners in such encounters. I mention this as an evidence of the close watch which was kept on everything concerning the First Division during these early days of the war. Like the only child, we suffered from too much attention, and found ourselves often irritated by the frequent visits of investigators, inspectors, and others from the higher command. This was in decided contrast to the later period of the war, and I have often thought of the urgent demands which were made on us from GHQ for immediate detailed reports about the smallest incidents, in contrast to the absence of such persistent pressure later on regarding large affairs, such as the incident of the famous so-called "Lost Battalion" of the Seventy-seventh Division in the Argonne Forest.

The leader of this German raid on our men was a Reserve officer who had been a schoolteacher in Alsace. He had made his plans for this particular operation many months beforehand, and it was purely a matter of good luck that he happened to be ordered to carry it out when the first American troops were in the line. It was the irony of fate that we captured this officer in the first day's fighting at St. Mihiel. Naturally our people were intensely anxious to retaliate, but the French higher command was opposed to any serious venture on our part. When Major Theodore Roosevelt had his battalion in the line at Les Jumelles, he bored a little from within and finally succeeded in securing the acquiescence of General Bordeaux to carry out an "embuscade," as they termed it. The French were always very partial to Roosevelt, because of their admiration for his father, and he was not slow to take advantage of the opportunities presented by their attitude, particularly when they might lead to adventurous fighting. In this instance his battalion was relieved from duty and returned to the Gondrecourt area before there was an opportunity to rehearse and carry out the operation, so it became necessary to secure the authority of General Sibert for the return to the line of a detachment of Roosevelt's battalion.

Major Roosevelt appealed to me to help him in this matter, and arrangements were finally made to go ahead with the enterprise. One morning I motored up to the village where his battalion was located, taking with me a French officer who was to assist in the rehearsals. I informed Roosevelt that the proposition had been approved and gave him the details of the plan. His enthusiasm knew no bounds and he embraced the French Lieutenant and proclaimed his complete satis-faction with the Army, the war, and the world in general. I did not explain then that General Sibert had given me instructions to see that Roosevelt did not personally participate in the affair, as the size of the detachment made it a suitable command for a Sergeant or a Lieuten-ant, and as Archie Roosevelt had been selected for this duty, the General did not think it wise to project two of the name into the first affair.[1]

The rehearsals were undertaken at once and everything proceeded with complete accord, almost an affectionate understanding, between the Roosevelts and the Frenchman, which presented an amusing con-trast to later developments. When the fateful night arrived, young Archie Roosevelt with his ally and a small detachment of men, stole out into No-man's-land, marking their route with a white tape, and surrounded an old building which the German patrols were known to visit regularly. There was some difference of opinion between Archie and the Frenchman on the way out. As I recall, for a time the patrol was lost and the latter officer thought it best to return to our lines. One thing led to another, until the debate in the dark became quite acrimonious, and Archie ordered the Frenchman back. In the meantime, a member of the patrol became separated from the others, and while no Germans were ever encountered, the detachment had the excitement of shooting up this missing member, when he attempted to rejoin them. This was the first American raid in the World War, and what Theodore said to me at this time about the French will not bear repeating.

After ten days at the front, I returned to Gondrecourt. All of our troops had completed their tour of trench duty by the latter part of November, and we then started upon the last phase of our training program. This was the gloomy and depressing period previously referred to as the Winter of Valley Forge. The rainfall was unusually heavy and the ground became soaked like a wet sponge; the streets of the little villages had few sidewalks, and the men usually ate their meals out in the open. Many had only one pair of shoes and, as I have already mentioned, some of them did not even have one pair. When we were not cursed with mud, we were frozen with the cold. All will remember the extreme severity of this particular winter.

The division was required to go through a series of open-warfare maneuvers, which necessitated the men's bivouacking at night. We lacked the transportation to shorten their marches and to carry them additional comforts such as firewood and extra blankets. The ground was frequently deep in snow and a chill wind seemed to blow continuously down the valley in which the division was located. The days were short and the nights long. It grew dark at four o'clock in the afternoon, and there were few places in which the men could assemble and be cheered by a warm fire and a bright light.

The officers labored to reduce the discomforts and hardships of their men, but many of them lacked the experience which is necessary to overcome such great difficulties. A number of the officers became much depressed as a result of the winter gloom and cold and because of the disheartening news which circulated regarding the progress of the war. A brief British victory at Cambrai had been turned into a great German success by a violent counterattack; Russia had dissolved, releasing the German divisions on that front for service in France; the Italians had suffered a tremendous defeat at Caporetto which had resulted in a rapid retreat to the Piave and the dispatch of

French and English divisions to Italy. Our old friends, the Chasseurs, were among the divisions selected for this new field of operations.

As an indirect result of this sudden troop movement through the south of France and along the Riviera into Italy, the supply of forage for the animals of the First Division was for a time completely cut off. The American Expeditionary Forces did not have enough forage in France, but even that which it did have lay at the base ports through lack of railroad rolling stock. The horses and mules in the First Division chewed up the woodwork of their stalls, ate their leather-and-rope halter straps, and on one maneuver so many dropped dead that the exercise had to be terminated. I believe seventeen animals in one regiment died from exhaustion on that day.

The country was covered with snow and ice, and I recall receiving word one night that a battalion of artillery in a little village nearby was without forage for their animals and without rations for the men. The horses were too weak to be moved and the division did not then possess transportation which could be utilized to haul rations to the men of this unit. The question to be decided was whether the animals would be left to starve while the men were marched to some point where there were rations, or was there any way we could devise to transport the necessary food. Unfortunately, I do not remember just what was done, but I have a distinct recollection of the dilemma in which we found ourselves at Division Headquarters regarding this incident.

During the latter part of December and the first half of January, we carried through a series of divisional maneuvers in trench warfare tactics. The suffering of the men at this time exceeded any previous or subsequent experience. They frequently stood up to their knees in mud, snow, and ice water for hours at a time, while the large elements of the command were being maneuvered into position.

They were also subjected to many experiments in training to prepare them for sudden enemy attacks with cloud gas. Tubes containing this gas were hidden in the snow and at a specified time would be suddenly opened to permit a wave of gas to blow down on the troops in the training trenches. To simulate the effects of gas shelling, details of Engineer troops would visit different portions of the assumed position and would unexpectedly break gas bombs in the vicinity of the troops. On one occasion a company of men had been posted as a reserve in a quarry. They had been standing for several hours over their shoe-tops in melting snow; no complaints were made; officers and men alike were stoical. Suddenly an Engineer soldier appeared and without warning threw several gas bombs in their vicinity. This was the last straw. They jumped on him and beat him up rather badly and for a brief period their officers did not intervene.

During the early part of the winter General Sibert was ordered to the United States, and General Robert L. Bullard assumed command of the division. General Bullard had commanded the Second Brigade of the division when it sailed from New York, but on his arrival in France had been placed on special duty organizing schools. Many other changes in officer personnel occurred during this time. A few days after our relief from duty in the trenches, practically every field officer in the infantry was ordered to school or some detached duty. Just before Christmas, General Summerall reported to the division and took command of the Artillery Brigade.[2] Earlier in the fall, Colonel John L. Hines arrived to command the Sixteenth Infantry.[3] Colonel Frank Parker, who had been on duty at Marshal Pétain's Headquarters, came to command the Eighteenth Infantry.[4] Colonel Hanson Ely was transferred from duty as Chief of Staff of the division, to command of the Twenty-eighth Infantry. Hamilton A. Smith, who had originally been Division Inspector, and later served at GHQ, now headed the Twenty-sixth Infantry.

The careers of the men just mentioned are very interesting in the light of their first assignments in the war. General Bullard later commanded an army corps and finally the Second Army. General Summerall was to lead the First Division in its greatest battles, and to command the Fifth Army Corps in the center of the Meuse-Argonne. Hines advanced from a regiment to a brigade, and then left us to command the Fourth Division. He finished the war as chief of the Third Army Corps on the right of the Meuse-Argonne field, and led his corps across the Rhine into position on the American Bridgehead. Colonel Ely was to capture Cantigny with his regiment, and then he advanced to the command of a brigade in the Second Division at

Soissons, and to fight with it until promoted in the midst of the Meuse-Argonne battle to the leadership of the Fifth Division. Colonel Parker followed General Hines in the command of the First Brigade, and was the chief of the First Division in its last advance before the Armistice. Poor Smith did not reap the reward of his splendid services, but fell in command of his regiment on the field of Soissons, at the turning point in the war.

Christmas in 1917 was a unique experience for those in our division. A large amount of money, about 40,000 francs I believe, was raised by the officers and men to decorate Christmas trees and purchase presents for all the children in the Divisional Area. There were many who were refugees from the provinces occupied by the Germans, and for each of these a complete outfit of clothing was procured. Christmas night in every little town the entire French population assembled to witness their first Christmas tree, and the children to receive their gifts. A deep, dry snow lay on the ground and decorated the trees. There was a full moon, and for a time one forgot the discomforts and tragedies of war in the emotional inspiration of the moment.

In my little mess, Madame Jouatte gave us a wonderful Christmas dinner. She roasted a large turkey and stuffed it with chestnuts and certain other things which she would not divulge. Accompanying the turkey and following it were all those dishes and delicacies we are accustomed to enjoy at Christmastime in America. She had for the moment completely shed her fixed resolve to do nothing which was not done in France, and she made for us an evening not soon to be forgotten. Young Hugo, Colonel Conrad Babcock, Colonel Voris, and myself were the permanent members of the mess, and I invited Campbell King and an interpreter, "Tony" Montgomery, to join with us in the feast.[5] An old piano, much out of tune, was brought into the dining room and a soldier furnished us with appropriate music.

The fun which developed was so in contrast with the gloom of the previous days and weeks that it rather went to our heads and we each insisted on dancing a few circles around the table with the excited Madame Jouatte. Colonel Babcock, in an excess of zeal, was doing a ballet step by himself, and in kicking unexpectedly to the side, he tapped the little toothless "femme de ménage," Marie, under the chin and she sat down screaming on the floor. Tony Montgomery lifted her to her feet and executed an artistic galloping dance step around the room, to the great delight of everybody, particularly of Marie.

These happenings seem very trivial and uninteresting today, but they were decided highlights in our life during the gloomy winter of 1917.

CHAPTER V

The Toul Sector

SHORTLY AFTER New Year's, General Bullard was informed that we were to enter the line as a division, about the middle of the month. Both officers and men were so worn down by the rigors of the winter and the strenuosity of the training program that this news did not cause much excitement. Everyone was relieved that the period of training was at an end, but all felt that we were not going to a very active sector. We were to march to the front under the direction of General Monroe of the Sixty-ninth French Division. His organization was to enter the line on the right of the sector selected for the First Division, and he was to control our destinies during the first few weeks. As this was to be the first appearance on the front of a complete American division, everybody took a hand and at no other period during the war did I personally experience so many changes in orders as occurred at this time.

Campbell King was Chief of Staff of the division, and I was the G-3. My duty was to prepare the orders and directions having to do with the operations of the division. In this instance, I wrote into the first paragraph of the order directing our march to the front, a statement of our status. I feared that General Bullard would change this, but he accepted it, and so it stands today. That the reader may understand the complications under which we labored, I quote here the paragraph referred to:

1. In conformance with the instructions of the 1st French Army, the Moroccan Division and the 69th French Division, the troops of this Division enumerated below will relieve the corresponding units of the Moroccan Division in the ANSAUVILLE subsector:

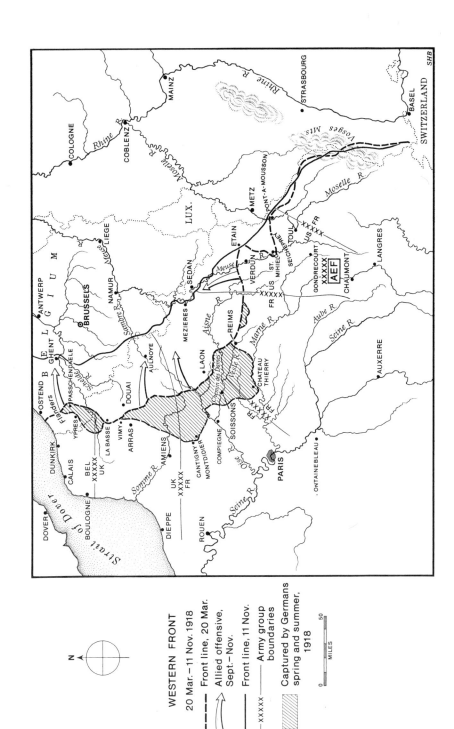

WESTERN FRONT
20 Mar.–11 Nov. 1918

- - - Front line, 20 Mar.

⇨ Allied offensive,
Sept.–Nov.

——— Front line, 11 Nov.

xxxxx ——— Army group
boundaries

///// Captured by Germans
spring and summer,
1918

0   50
MILES

SHB

The foregoing makes no reference to the orders from the American General Headquarters, but these were not lacking.

The Ansauville subsector lay due north of Toul, midway between St. Mihiel and the Moselle River. It was about forty kilometers north of Gondrecourt. There not being available any automobile buses at this time, the division moved to the front by marching, and the general control of these marches was lodged with the commander of the Sixty-ninth French Division. His staff officers furnished me the data as to the routes and villages to be utilized by the American troops, as the basis for our orders. No sooner had the latter been issued than word was received of a number of changes. As fast as these alterations were announced, new ones were received. This continued throughout the march, which extended over a period of five days.

The first movement was scheduled for January 14th, and the day set was preceded by a terrific blizzard. The troops and trains moved out shortly after sunrise and started their march on roads heavily glazed with smooth ice. A cold wind blew down from the north, penetrating the thickest clothing. Fortunately, we had arranged for very short marches on the first day, but even so some of the columns were barely able to reach their destination, and many of the wagon trains failed to join their units that night. Though rough-shod, the mules could not get a footing on the ice, and we passed team after team standing along the road trembling, refusing to respond to the urging of the drivers. The escort wagons would start sliding on the gentle slope from the crown of the road and would frequently overturn in the ditch, where they had to be unloaded and carried back on the highway by hand.

The troops themselves suffered from the bitter cold and were exhausted by their efforts to make progress against the strong head wind along the slippery surface of the highway. I saw a company of Engineers march over the crest of a steep hill and slide pell-mell to the bottom — most of the men, overbalanced by their heavy packs, rolling into the ditches alongside of the road. Instead of reaching their destination in the early afternoon, most of the units did not arrive until long after dark.

During the first night the temperature rose and a heavy thaw set in, which caused the Meuse River to overflow its banks and flood the low country south of Commercy. The regiments which were routed through this region were compelled to march nearly a mile through water from one to two feet deep. It was very difficult to keep to the road and some of the men unknowingly stepped off of the highway and went down in the water up to their necks. When they reached their crowded billets that night they were without fires and had to sleep in wet clothing. Though all were exhausted and miserable, I do not recall hearing a murmur of complaint.

At one stage of the march on this day I found that the road had been rendered impassable by the flood, and hastened back to indicate a detour for the Sixteenth Infantry, around the dangerous stretch. I found General Hines, then Colonel of the Sixteenth, traveling through the mud in a motorcycle sidecar, just north of Void. We arranged for the change in routing, and while we were talking a young officer, a relative of mine whom I had not seen for eleven years, waded up the road and greeted me. Too engrossed with the difficulties of the moment, I barely spoke to him and did not have another opportunity to see him until months later during the fighting at Cantigny. This next meeting was under even more unfavorable circumstances, and while it had its amusing side, it was unfortunately connected with his becoming a casualty. I mention this little incident as an indication of the highly impersonal status which existed in our Army during active operations in France. It was all a terrible business, and those engaged had little opportunity to give time to personal matters.

On the 18th, the leading battalions entered the sector and began the relief of the organizations of the French Moroccan Division. This was the same division I had accompanied in the fighting at Verdun the previous August. The men were of the rough soldier-of-fortune type and greeted our fellows with the casual tolerance of war-worn veterans. They helped us wherever they could, but lost no opportunity to jolly our men with the pleasant prospect of service in dilapidated trenches and dugouts, usually filled with water and mud. The companies of the Moroccan Division were very small as compared with our large units, and we found it exceedingly difficult to provide

adequate shelter. As a matter of fact, tactical considerations frequently had to give way to other questions of expediency. As I will
explain later, the matter of shelter became increasingly difficult with
the inauguration of a radical change in the plan for the defense of this
front.

Division Headquarters was located in Ménil-la-Tour, a small, cheer-
less village, eight kilometers north of Toul. There were few billets in
the town and our staff was quite large. In addition, we were encum-
bered by a number of visitors from GHQ, all of whom had to be
provided with messing and sleeping accommodations. The staff work
during this period was exceedingly difficult, as we were without experience in the administration of a stabilized sector, and the plan of
defense on this portion of the front was an elaborate and complicated
affair, the growth of several years, during which a succession of divisions had occupied the sector. The work had generally to be carried
on with four or five observers from GHQ standing at one's elbow to
watch how it was being done. This did not tend to quiet the nerves
and promote the assurance of the division staff during their novitiate.
The staff officers of General Monroe, under whose command we
served during the first eighteen days, were ever willing to help — too
willing as a matter of fact. They apparently, and rather naturally, had
little confidence in our ability to meet the new and novel conditions
imposed, and saw things only from the point of view of a Frenchman,
which is quite different from that of an American, particularly as to
methods.

General Bullard assumed command of the Ansauville subsector on
February 5th, and almost the same day we received directions which
completely changed the long-established system of defense. This
change was a result of the capture of certain German documents
which outlined the elaborate course of training which German divisions on the Western Front were then receiving in preparation for an
attempt to launch a great offensive and carry the fighting out into the
open. To meet this menace, which was termed a "Maneuver of Rupture," we were to organize our troops in depth, that is, to thin out the
front line and dispose the troops in a series of successive echelons.
The German plan contemplated the secret concentration of a large

mass of troops by a succession of night marches, the last march to carry the attacking divisions into their assault positions on the night before the attempt to break through. Large numbers of trench mortars or mine throwers were to be concentrated in the forward zone and were to deluge the advance positions of the Allies with their fire just prior to the attack. A short but violent artillery preparation was to precede the assault for the purpose of cutting all wire and other communications, blocking the roads, and demoralizing the garrisons. Large numbers of gas shells of the nonpersistent type were to be fired into certain areas through which the German infantry was later to pass, and gas shells of the persistent type were to be fired into those areas which it was intended to isolate, without directly attacking. Light-horse artillery and portable trench mortars were closely to accompany the shock troops. Battalion and regimental commanders, for the first time in several years, were to be mounted.

The whole plan contemplated a preliminary assault, "short and brutal," which was to overwhelm the forward positions of the defending troops. Points strongly defended were to be isolated by the rapid penetration of the German infantry through the weak points in the line, thus cutting off those who held out. It was calculated that the leading assault divisions would make an advance of twelve kilometers during the first twenty-four hours. Following closely in rear were to be supporting troops, whose mission was to push on and exploit the success by the rapidity of their marches — there was to be no halt for the purpose of consolidating captured positions.

We received this information in February, and on March 21st the enemy successfully launched a tremendous offensive against the left of the British armies, which for a time threatened to bring the war to a sudden conclusion disastrous to the Allies.

During the previous two years of the war, the French and British had always contemplated offensive action and, as a result, their positions were, as a rule, not elaborately organized for defense, as were the enemy's, with concrete pillboxes, Hindenburg Lines, and other more or less permanent fortifications. Most of the shelters or dugouts, for the Allied infantry, were distributed in the advance trenches and there was little shelter for the infantry along what must be the main line of resistance in case of a great defensive action. To organize our position in depth it became necessary to abandon a majority of the existing dugouts, and as it required weeks, and sometimes months, to construct shelters which would be proof against artillery of moderately heavy caliber, we were confronted with the necessity of disposing the infantry of the First Division in positions where there was no shelter to protect the men against the rigors of the winter season, not to mention the destructive fire of the enemy's artillery. To meet this drastic change in plans it became necessary for our worn-down troops to work long hours each day on the preparation of the new positions.

The sector occupied by the division lay in a low, swampy region, completely dominated by a number of high points within the German lines. The most notable of these was the famous Montsec, an isolated hill which rose 150 feet above the plain of the Woëvre, and from which the Germans, in their concrete, underground observation stations, could overlook every movement of their enemies. The swampy nature of the soil made it extremely difficult to drain the trenches, and the Moroccan troops, as is characteristic of shock divisions, paid little attention to measures for improving the defenses. Any increase of circulation or movement on the roads, or in the lines, would inevitably draw increased artillery fire from the enemy, and we found it very hard to restrain our soldiers from passing to and fro along the roads and trails in the sector. Unaccustomed to the habits and arrangements for life in one of these strange underground rabbit-warrens, the officers could not foresee their requirements, which resulted in frequent movements to the front and rear to secure the needed instructions or supplies. As a result, the Germans quickly became aware of a change in the aspect of the sector and their artillery became increasingly active.

It was hard to provide against the possibility of gas shelling. The exits of the dugouts were not so constructed as to protect the inmates against the effect of gas, particularly the new Yperite, or mustard gas. Our men had not yet become so trained as to accurately detect the difference between a gas and an ordinary shell, which resulted in frequent false alarms. Walking back from the front line at dusk one winter evening, I put on my gas mask to train myself to breathe freely while exercising. It was difficult to find one's way, as the windows of the mask quickly became fogged. At the celebrated "Dead man's curve" near Beaumont, I passed a column of escort wagons. One of the teamsters, observing me wearing a mask, emitted a blood-curdling yell; "My God! Gas!" They all snatched at their masks, belabored their teams, and raced tumultuously down the road.

During this period we were visited by most of the Major Generals who had been sent out from the United States to make a brief inspection of conditions in France, preliminary to the final training of their divisions in America. We were thus burdened with the necessity of entertaining them, escorting them about the sector and explaining our organization and plans. This proved a trying task in the midst of efforts to securely establish the division. These officers brought us the first detailed account of what was being done in the United States. The great cantonments, the successive drafts, and the Liberty Loan campaigns — all these had developed since our departure. We learned of new organizations and new officials. In the midst of our labors on the new American front and in the gloom of the winter, we heard tales of instructors in singing and boxing, of psychiatric experts, and of many other strange additions to Army life.

Every specialist and scientist who could obtain authority to visit France seemed to appear at the Headquarters of the First Division, where they argued determinedly for more consideration in favor of their particular activities. The great doctor who was an authority on orthopedic matters desired that we organize special battalions of flat-footed soldiers; the man developing the Violet Ray was anxious that we should employ its weird characteristics to advantage in signaling; the Chemical Warfare men wished to issue canary birds to detect the presence of gas; the soldiers themselves were enthusiastic over the carrier pigeons, because there was always a chance of stealing one for a supper party. So imbued was everyone with the idea that modern warfare was a highly scientific affair that they attempted to inflict on us, en masse, a weird variety of appliances and schemes, many of which were excellent, but which we lacked time to assimilate.

Within the lines we found curious activities connected with the defense of a sector. There were water troops, railroad troops, Annamites engaged in quarrying, special French antiaircraft detachments, heavy guns manned by sailors, guards who watched the bridges and culverts and were prepared to blow them up in case of attack, and many other services which have their counterparts in the general utility organization of a large community.[1]

As this portion of the front had been quiet for a long time, those detailed on these special jobs were very glad to hold them and live quietly in comparative safety. To avoid the possibility of relief and transfer to a more active portion of the line, the men so engaged were not inclined to advertise their duties or their whereabouts. They drew their rations regularly at appointed places, and otherwise were as unobtrusive as possible. As the German artillery fire increased and casualties became more frequent, these men would suddenly appear from some hitherto unknown assignment. One French soldier reported at Division Headquarters and inquired as to when he was to be relieved. It developed that he had been on duty for two years as the guard at a stone dam, which raised the level of the water in the Etang de Vargevaux. His sole duty had been to report any faults in the dam, and to blow it up in the event the enemy infantry penetrated to that vicinity. There was good fishing in the lake and comfortable shelter in an old mill. Shells rarely fell in that vicinity; but recently he had had several narrow escapes, and now appeared for the purpose of securing a transfer.

During the first few weeks our patrols had some small encounters with the Germans. We captured one or two of their men, and they killed several of ours and captured four. When the last incident occurred a newspaper correspondent hurried south to Chaumont with the news that an American patrol had been ambuscaded, several wounded, four killed, and four captured. As the dead lay in No-man's-land and there were no communicating trenches leading up to the front in this section, it was not possible for us to determine until after dark which men had been killed and which captured. The arrival of the press man in Chaumont, however, stirred up the authorities there, and The Adjutant General, by telephone, demanded the names of the dead and of the captured. Campbell King explained over the phone that this information could not be furnished until after dark, and that even then it would require several hours for the patrols to work their way out to the scene of the fight and get back to a point where their report could be telephoned to the rear. This explanation was not accepted as satisfactory, and the order was renewed to obtain the information immediately. King assured them that to carry out this order would inevitably result in additional casualties, and it was only after considerable discussion that a temporary stay of execution was secured. This happening is an illustration of that natural lack of appreciation by staff officers far to the rear, who had never themselves served under the conditions with which we were then confronted. Those concerned at GHQ were exceptionally bright and efficient officers, but all had been plunged into new duties so suddenly and with so little prior experience in major warfare that it was literally impossible for them to fit into their new duties without at some time failing to visualize the true situation. That they accomplished what they did was a wonderful achievement, and the rapidity with which they rose to an understanding of the vast problems of the AEF was nothing short of miraculous. However, the First Division, as the only child, had a heavy burden to bear for many months.

My time during this period was divided between working on the new plans for the dispositions of the troops, and familiarizing myself with the sector by frequent tours of the front. On one of these reconnaissances I was endeavoring to locate the new positions of the important machine guns for the defense of Seicheprey — later to become celebrated by reason of the fight which occurred there between the enemy and the Yankee Division. The location and field of fire of these guns was indicated graphically and rather attractively in colors on a map. I had found all of them except one pair on the slope just in rear of the ruins of the minute village. Under cover of a low fog, I found it possible to walk along the top, rather than be delayed by following the sinuosities of the trenches. Finally I reached the point where the guns were shown to be located and found them properly placed, with a little soldier standing rigid between them, staring out over the parapet. From my position on the bank of the trench immediately in rear of him, I inquired where the other men of the crew were. Without turning his head and in a very strained tone, he replied, "There ain't none." His helmet seemed to rest on his ears; his overcoat sleeves extended beyond his fingertips; and the lower portion of the coat dragged on the ground. He was not a very prepossessing soldier.

I insisted that there must be some other men assigned to duty with the two guns, but he seemed too scared to reply, so I undertook to reassure him by indulging in a few friendly inquiries. He said he had come from "Hammervil" (Hamonville) the previous night. I asked him where he had come from in the United States and he replied, "Camp Lewis." (He was evidently a recent replacement). Having no knowledge of Camp Lewis, I inquired where his home was, and he told me it was in San Francisco. I then wished to know whereabouts in San Francisco, and he said he lived on the corner of Golden Gate and O'Farrell. All the while he had continued to stare to the front and spoke in a jerky, constrained fashion. Thinking I might give a little personal touch to the conversation, I remarked that I had been in San Francisco just before the war and drove by his home each morning in going to my office. I concluded the conversation by inquiring as to what his business was. Still staring over the parapet, and shivering from cold or embarrassment, he replied, "Sir, I am a ladies' dressmaker."

Later on, within a few yards, I located the Corporal and the other men of the crew belonging to these particular machine guns. They were under shelter, as was entirely proper, and the Corporal was much incensed that his representative had denied any knowledge of them. I reported what had happened to General Bullard, as evidence that the formidable array of signs and colors on a map did not necessarily indicate that a highly trained or born soldier was always at hand to carry through the plan in case of emergency.

One afternoon while on a tour along the lines I was sitting with our French Liaison Officer, Captain Seligman, in the shelter of a bush on a hilly slope overlooking our forward trenches. In a desultory fashion the Germans were firing 200-millimeter trench-mortar shells into the Bois de Remières. It was unusual to find trench mortars or mine throwers of such heavy caliber being employed along a quiet portion of the front. Seligman and myself talked this over and I endeavored to learn from his long experience what this might foretell.

At first he would not risk an opinion, but finally expressed the thought that this was possibly registration fire. That is, the Germans were carefully targeting their mortars in order that, at some future time, they might be able to fire suddenly and accurately on certain specified localities. We talked to several of the local commanders and they told us that there had been some fire of the same nature the previous afternoon. The following day Seligman and myself returned to this section of the front and again we observed the falling of a few of these heavy shells.

Confirmed in my belief that Seligman's statement of a possible meaning for this activity was the correct solution, I returned to Division Headquarters and drafted a memorandum of instructions for the troops, which anticipated a possible German assault or raid on the Bois de Remières. In these instructions the infantry commanders were directed to draw back their companies from the forward trenches during the hours of darkness and not to resume their regular positions until after dawn. The artillery was also instructed to prepare a special barrage to cover the front of the Bois (woods). General Bullard accepted these proposed instructions and directed that they be issued. In view of what happened later, I quote below the memorandum referred to: *

At dawn on the morning of March 1 the enemy deluged the Bois de Remières with a fire of trench mortars of the heaviest caliber. The vacated dugouts under the front-line trenches were demolished, the trenches blocked, and all wire communications cut. The American artillery barrage fell promptly and blasted the snow-covered ground in front of our wire. The entire right half of the sector was shelled by 77-mm. and 150-mm. guns. After a brief and violent bombardment the German fire lifted from the forward portion of the Bois de Remières, and two detachments of the enemy, totaling 220 men, rushed the salient of the woods. Included in this force was a section of Flammenwerfer (flame-thrower) troops. These men, with their apparatus strapped on their backs, poured streams of fire in each dugout. Fortunately, our men had been withdrawn from this portion of the

* *Note* [probably by Sergeant who typed manuscript]: Col. Marshall has not been able to get this memo from Gen. Summerall as yet.

position and from their new locations they now gallantly counterattacked, despite heavy casualties from the previous bombardment. The German raiders were surprised by the attack from this unexpected quarter and were badly cut up, their leader was killed, their Flammenwerfers abandoned on the ground, and a few of their number were captured. We lost a few prisoners as a result of one Lieutenant's moving his platoon forward in advance of dawn, and just prior to the assault.

This was the first nearby encounter of American troops with the Germans. Our men fought beautifully and viciously, and covered themselves with glory. The result was apparently tremendously reassuring to the higher French officials. Raids are exceedingly hard to meet. One side is completely prepared with a tremendous preponderance of guns, previously registered, and men specially rehearsed for a precise duty. The opponent is always struck at a weak point and, by the nature of the operation, is to a certain extent surprised. For this reason everyone was particularly pleased that the men had emerged from this initial encounter decidedly the victors.

The following morning, M. Clemenceau, now Premier and Minister for War, accompanied by General Debeney, the commander of the First French Army, arrived at our Headquarters to bestow the Croix de Guerre on those who had particularly distinguished themselves.[2] There was no suitable place in the sector for the ceremony, which of necessity had to be conducted under the cover of woods or in a building. A narrow road in a large forest was selected and a battalion of reserve troops formed in line along this road. Deep ditches and boggy fields prevented any movement off the road, so M. Clemenceau had to leave his car and make the presentations within a few feet of the line of troops. A light snow was falling which added to the picturesqueness of the occasion.

It was difficult to draw the men to be decorated back from the front in time for the ceremony. They arrived covered with mud and other traces of the fighting in which they had won their new honors. One man was missing. After Clemenceau had made the awards and had congratulated the recipients on their splendid and courageous performance, he made his way with difficulty to the running board of his car. As he was stepping inside, a tall, gangling soldier appeared running down the road, waving his arms, and calling, "Wait a minute, I am ————." He was the missing man. The Minister laughed heartily over this dénouement, descended from his car, and pinned the Croix de Guerre on ———— 's breast, shaking his hand and saying, "I am delighted to decorate you. You were late today, but that does not matter, for you were not late yesterday."

Two German raids had now been directed against the front of the First Division and the time had arrived for our men to take the initiative. Accordingly, General Bullard discussed the matter with the Infantry Brigade commander, General Duncan, and it was decided to carry out two raids simultaneously — one in front of Seicheprey by the Eighteenth Infantry, and the other to be directed at the outskirts of Reichecourt by the Sixteenth Infantry. The detachments were to consist of about twenty men each, Captain Quisenberry and Captain Sidney Graves to be the commanders.[3] After much discussion and one or two long conferences between the regimental commanders and the brigade and division commanders, it was decided that the raids should be of the silent character, that is, the raiding parties should approach the German wire by stealth, wearing black jerkins and, with hands and faces blackened, slide long Bangalore torpedoes under the wire, and at the agreed moment explode them to cut the necessary gaps, the artillery at the same instant to open up with its barrage. The two groups were billeted in the rear area of the division, where they could rehearse their maneuver on ground marked out to represent the German trench system concerned. Reinforcing French artillery was sent into the sector and given instructions to coordinate its fire with that of the First Artillery Brigade, under General Summerall.

Plans and preparations had all been completed by the evening of the day before the raid was to occur. Suddenly a heavy snow fell and the raiders were confronted with the dilemma of attempting to steal across a white No-man's-land without being detected. The detailed plan could not be changed at that late date and some other remedy had to be found. Major Wilson, the Chief of the Supply Service of the division, was told to procure white clothes for the forty men concerned. Where they were to be obtained was his problem, and he left in an automobile, damning the eccentricities of modern warfare. While we were at breakfast the following morning he returned from Nancy and triumphantly carried into the mess his white uniforms. They were women's nightgowns of various patterns and degrees of frilliness — the largest he could obtain. When the husky soldier men received this garb their morale fell to the zero point. One huge doughboy stated that he was willing to sacrifice his life, but he'd be damned if the Germans should find his body in a woman's nightgown. Everyone was both worried and convulsed over the mixed seriousness and absurdity of the situation, when the sun came out and melted the snow.

On the night selected the raiders were transported to the front in trucks and made their way on forward in the dark to the front-line trenches. A code had been specially arranged to permit the rapid transmission of the result of the raid to Division Headquarters over special telephone lines carried into the front trench. H-hour was set for several hours after dark, and as the moment approached we were all on edge to hear the roar of the guns which would announce the passage of the raiding parties through the enemy's wire. Word came back that the Engineers with the Bangalore torpedoes had not yet reported at the front, though it was known that they had left the support lines an hour or two earlier. Finally, a few minutes before H-hour, reports came from the commanders of the raiding parties that the Engineers had just arrived, too late to cross No-man's-land before the barrage would fall. It was impossible in the short time remaining to send instructions to the scattered artillery units that the raid would have to be abandoned. Open messages over the telephone were not permitted, because the enemy had listening-in sets all along the front. There remained nothing to do but sit and listen to the crash of the guns as they opened up at H-hour. We succeeded in stopping their fire before they had completed the arranged program.

General Pershing and several high ranking staff officers had come to Division Headquarters, to follow the course of the raiders, and their presence in this unfortunate predicament was embarrassing, to put it mildly. The French corps and army commanders made telephonic inquiries shortly after H-hour to learn the result of the raid, and no one was particularly anxious to be charged with the duty of making a reply. The two commanders, Captain Quisenberry and Captain Graves, were heartbroken, and the Engineers responsible for the mishap were reduced to tears. On investigation, it appeared that the Bangalore torpedoes, which were about fifty feet long, and very fragile, had proved so difficult to carry in the dark over the trenches and through the wire entanglements, and the Engineers became so disturbed over their slow progress that they attempted to cut across by the most direct routes and were lost in the dark. There was nothing much that could be done — everybody had tried his best — but their inexperience in such matters had caused them to underestimate some of the difficulties.

It now became necessary to carry out another raid immediately, even though the artillery bombardment must have given the Germans warning of some such probability. The French artillery reinforcements were already with us, and as there was little shelter for the crews, they could not be held for more than a few days longer. General Bullard charged me with the arrangement for this new effort, and it was decided to cut the wire by artillery fire on the day before the raids were to be attempted, then to make one raid in the morning, very carefully arranged from the viewpoint of the security of the participants and without much hope of obtaining any prisoners. Assuming this would appear to the enemy as the climax of our effort, the second raid would be launched as a surprise shortly after dark that evening. Captain Quisenberry had the more dangerous duty and thankless task of making the morning raid. The two detachments were again located in rear area of the division to rehearse the new plans. I went over the arrangements with the two commanders and attended some of their rehearsals. Every precaution was taken to avoid any more unexpected delays and the Engineers were eagerly pressing to be allowed to carry out the raid themselves.

On the morning selected, Captain Quisenberry's detachment, under the cover of a heavy barrage, crossed No-man's-land, entered the German positions and, as expected, found them vacated except for one dead German. The return trip was safely made, and it was not until they were well within our lines that one of the party was killed by a shell. The same night, shortly after dark, young Graves led his men across No-man's-land, and, covered by a heavy barrage, passed through the gap in the wire into the German lines; again no prisoners were taken, but this time they engaged in fighting with several Germans, all of whom I believe were killed. In the light of what occurred later, I rather imagine that some of these Germans might have surrendered, but our men were so new and keen at the game, that they did not give the other fellow an opportunity to declare his intentions.

The young officers who had the honor of leading the first American raiding parties were both spendid soldiers and early noted for their courage and qualities of leadership. Poor Quisenberry was killed two months later at Villiers-Tournelles in Picardy, a shell cutting off both his legs. Graves remained with the division until after Cantigny, and was then returned to the United States and sent to Siberia, but not before he obtained the Distinguished Service Cross for an exhibition of gallantry in Picardy.

Among the visitors to our Headquarters was Colonel John McA. Palmer.[4] He had sailed for France with General Pershing, as the Chief of the Operations Section at GHQ, but ill health had interfered with his duties and he was on sick leave at this time. Colonel Palmer spent a day with Colonel Hines, commanding the Sixteenth Infantry, and that night he told the members of the division mess of the exposed position of Colonel Hines' quarters. Explaining how the Germans fired at this shelter every day, Colonel Palmer described how he had entered the dugout that afternoon, and was standing at the window washing his hands when a German shell exploded just outside. He never got any further with his description, for, at that very instant, five terrific explosions shook our Headquarters, the lights went out, the members of the mess dispersed, and I never saw Colonel Palmer again until October 1918, during the Meuse-Argonne battle — not that he got out of the way any more rapidly than I did. In the kitchen I found the American cook dragging a broom handle along the slats of a wooden shutter. He explained that he was making a sound like a machine gun to scare off the aeroplanes. Some German bombers had dropped five of the largest-type bombs into a field several hundred yards from our office, but we received the definite impression that each projectile had landed in the yard.

CHAPTER VI

The Move to Picardy

ORDERS WERE RECEIVED in March directing me to proceed to Langres, where our AEF General Staff College had been established, and deliver a series of lectures on the practical working of the American division as then organized. Leaving Ménil-la-Tour on the 20th, I motored south through Neufchâteau and reached Langres that evening. On the following day came news of a great German offensive launched on a broad front in the general direction of Albert. At first the official communiqués gave favorable reports on the resistance offered by the English armies, but at the end of thirty-six hours it became apparent that the enemy were rapidly crushing the hostile opposition and penetrating deeply into the Allied position. The reports grew steadily worse and worse and the English instructors on duty at Langres became noticeably worried and depressed.

When I completed my second lecture I was called into the office of the director of the School and informed that two of the British officers had received orders to report back immediately to their own army. The particular courses of instruction with which these two gentlemen were charged were to be turned over to me. Authority had been obtained by telephone to hold me at Langres and I was directed to confer with these officers at once regarding their work, as they would leave that afternoon by automobile.

While discussing the program of instructions and the problems they had planned, the director of the College sent me word that another of the English officers had been recalled and that I would take over his work. Before the afternoon was finished, I had been charged with the conduct of the courses prepared by four English instructors, and these officers had made their departure for the battle front. There was not much time for personal thoughts with this variety of new duties to be assimilated, but I did have a feeling of great depression over being separated from the First Division just as the active fighting began.

The next morning while at breakfast with General McAndrew,[1] the commandant of the Langres Schools, and General Bjornstad, who was the director of the General Staff College, telephonic orders were received for me to be sent back to my division immediately, and I left within the hour.[2] On my arrival at Ménil-la-Tour late that afternoon, I learned that we were to be relieved by the Twenty-sixth Division and that the officers of the latter division were then making a preliminary reconnaissance of the sector. As soon as relieved the First was to entrain for an unknown destination northwest of Paris. As the only American division whose training had been completed, we were going to the battle, which by this time had assumed the proportions of a great catastrophe. Everyone was jubilant, but all were intensely busy making their preparations for the relief and the entrainment.

The Twenty-sixth had but recently been withdrawn from the front on the Chemin des Dames, where the regiments had received their first experience in the trenches, each serving under the control of a French brigade commander. Assembled to the north of Chaumont, they were about to engage in an open-warfare maneuver with the Forty-second Division, which had similarly been withdrawn from its first front-line experience, to the east of Lunéville. The sudden change of orders interrupted this maneuver and started both divisions back into the line to replace troops which were in condition to engage in the battle. With many complications, due principally to the lack of transportation in the Twenty-sixth Division, we accomplished the relief in record time, and the troops of the First were collected in billets in the Toul region, except one brigade which was already in the Gondrecourt area. Commencing on the evening of April 4th, the loading of the troops was completed by noon of the following day and the last of the fifty-seven trains got under way. The motor transportation proceeded under its own power. Colonel Erickson of the G-3 Section, with our French Liaison Officer, Captain Seligman, left in advance of the division staff to locate the destination of the division and to arrange for the first marches of the troops after their detrainment.[3] General Bullard fell ill just prior to our departure and we were forced to leave him in the hospital near Toul. The division staff made the trip by automobile and rendezvoused the first night at Fontainebleau. We were careful to avoid the region immediately east and north of Paris, as it was certain to be congested with the transfer of French reserves which were being rushed to the threatened front.

That night at the Hôtel Angleterre, across the street from the Fontainebleau Château, we indulged ourselves in a rather elaborate dinner, as all seemed to feel that there might not be a similar opportunity for a long time to come — if ever.[4] I selected a table where Mrs. Marshall and myself lunched years before. We had been especially coached to order filet of sole, as the hotel was supposed to be famous for the excellence of this dish. I ordered it again on this particular evening and tried to enjoy it with the same relish I had on the previous occasion.

In the morning we made an early start and, heading northwest to avoid Paris, we located the improvised Regulating Station through which the trains of the First Division were then passing. There Colonel Erickson was greeting the commander of each train with orders giving him his destination and the marches he must carry out after detraining, to reach the assembly zone assigned the First Division, centering around Chaumont-en-Vixen. The trains arrived with ten-minute intervals, and in addition to those of the First Division there were others transporting two French divisions.

After obtaining Colonel Erickson's information we proceeded on to the Headquarters of the Fifth French Army, under the control of which the First Division was then passing, and called on General Michler. From him we learned of the progress of the battle and were informed that the division would have a few days in which to concentrate and make its final preparations prior to entering the line. Headquarters were established at Chaumont-en-Vixen, and arrangements at once made to put the division through a terrain exercise in mobile warfare adapted to emphasize the lessons which had just been learned by the French in opposing the enemy's great offensive.

General Michler was greatly concerned over the poor condition of our animals, which had not yet fully recovered from the hardships of the fall. Shortly after our arrival he inspected our artillery regiments and made frequent references to the apparent weakness of the horses. General Summerall, who commanded the Artillery Brigade, had been strenuously endeavoring all winter to condition his horses and he was not prepared at this time to acknowledge the existence of any weakness which might delay our entry into the fight. As he assured General Michler that the teams could do their work, a mounted orderly passed close by and his horse — as though he had overheard the conversation — sank to the ground and expired in our presence. Even this did not faze General Summerall, who is one of the greatest living exponents of the principle that much more can be done than ever seems possible, if there is the will to do it.

General Pershing arrived to inspect the division and witness the terrain exercise. At its conclusion General Michler gave a critique to the assembled field officers and endeavored to indicate the points which he thought required improvement. All the officers of the division were then assembled at Chaumont-en-Vixen, where they were addressed by the Commander in Chief. His remarks at this time, preliminary to our entry into the battle and with the expectation that we would soon be employed in a great Allied counterattack, made a profound impression on all those present. I quote here a portion of his speech:

> I did not come here to make a speech; I am not given to speech-making, so only a word more and I shall close. Let me say then that I have every confidence in the First Division. You are about to enter this great battle of the greatest war in history, and in that battle you will represent the mightiest nation engaged. That thought itself must be to every serious man a very appealing thought, and one that should call forth the best and the noblest that is in you. Centuries of military tradition and of military and civil history are now looking toward this first contingent of the American Army as it enters this great battle. You have behind you your own national traditions that should make you the finest soldiers in Europe today. We come from a young and aggressive nation. We come from a nation that for one hundred and fifty years has stood before the world as the champion of the sacred principles of human liberty. We now

return to Europe, the home of our ancestors, to help defend those same principles upon European soil. Could there be a more stimulating sentiment as you go from here to your commands, and from there to the battlefield?

Our people today are hanging expectant upon your deeds. The future is hanging upon your action in this conflict. You are going forward, and your conduct will be an example for succeeding units of our army. I hope the standard you set will be high — I know it will be high. You are taking with you the sincerest wishes and the highest hopes of the President and all of our people at home. I assure you, in their names and in my own, of our strong beliefs in your success and of our confidence in your courage and in your loyalty, with a feeling of certainty in our hearts that you are going to make a record of which your country will be proud.

Few Americans will ever realize the situation of the Allies at this particular period of the war. The Fifth British Army, virtually demolished, had been replaced by French reserves and these in turn were suffering severely. The enemy had made a penetration of sixty kilometers and had cut the principal railroad artery between the British and French. Amiens was under gunfire and with its fall rail communication between the two Allies would practically cease. During the onrush of the Germans there was one period of twenty-four hours when serious consideration was given to the plan of carrying the French line due west to the coast, and abandoning all effort to keep in touch with the English. The most severe loss, however, was in the morale of the English infantry, which for a time was very low.

In this critical situation General Pershing rose to greatness. Surrendering the direct control of his own troops, which he had so vigorously maintained in the face of repeated endeavors to prevent the formation of an American army, he released them to be scattered over four hundred miles of front. Temporarily jeopardizing his own and even American prestige, he laid all his cards on the table and directed every move toward the salvage of the Allied wreck. In the midst of a profound depression he radiated determination and the will to win. His manner and his expression, more than his speech, fired the officers of the First Division with the determination to overcome the enemy wherever he was encountered.

Those who marched to battle for the first time in the summer or fall of 1918, as did the great majority of the AEF, have never experienced the feeling of men who went forward to meet an enemy in overwhelming numbers, crushing all within his path. Those days in the spring of 1918 left an impression on the men of the First Division which plainly marked them apart from the others throughout the war. Accustomed to great hardships, to long hours of work, no play, and the gloom of a French winter in the trenches, held in the line for months at a time without relief because of the paucity of reserves, the weaklings were eliminated from the division, and there was born in it a contempt for difficulties and hardships and horrors.

Late one afternoon the orders came for the division to march to the north, and early the next morning the long columns of troops moved out in the general direction of Beauvais. Every unit was accompanied by a correspondent, most of them famous in their profession — Irvin Cobb, George Pattullo, Junius Wood, Carroll, and a host of others. We had no transportation to spare and these worthy scribes were compelled to walk, and thus gathered considerable local color en route. They had been with us off and on since our arrival in France, and now had every expectation of being present at our baptism in battle. Irvin Cobb had previously become celebrated for his march in carpet slippers south through Belgium into France with the German Army, but I understand he got more action out of his walk with us than he did those August days of 1914.

The passage of the division through the region of Beauvais was quite a staff problem. The town was a great road center and there did not remain sufficient direct parallel routes to the north. In addition the national highways entering the town had been posted as "Routes Gardées," that is, they were barred to all but motor traffic. Our foot troops and our animal-drawn vehicles therefore had to keep clear of these roads and confine themselves to the small country highways. When one pauses to consider that a division requires about thirty kilometers of road space, the complications in making this particular march may be partially understood. After we had passed to the north of Beauvais I learned that the movement had for years past been a favorite march problem in the Ecole de Guerre (French War College), but in prewar days the "Routes Gardées" had not been thought of, and the wartime movement was therefore much more difficult than the peacetime problem.

After three days of marching, the Headquarters of the division rested in Froisy, a small village south of Breteuil. We remained there for two days while the officers made a reconnaissance of the portion of the front to be assigned to us. We were to relieve two French divisions northwest of Montdidier, on a portion of the line which later was designated as the Cantigny Sector. The battle zone in Picardy presented a different aspect from the swampy, desolate region north of Toul. Heretofore unmarked by war, the fields bore promising crops and the many châteaux and little villages wore an air of prosperity in decided contrast to those sections of France which had long been located close to the lines. Long stretches of level country were broken by gentle hill slopes. The roads had been in excellent condition but were already showing signs of the heavy traffic to which they were subjected. French labor troops were piling broken stone alongside of every kilometer to assure the constant repair of these important factors in strategical and tactical operations. The onrush of the enemy had carried the fighting into a region devoid of organized aviation fields, and the level meadows north of Beauvais had been hastily fitted out for this purpose. Extensive camps had been erected with a tent for each aeroplane and canvas shelters for the aviators. There was assembled immediately in rear of our new sector, a collection of the most famous French aviators and it was an interesting experience to ride through these camps where the combat planes were continually arriving or departing with many spectacular loops and other dangerous gyrations. The horizon was dotted with observation balloons and the continuous roar of the distant guns filled the air.

A few kilometers to the north was the new junction point between the French and British armies and immediately in rear of this most critical portion of the front lay our old friends of the Moroccan Division in the place of honor as an Allied reserve. As we entered the line they were called on to deliver a desperate counterattack against the Germans who had renewed their assault at Villers-Bretonneux, to cut the railroad near Amiens. In the short fight which followed, the Foreign Legion was well-nigh decimated and many of the officers I had met the previous August made the final sacrifice.

We commenced the relief of the French units on the night of April 24th, and by the 26th the First Division was established in front of the enemy. There were no trenches, the men being distributed in individual pits or "foxholes," and the Headquarters located in any convenient cave or cellar. This lack of covered communications and the continuous violence of the artillery fire made it almost impossible to circulate in the sector during daylight hours. Our casualties made a formidable daily list, considering the fact that there was no advance by the infantry on either side. The losses in officers were particularly heavy, as it was necessary for them to move about to oversee their men. The captains of machine gun companies, whose personnel was more scattered than others, had a particularly trying task, and most of them were killed or wounded during the first ten days. After the machine-gunners, the field officers suffered most, and we had two Lieutenant Colonels killed and two others wounded in a very short time.

The reason for this remarkable artillery activity is rather interesting, as it was the direct result of the Allied dilemma at that time. The French reserves, which had been hastily thrown into the line previously held by the Fifth British Army, had suffered severely in bringing to a halt the German advance. I inspected the position of one French battalion which we were to relieve, and found that only two officers had survived the previous ten days' fighting. There were few other reserves available, while the enemy was known to have a large number of divisions still available for the resumption of the battle. It was to prevent the deployment of these German reserve divisions that the Allied artillery was called on to maintain an excessive rate of fire throughout the hours of darkness. Ordinarily fire of this character, called "counter-preparation fire," was only ordered at the moment an attack was expected, because the amount of ammunition consumed in this way would have been too great and the demands on the gun crews too severe to permit of its more general employment. In the existing situation of the Allies it was felt that the infantry then on the line would not be able to resist another great German advance, and, as I have already said, there were insufficient reserves. Therefore, we were called on to employ a modified form of counter-preparation fire from 11 P.M. until dawn. This would make it virtually impossible for the enemy's assault infantry to be moved into position without incurring demoralizing losses. At the same time, it was a desperate remedy, as the large reserves of ammunition would be quickly depleted, the guns worn out, and the crews exhausted. We averaged more than one exploded 75 mm.-gun per day, and fired at times as high as 30,000 rounds per day, with our three regiments of artillery. In addition to these guns were those of the Army Corps and of the Army, located in our sector, all firing throughout the night. This activity produced a similar activity on the part of the enemy and he thoroughly covered our sector with his fire. While incoming shells in daylight were not nearly so numerous as at night, nevertheless the roads and villages were kept under more or less continuous bombardment. As there was no barbwire to obstruct free passage through the fields, I found it much safer to move about the rear portions of the sector on horseback, as in this way I could keep clear of the roads and trails and make a rapid change of position to avoid suddenly shelled areas.

The Post of Command of the First Division was located in the wine cellar of a small château at Ménil-St. Firmin. The house had apparently been vacated by its occupants on less than an hour's notice. Silver, linen, clothing, and other intimate personal effects had been abandoned. I was assigned the room which had been occupied by the lady of the house, and I found it filled with her personal possessions. A partially completed letter lay on her desk, and the contents of the wardrobes showed that she had made a hurried endeavor to carry off with her some of the clothing which they contained. These intimate indications of the tragedy of war are difficult to appreciate by those who have never felt its brutal hand.

We soon accustomed ourselves to life under these changed conditions, but the daily casualty lists created a feeling in each man's mind that he had but a small chance of coming through unscathed. In making our reconnaissances of the front, we usually started out from Division Headquarters at one o'clock in the morning and motored forward about a mile, leaving the car by the roadside. The chauffeur usually awaited our return in the shelter of a shell hole. We would then pick up a guide from the nearest regimental or battalion head-quarters and proceed in the darkness on up to the front line. During the night we could check up most of the dispositions of the troops, but it was only possible to size up the terrain in the short period at dawn just before sunrise. If one delayed at the front until after sunup he was compelled to remain there in a shell or foxhole until darkness that evening. The absence of barbwire entanglements along the edge of No-man's-land made it possible for one to wander unknowingly into this zone, and on into the enemy's lines. Before dawn one morning I was picking my way along in the darkness, when I encountered a smashed aeroplane, which had previously been reported as having fallen in No-man's-land. This served as a sufficient landmark to guide me back into our own lines. The ordeal of the chauffeurs during these reconnaissances was particularly trying, as they were required to wait alone for long hours, usually under heavy shell fire, at some point which they had never seen in daylight.

In our wine cellar at Division Headquarters, Campbell King, Colo-nel de Chambrun of the French Army, and myself occupied the same sleeping compartment. De Chambrun had the upper half of the im-provised double-decked bunk in which I slept. He usually retired about ten o'clock, while King and I rarely found it possible to turn in before midnight. The Watch Officer sat just outside our compart-ment, and received all telephone calls, waking us up if anything impor-tant came in. As the situation was strained and continuously danger-ous, there were frequent alarming messages, especially just before dawn, which is the usual time selected for attacks. We would usually discuss these reports while lying in our bunks and then either King or myself would have to get up in the cold and take whatever action might be required, which ordinarily had to do with increased artillery fire in front of some portion of our line. One night was particularly hectic. About 11 P.M., a report came in from Villers-Tournelles that the enemy was pouring mustard gas shells on the town. Soon the wires were cut and from then until dawn we had something of a crisis. High explosives were mixed with gas shells, and the two combined caused a tremendous number of casualties in the Eighteenth Infantry, which was located in the region. Altogether I believe 900 men were put out of action in that one regiment during this particular night. Their food was ruined by the gas and it became necessary to reach them with a new supply of rations before dawn. The road into the town was beaten by the continuous fire of a number of German guns, which made it a perilous trip for the ration carts. About five-thirty in the morning, I went forward to confer with Colonel Parker, the regimental commander, and to personally examine into the situation. For a quarter of a mile outside of the little village, the soggy, wet ground was peppered with fresh shell craters, most of them containing mustard gas. Walking in a gas mask in the heavy ground, picking one's way among these craters, and frequently lying down to avoid the bursts of incoming shells was a very trying physical ordeal. I found Colonel Parker's shallow dugout in the cellar of a little house off the main street of the village. He and his staff had been wearing gas masks continuously for seven hours and showed signs of the great strain they had undergone. While we were talking, a heavy-caliber shell landed on the adjacent dugout and killed all the occupants but one, who came bounding down the steps of our shelter with a wide dazed smile on his face. He was the regimental draughtsman, but I doubt if he ever drew another straight line after that. This was our first experience with mustard gas, and it proved to be a particularly hideous phase of warfare. It immediately became necessary to move the troops out of the cellars of the village and into the open fields where there was no shelter.

During this period of our service, the most dangerous duty probably fell to the Quartermaster Sergeants and teamsters who went forward each night with the ration carts to revictual the infantry. Confined to roads and anticipated by the enemy, they had to make their way up along the most heavily beaten zones in the sector. The casualties among these men and the poor mules who hauled the carts were very heavy. No publicity or glory attached to this service, but those who carried it through always had my profound admiration. Apropos of these unsung heroes, I found one day an elaborately decorated grave in a woods where the supply echelon of an infantry regiment was located. Over the grave was a large wooden cross with the following inscription:

> Here lies poor Nellie of the Supply
> Company of the Sixteenth Infantry.
> Served in Texas, Mexico and France.
> Wounded and killed near Villers
> Tournelles. She done her bit.

"Nellie" was an army mule.

CHAPTER VII

Cantigny

T HE ACTIVITY of the artillery and machine guns continued throughout the month of May and there was seldom a lull in the bombardment. The casualty lists grew rapidly from day to day and we lost some of our best officers and men.

King and myself were awakened one night by the Watch Officer, with a telephone message from a village far in rear where some of our trains were located. We were told that German aeroplanes had just bombed the town and one projectile had struck Colonel Clayton's (the Division Quartermaster) billet, had killed him, a Major, and a Captain, who were his assistants.[1] The enemy was particularly active in the air and endeavored to prevent the rest of troops in the rear zone by nightly air raids. They paid particular attention to any buildings or localities where our various Posts of Command might be located. Divisional Headquarters usually received several showers of bombs each clear night, and on one occasion over two hundred were dropped in our immediate vicinity.

The enemy undoubtedly suffered even more from our harassing fire. Prisoners captured by the division stated that the tour of duty in the front line had been limited to four days because of the severity of the service, and the men carried in with them their four day's rations, as it was impossible to send up food at night because of the Allied artillery fire. We also learned from these prisoners that the Grippe, or "Spanish Influenza," had appeared in the German Army, and a very large percentage of the men were affected. This was evidently the "Flu," or its forerunner, which did not strike into our troops until the following fall.

Early in May orders were received for us to prepare to make an attack east against the heights extending north from Montdidier. This operation was to be in the nature of a counterattack, to be launched as soon as the Germans had committed themselves to an anticipated drive in Flanders, directed against the Channel ports. The First Division was to play the leading role and with a French division on either flank. The latter were to execute a partial wheel to the right and left, their outward flanks pivoting on the original line. Back at French Corps Headquarters I learned from General Deport that this assault to the east was to be followed twenty-four hours later by a general advance northward by the Third French Army, stretching to the east from Montdidier.

Orders were soon issued outlining the part each brigade and regiment was to play in the attack and all commanders became actively engaged in their preparations. It was felt that the complete lack of "boyaux," or communicating trenches, would make it difficult to lay the necessary telephone wires and carry out final preparations for the assault, so we undertook the construction of two parallel communicating trenches each about one and a half kilometers in length, to be connected with each other by a trench one-half kilometer long. It was realized that at the first indications of this work the Germans would concentrate a heavy artillery fire on the area involved, which would cause heavy casualties in the working parties, if it did not prevent the construction of the trenches. To avoid this the Engineers made careful plans to dig these trenches one at a time, and to complete each length in a single night. This required very elaborate and precise arrangements, because the continuous harassing fire would certainly interfere with the deployment of the working parties in the dark, and the collection of such a large force of supporting troops in the forward zone might jeopardize the defense of the sector in the event of a sudden attack.

On the night selected to commence this work Engineer noncommissioned officers as foremen were distributed along the trace of the proposed trench and Engineer guides led the infantry working parties to their assigned positions. Before dawn, a kilometer and a half of trench had been dug and most of it completed to a depth of four feet, and the fourteen hundred workers safely withdrawn after having suffered but few casualties. With the clearing of the morning mists the German observers, in their balloons and aeroplanes, quickly located this new development inside our lines, and their artillery at once directed an harassing fire along the entire length of the trench. That night we repeated the performance by digging the parallel communicating trench to the north. Again the enemy directed his fire on this new sign of our activity, which everyone on our side carefully avoided. The third night the trench to connect these two parallels was constructed, and with its discovery in the morning the Boche distributed his fire over this entire region.

The selection of emplacements for the artillery which was to reinforce us in the attack was a difficult problem, as the batteries had to be absolutely concealed from the enemy's view; otherwise their appearance in the sector would apprise him of our plans. As the enemy's forward positions were located on high ground and ours on a gentle downward slope, there were few places where guns could be installed and ammunition accumulated, without their presence being detected. The entire sector was a beehive of industry throughout the hours of darkness; additional trenches and dugouts were being excavated; telephone lines laid; artillery ammunition distributed, and many other necessary preparations made for the coming attack.

It was expected that the enemy would renew his assault in Flanders about the 18th of May, and this would mean that our counterattack would probably be launched the following day, but as the time approached the Allied Intelligence Services could obtain no indications of the expected renewal. The days passed without a hostile advance, and out of a clear sky came orders for us to abandon our plans and to prepare an operation for the capture of the heights of Cantigny, without the assistance of any French divisions. Our elaborate communicating trenches, recently constructed, did not extend toward Cantigny and would be of no assistance to us in that attack. The other work of preparation was of little help. An early date had been set for this new and distinctly American operation and we were rushed to make the necessary preliminary arrangements. The Twenty-eighth Infantry had just relieved the Eighteenth Infantry in front of Cantigny and the former regiment was assigned the new mission. Its commander, Colonel Ely, at once undertook the construction of the necessary trenches, parallels of departure for the attacking troops, and the dugouts which must be used by the various headquarters during the assault. By direction, this was to be an operation with a strictly limited objective; the troops were not to penetrate far enough into the enemy's positions to put his artillery out of action, and it was, therefore, necessary to anticipate a violent artillery reaction following the assault. Under such circumstances a much more elaborate preparation is required for the aftermath of the battle than is required for an operation more on the order of open warfare. The hostile artillery frequently dispersed the working parties during the night and caused many casualties. A rainy spell set in, which added to the difficulties. Once the men had dispersed to seek shelter from hostile fire on a dark night, it was a trying problem for the officers to collect them again and get them back to work.

Before completing the plan for the operation, Captain Crochet, Major Sherman, and myself made a reconnaissance of the terrain in front of Cantigny. We had to start in the dark, and failed to find the guide who was to meet us at an agreed point. Directing our movements with a luminous compass, we worked our way forward but did not come in contact with any troops for some time. We were uncertain of our whereabouts, when we located a French soldier in a foxhole and learned that we were in the front line of the French division on the left of the First. This seriously delayed us and we did not locate the American troops on our left front line until shortly before dawn, which gave us little time to look over the ground before daylight.

From a little clump of trees, termed on the map "Le Boquetaire," on the edge of No-man's-land in front of Cantigny, we studied the lay of the ground until shortly after dawn. A level, grassy plain extended between our position and the village; a little further to the south a ravine broke the level of the plain and extended around the southern portion of Cantigny. We were too far forward to suffer from hostile artillery fire, as the enemy could not fire on us without the possibility of causing casualties within his own lines, but there was some machine-gun fire.

After familiarizing ourselves with the ground we started our withdrawal, but the sun came up too quickly for us and we were confronted with the necessity of either remaining in that locality until
nightfall or exposing ourselves in an endeavor to get back to Division
Headquarters. As there was much work to be done without delay, we
undertook to crawl over the low ridge immediately in rear. Work had
been commenced on a communicating trench but we found that it
seldom exceeded one foot in depth. We followed the trace of this
trench on our hands and knees for some four or five hundred yards
and frequently had to lie flat or to do our crawling with our hands and
toes, as a German machine-gunner located our movements. I think
each of us was considerably disturbed over the possibility of being
shot in a rather ignominious fashion and we were all very glad when
we reached the cover of the ridge.

On this reconnaissance I was particularly impressed with the contrast between the living arrangements of the French soldiers and the
American soldiers under such circumstances. I found the Frenchmen
in their little foxholes, or short sections of trench, cooking an appetizing breakfast in their mess tins and cups, using solidified alcohol. Two
or three men would apparently pool their rations and concoct a very
satisfactory hot meal. The American soldiers also had solidified alcohol, but they usually left the top off of the can the first time it was
used and the alcohol evaporated, leaving them without means of heat-
ing their food for the next meal. Food had been sent up from the rear
in special containers called "Marmite cans," which were supposed to
keep it hot but did not do so. I saw one man with a mess tin filled with
cold stew and mashed potatoes, over which he had poured molasses.
This seemed to be the favorite method of preparing the meal, but
they gulped it down without much relish. In defense of this system, I
heard that one of our soldiers had stated that "they might as well mix
it up outside as inside."

Four days before the Cantigny fight the Twenty-eighth Infantry
was withdrawn from the front to give it an opportunity to rehearse its
battle maneuver. A platoon of fourteen French tanks and a section of
flame fighters were assigned to the regiment. A section of terrain
about twelve miles in rear of the sector, which resembled the sur-

roundings of Cantigny, was staked out and here the troops rehearsed their various parts for two days. The Eighteenth Infantry had relieved the Twenty-eighth and was having a hard time completing the trenches and other jobs which had been started by their more fortunate predecessors. We were heavily reinforced by French artillery which was intended to suppress the German artillery fire during the advance and particularly after our men had gained their objectives. In all about one hundred supplementary guns were placed in position and instructions given which would coordinate their action with the First Division.

In filling the forward dumps with ammunition, pyrotechnics, and other essential supplies, there were several mishaps, the most important of which was the explosion of a large dump containing all the pyrotechnics and small-arms ammunition and water cans intended for the Twenty-eighth Infantry. Through error these had been unloaded at the same place, and had not yet been distributed when a German shell landed in their midst. A still more unfortunate happening occurred about this time, which threatened the success of the operation. A young Engineer officer, named Kendall, had just joined from a special school in our SOS. He was given the task of distributing the heavier intrenching tools along the jumping-off trenches. Loading up an infantry working party of fifty men with sacks of these tools, he started forward after dark two nights before the attack, leading the detachment.

The tale was told me the next day by the Infantry Lieutenant with the party. He had followed in rear to keep the men closed up. After stumbling along in the pitch dark for more than an hour, the column made a long halt. His suspicion that all was not well became aroused and he worked his way forward to the head of the column to investigate the reason for the halt. There he found a Sergeant, who told him that Lieutenant Kendall had been uncertain of his whereabouts and had gone forward, telling the Sergeant to await his return. The Sergeant thought they were in No-man's-land, and after a whispered discussion they moved on a few paces and both of them fell into a trench. At this instant they were fired on at close range from their right and the flashes of the rifles revealed the outlines of a party of

about ten Germans. Returning this fire and at the same time withdrawing, they came under fire from their left rear. The Lieutenant
left the Sergeant to attend to the first group of the enemy, while he
himself deployed some of the men to stand off the second group. In
some miraculous fashion the detachment extricated itself from this
dilemma and withdrew in the dark away from the enemy. Just as they
escaped from further molestation by the Boche, they were fired into
by their own troops, and were only identified by the violent swearing
in which they all engaged.

Without suffering a single casualty the Infantry Lieutenant
brought his men back into our lines, but they had left their sacks of
tools in No-man's-land and the German advance trench. Furthermore, Kendall completely disappeared and was not heard of until his
grave was located on the far side of Cantigny, long after the Armistice. It developed that he probably had in his dispatch case a map
giving the location of all the trenches and dumps which had been
prepared for the assault. This, in connection with the fifty sacks of
tools, it was feared would disclose to the enemy our intentions, with
the inevitable disastrous result.

Just at this busy time, my connection with the First Division came
very near being terminated, at least temporarily. Coming up out of the
Division Headquarters dugout on the late afternoon of the 26th, I got
on my horse and started him at a canter up a trail leading from
Division Headquarters. In my haste to get under way I had carelessly
hurried the horse into a lope before I had adjusted myself in the
saddle or straightened out the reins. He slipped, or stumbled, went
down, and rolled over twice, my left ankle remaining in the stirrup
and sustaining painful fracture. Crawling back on the horse, I returned to Headquarters and was carried down in the dugout. The
doctor strapped up my foot with adhesive tape and I continued my
participation in the affairs of the division with the injured foot resting
on a table or a chair. During the next week I did not have my clothes
off and worked from sixteen to eighteen hours a day. The ankle
ached so severely that I could not rest comfortably, and there was
plenty of work to do for anyone who was awake.

The Twenty-eighth Infantry reentered the lines the nights of the

26th and 27th. There were attached to the regiment for the operation additional machine-gun companies and Stokes mortar and one-pounder detachments. The troops of the Eighteenth Infantry remained close in rear to act as supports or reserves, and Roosevelt's Battalion of the Twenty-sixth Infantry on the right of the Twenty-eighth was to cooperate closely with the advance. All was in readiness and everyone immensely keen to get off.

To afford the gunners of the newly arrived French batteries and trench mortars an opportunity to register their places without fore-warning the enemy of a possible attack, it was arranged to start registration fire in the early morning at the first moment the light would permit of the proper observation of results. Four-forty-five was selected as the hour for the commencement of this firing and one hour allotted for the purpose. The general bombardment was then opened to destroy the enemy's trenches and gun positions, and to demoralize the garrison. An hour later the infantry would go forward, closely following the artillery barrage.

On the 27th we received the disturbing news that the Germans had launched a powerful attack on the Chemin des Dames and were making quite rapid progress. Late that evening word came that some of the French artillery regiments which had been loaned us would have to be withdrawn the following morning as soon as the infantry had reached its objectives, in order that they might be sent to the scene of the renewed enemy offensive. This was a heavy blow, as we were to depend on these guns to suppress the enemy's artillery fire, which would undoubtedly be directed at our infantry in their un-sheltered positions on the final objectives.

The correspondents all assembled at Division Headquarters that night to be informed as to the plans for the next day's battle. There had been frequent complaints in the past that too much secrecy had been observed in our treatment of the newspapermen. On this par-ticular occasion, they were given the complete plan and full liberty as to their own movements. Hopper,[2] the representative of *Collier's* mag-azine, made a specific inquiry of me as to where they might go and I told him that the only prohibition General Bullard placed on their movements was that they should not precede the first infantry wave into Cantigny. At this reply, everyone laughed at Hopper, and he seemed somewhat startled with his opportunities for observation, but the following morning he played his part so well that he did go into Cantigny immediately behind the first wave of the infantry and was much embarrassed by the tender of surrender from a party of Germans, he only having a pencil with which to receive them.

The morning of May 28th broke clear and the preliminaries of the attack were carried through with precision. The general artillery bombardment opened with a tremendous roar and Cantigny itself took on the appearance of an active volcano, with great clouds of smoke and dust and flying dirt and debris, which was blasted high into the air. At six-forty-five the long waves of the infantry moved out in perfect alignment, preceded by a dense barrage. The front of attack was about a kilometer and a half and extended a considerable distance to the north or left of the village. The old-fashioned clumsy French tanks made their way abreast or in advance of the infantry and quickly drove under cover any German machine-gunners who exposed themselves. Without mishap and with comparatively no casualties — estimated between 35 and 75 — the troops swept forward through the village and beyond to their final objectives. We had caught the Germans in the middle of a relief, and prisoners poured from every undestroyed dugout. The reports of the progress of the fighting came into Division Headquarters by telephone every five minutes, which kept us in the most intimate touch with what was happening. These were telephoned by officers of the G-2 or Intelligence Section, who were located in the front line overlooking the disputed ground.

The success of this phase of the operation was so complete and the list of casualties so small that everyone was enthusiastic and delighted, but this reaction was of short duration, for troubles were coming thick and fast. Orders for the withdrawal of more French artillery arrived before the advance had been completed, and we discovered that at least one French regiment had started its withdrawal without having fired a shot. The German guns, unsuppressed by our lack of counter-battery fire, opened a violent bombardment on the newly captured positions. More and more French artillery was relieved, with orders to join the armies south of the Chemin des Dames, until all the reinforcing artillery had been removed by midnight of the 28th.

This action by the French higher command played havoc with us, but was entirely proper, as the German advance toward Château-Thierry had broken through all opposition and was rushing south with unparalleled rapidity. Cantigny was but a small incident, while the great disaster further south which was befalling our Allies was hourly assuming more serious proportions.

Following the violent bombardment on the afternoon of the 28th, the German infantry endeavored to counterattack and drive the Twenty-eighth out of Cantigny. This effort was broken by our combined small-arm and artillery fire. A second counterattack was reported the same evening, and on the 29th the enemy twice again drove his infantry against our positions without success. Meanwhile the men of the Twenty-eighth, Eighteenth, and a few detachments from the Sixteenth Infantry, were suffering large numbers of casualties from the hostile artillery. In addition to those who were actually wounded, many of those untouched became in effect casualties from the shock of the explosion of heavy-caliber shells. Cantigny was kept under continuous bombardment by 210-mm. guns. A 3-inch shell will temporarily scare or deter a man; a 6-inch shell will shock him; but an 8-inch shell, such as these 210-mm. ones, rips up the nervous system of everyone within a hundred yards of the explosion.

All the newly laid wire communications into Cantigny were quickly destroyed and the enemy's fire was too severe to permit their repair except at the expense of many casualties among the Signal Corps men. Runners and couriers could not get back during daylight hours. The aviators were unable to report the condition of the front, as it was obscured by high clouds of dust. Frequent reports, highly alarming and often unjustified, poured into Division Headquarters. A few men made their way back with clothing in tatters and reported themselves as sole survivors of their companies. To these we gave hot coffee and food and then sent them back to the fight with renewed courage and less exaggerated ideas as to the extent of the losses.

For three days the attacking troops were subjected to counterattacks and to a bombardment which exceeded any experience they were to have later on in the great battles of the war. The heights of Cantigny were of no strategic importance, and of small tactical value. The issue was a moral one. This was our first offensive, which had been ordered primarily for the purpose of its effect on the morale of the English and French armies. For the First Division to lose its first objective was unthinkable and would have had a most depressing effect on the morale of our entire Army as well as on those of our Allies. For similar reasons, the Germans were determined to overthrow our first success and demonstrate to the world that the American soldier was of poorer stuff than the German. A captured order of Ludendorff's confirms this statement, as he gave special instructions to smash the Americans wherever encountered. The losses we suffered were not justified by the importance of the position itself, but they were many times justified by the importance of other great and far-reaching considerations.

In the midst of our trials and tribulations, there were two rather dramatic occurrences at Division Headquarters. On the afternoon of the second day a most alarming and disturbing report was received from the front by wireless and also by courier. We were hard put to meet the new developments of the situation and labored throughout the night to overcome the difficulties. On the third day the hostile artillery fire continued violent, but we seemed to be escaping without any renewals of the enemy's counterattacks. Late in the afternoon a pigeon message reached Headquarters. It was similar to those of the previous evening and just as alarming. We had been congratulating ourselves that the daylight hours had passed without the development of any crisis, but the news in this message operated as a decided depressant. General Bullard stood at one end of the Operations compartment in our wine cellar, thoughtfully turning over in his mind this new development. The other officers all sat or stood in complete silence. I took the little tissue-paper message from my assistant, who had read it aloud, and carefully scanned it. It had no date, but showed that it had been written at 6 P.M. Looking at my watch I found that it was then 5:55 P.M. If the watches at the front were correct, the bird had made its trip and the message had been relayed to us five minutes before it was shown to have been started. Rapidly comparing it with the wireless and courier messages of the previous evening, I was able to announce, to the profound relief of everyone, that the news was twenty-four hours old, and the particular crisis it referred to had been successfully passed.

It developed later that the birds at the front had become mixed in their baskets, with the result that a lady and gentleman pigeon had developed such an affection for each other that one or the other of them — the bird we had received — had delayed in the vicinity for nearly twenty-four hours after its release.

That same night about one o'clock, a runner from Roosevelt's battalion came into Headquarters with a German carrier pigeon, which had been shot on the parapet of the front-line trench. We woke up the officer who understood German and he took out the little message from its container on the pigeon's leg, and translated it for our information. It was from the Colonel of a German regiment, addressed to his Division Commander, and read about as follows:

> I found the bridge at ——— in flames but successfully crossed with the regiment and am pushing on towards ———, in compliance with your orders.

Consulting the map we found that this was positive indication that the enemy had advanced about thirty kilometers south of the Chemin des Dames and was apparently continuing his progress with little resistance. The pigeon had flown a hundred miles off his course and had alighted in our division with this indication of the extent of the disaster which was soon to culminate at Château-Thierry. We immediately telephoned the contents of the message to our French Corps Headquarters, and it was from there relayed to Marshal Pétain's staff. Early the next morning Corps Headquarters informed us that this little pigeon had furnished the first identification of a German division which had previously been on the Russian front.

On the nights of the third and fourth days of the battle the Twenty-eighth Infantry was relieved by the Sixteenth, which had previously been in reserve. General Bullard was loath to employ his last fresh regiment as there was every indication that an extensive German offensive would soon be launched in our vicinity. Thirty-five enemy divisions had been approximately located in rear of our portion of the front.

We held Cantigny. The Germans never afterwards reoccupied the village. The price paid was a heavy one but it demonstrated conclusively the fighting qualities and fortitude of the American soldier. Little has been heard or is known of this action. The enemy's rush on Château-Thierry and the dramatic entrance of our troops at that point, at the psychological moment, naturally attracted the undivided attention of the public in America.

It was not the ordeal of personal combat that seemed to prove the greatest strain in the last war. It was the endurance for days at a time of severe artillery bombardment by shells of heavy caliber, that proved the fortitude of troops. To be struck by these hideous impersonal agents without the power personally to strike back was the lot of the American soldier at Cantigny. On other fields later on, he overran the enemy, advanced deep into his positions, and suffered far heavier casualties. But the conditions were utterly different and the strain on the individual less severe.

This little village marks a cycle in the history of America. Quitting the soil of Europe to escape oppression and the loss of personal liberties, the early settlers in America laid the foundations of a government based on equality, personal liberty, and justice. Three hundred years later their descendants returned to Europe and on May 28, 1918, launched their first attack on the remaining forces of autocracy to secure these same principles for the peoples of the Old World.

CHAPTER VIII

Final Weeks in Picardy

GENERAL PERSHING established a temporary Advance Headquarters in a little village about twenty kilometers west of us, shortly after our arrival on the Picardy front. He felt it necessary to keep in close touch with what was happening in that region, and with his divisions which were then arriving to train in rear of the English to the north of us. During the fighting at Cantigny he was several times at our Headquarters, and on one occasion appeared in our dugout during a most critical and worrisome moment in the operation and surprised us all in laughter over a joke. A member of the Operations Section had given me a copy of *La Vie Parisienne,* and we were laughing somewhat hilariously over a rather risqué French bon mot. Instead of reproving us for such levity in the midst of a serious situation, he was probably reassured, as things could not be quite as bad as reported if we could find it possible thus to relax.

The troops around Cantigny were so exhausted and depleted by the third day of the fight that their relief became imperative. General Bullard was reluctant to put in his last remaining regiment, because there was a serious threat of a heavy German offensive on the Picardy front. When this could no longer be avoided, the Sixteenth Infantry was called on to take over the newly captured positions during the night. There was little opportunity for preliminary reconnaissance by the officers and there was a grave probability of these troops suffering heavy losses in moving forward for the relief. It was decided to reduce the garrison about one half, and to facilitate the operation a sketch map was quickly made which showed the front to be occupied by each of the new companies going in. The company limits were selected with a view to their being easy of location in the dark, and were clearly indicated on the sketch. Each officer in the Sixteenth was provided with one of these sketches, despite the risk of their falling into the hands of the Germans, and to the relief of everybody, the Sixteenth, under Colonel Bamford, occupied the new positions with a very small loss.[1]

The personnel of the organizations withdrawn was much mixed and it was necessary to transport them to villages some fifteen kilometers in rear and there sort them out on the following day. The fire of the heavy-caliber German guns had badly racked the nervous systems of both officers and men, and it required a hard heart not to permit them to relax and rest for many days after the terrific ordeal from which they had just emerged. The sky was clear and warm sunlight bathed the fields, filled with poppies and other spring flowers, making the little villages appear havens of comfort. By the hundreds the men cast themselves on the grass and slept or regaled themselves with the peaceful beauty of their surroundings. Exhausted in body and soul, nerves still racked by the concussions of the great shells, they all seemed to be reveling silently in the quiet and restful atmosphere. But the grim demands of war would not permit even twenty-four hours of rest for their fagged minds and exhausted bodies. As they constituted the only remaining reserve, and with the immediate prospect of another great German offensive, it was necessary to drive them to the work of cleaning and renewing their equipment, reorganizing their shattered ranks, and generally preparing for an early return to the fray, which occurred a few days later. The division was required to extend its lines to the north — doubling its original front — in order to relieve the French division on its left. This worked the most severe hardship on the machine-gunners, who in many cases had suffered a 60 percent loss and who were not even given a single night's rest, but were transferred into new positions on the extended front.

With the passing of plans for offensive action by the division and the assumption of a definite defensive role, the corps commander moved his Headquarters back to Breteuil, and assigned to the First

Division the former Corps Post of Command at the Château de Tartigny. Here we found ourselves established in comparative luxury. The building was something of a miniature Versailles, with a stone court on one side and a delightful park on the opposite. My billet was the room previously occupied by the corps commander, and from its windows afforded a beautiful view along the axis of the drive through the park. General Bullard occupied the former boudoir of Madame Tartigny, a beautiful room in gold and white, with many mirrors and a gilt bed. As it was not so much exposed to bombardment as our former shelter at Ménil-St. Firmin, we elected to sleep above ground, though an emergency shelter had been prepared in the cellar.

The improvements and added comforts in our surroundings affected the entire staff, and everyone wore a cheerful expression. However, the night bombing by the German planes grew more serious and the château seemed the focus of this activity. Those officers attached to Headquarters, whose duties did not directly pertain to combat, were quartered five kilometers in rear at the large town of Breteuil, but, unfortunately for them, the Germans turned one 8-inch gun on that locality and showered the town with bombs every night. In order to obtain some rest, these officers decided to sleep in the woods, as the weather was propitious and the Germans had not bothered these localities, but the Boche double-crossed them their first night in the open, by devoting all his attention to the woods. Out of this came an amusing incident. The Colonel commanding the trains had provided himself with a white pillow to which one of his young lieutenants took decided exception, claiming that it presented a target in the dark for the Boche aviators. It was reported that they had a rather heated argument in which the Colonel was unable to exercise the prerogatives of his rank.

As the first week in June drew to a close, the information of the enemy indicated preparations for an attack along our portion of the front and extending south through Montdidier. Every precaution against this threat was taken, but little could be done for the small detachments which composed the outposts, stationed from one to three kilometers in advance of the main line of resistance. On this duty an infantry company was assigned to approximately one kilometer of front, and disposed three of its four platoons in the first line, with the remaining platoon in support. Confronted with the probability of being attacked by ten times their number, these units had orders to fight in place or to counterattack. They were explicitly forbidden to withdraw, even though it was apparent they must be overwhelmed. Brutal as this arrangement may now seem, it was essential if the main line of resistance was to be maintained. Until the leading waves of the German infantry were at least partly checked and disarranged by our outposts, the deluge of artillery fire which was certain to fall on our main positions would make it well nigh impossible for those troops to break the momentum of the attack. In the previous battles that spring, the enemy generally overran the main lines and then quickly overwhelmed the artillery in rear and broke out into the open. The orders from Marshal Foch, and in turn from the commander of the group of armies, and of the army in which we were serving, plainly directed that not another foot of ground should be given up.

On the morning of June 8th, the corps commander, General Vandenburg, visited General Bullard and told him that a prisoner had been captured a few hours before who stated that the German assault troops were moving into position and the offensive would be launched on the morning of the 9th. That afternoon the French General commanding the division on our right paid us a visit. Shortly after his arrival Colonel Campbell King came into my office and told me to report with him to General Bullard. He also said that the French General had asked to see our plan of withdrawal and had been told that we had not prepared any. I found him with General Bullard in the latter's bedroom, and he spread on the table a copy of the directions he had just issued to the troops of his division to guide them in the event of attack on the morrow. His orders plainly and definitely provided for the withdrawal of all of his advance troops. The plan called for the infantry in the front-line trench to send up a rocket signal as soon as the German infantry debouched into No-man's-land. The French were then to begin a retrograde movement, while their artillery was to open fire on the enemy and this fire was to be in the nature of a retrograde barrage so that it would continue to bear on the advancing hostile infantry. The outposts were to stop at the main line of resistance and there make the fight. If it were possible of execution, this certainly would have been the most economical method of demoralizing the Germans in the earliest stages of their attack, but any man who has gone through a battle in trench warfare knows that there is small probability that the exact moment of assault could be detected. Preceded by long and violent artillery fire of preparation, including gas, resulting in clouds of dust, and causing the defenders to seek every shelter available, it was always a problem as to just when the real advance was beginning. Another factor, however, made this plan seem not only impracticable, but highly dangerous. Once troops had started to the rear under such circumstances, suffering heavy losses by artillery fire, confused by the terrific conditions incident to such moments, there was no telling just where they would stop, and there was the serious probability of the troops in rear being affected by the retreat of their comrades into their positions.

The French commander desired General Bullard to issue similar orders to the First Division, stating that they would be in keeping with the instructions from the higher command. In reply he was told that even if considered desirable it was too late to issue any such instructions, and that it was not believed that if issued in time they could be carried out by our troops. We pointed out the difficulty of insuring the sending up of the signal rockets at the right moment, the possibility of the men's becoming so disorganized in their retirement that they might carry this same spirit of disorganization into the main line of resistance. To this last, which I had stated, he took very decided exception, and, turning on me, said, "Young man, you should not say such things of your troops." He also remarked that we were somewhat inexperienced in this warfare and that he had had three years or more of fighting.

General Bullard at this time was sorting out some maps and produced one, unfortunately not the one he intended, which immediately attracted the attention of his visitor. It had on it a number of areas colored bright green to indicate the localities on which our heavy artillery was to fire under certain circumstances. It happened that most of those green spots lay within the sector of the division on our right, which was then occupied by French troops. This plan had been prepared to be put into execution should our Allied neighbors withdraw or be driven back during the attack. Naturally, it created a most unpleasant impression on the mind of the visiting General. He took immediate exception to it and General Bullard was not in a position to offer a tactful explanation. From this, the discussion passed on to consideration of the standing orders of the higher command. We had said that these orders forbade another foot of ground to be given up. He replied that we were taking this too literally, not understanding how to interpret the very general instructions of the commanders of armies and groups of armies. He also did not think we had quoted the instructions correctly; so I left the room and secured our copies, which sustained General Bullard's contention.

The conference had grown very difficult. The French General was angry and growing intolerant. Apparently due to my lack of years, he was most severe with me. As he rose to take his departure, after having been told finally by General Bullard that our orders to fight in place would stand, he remarked his concern over the situation and said, looking at me, as I held the guilty map, "You must remember that I am concerned as to the safety of my left flank." This seemed a little too much and I was indiscreet enough to reply, "But your troops are to retire, mon Général, and ours are to fight in place. General Bullard is the one to be concerned as to his flank."

Following this stormy session we went about making the final arrangements for the expected deluge. Late that night orders came from the Army Corps for our artillery to open with counterpreparation fire — that is, a heavy and continuous fire to be directed on the areas where the enemy's assault troops must form up — at an early hour in the morning, I have forgotten just when. Before this moment had arrived, the German artillery fire of preparation broke forth with a roar, and immediately everything turned loose. The morning of the 9th was clear and bright, facilitating observation. Reports commenced to arrive that the Germans were assaulting various portions of our front, but whether in force or with what success, we could not learn. From the division on our right also came reports that its entire front was being assailed.

With broad daylight the situation grew clearer, and it became apparent that the First Division front was not the object of the enemy's main infantry assault, but that he had launched three or four local attacks with groups of two or three hundred men each. These had been met in every instance by the outpost troops with a determined resistance, and, wherever necessary, with prompt counterattacks by the pitiful little support platoons. In one place it was reported that our counterattacking troops had crossed No-man's-land and gained a lodgment in the enemy's front-line trenches. These men knew that they could not retire and that, therefore, they must make the best of a terrible situation. As a result, they fought so desperately and determinedly that in no place was the enemy successful, and, in the one instance referred to, they even followed him back into his own trenches. To the south, on our right, a different situation unfolded itself. From our observation posts the advance of the Germans into the French lines could be seen. True they had been attacked in much greater force, but due at least partially to the withdrawal plan, the enemy gained before afternoon a depth of two and a half kilometers in portions of that French division's sector. Further south, and stretching on around Montdidier, and thence eastward toward Noyon, the main battle raged, and the enemy drove forward to a maximum advance of nine kilometers.

General Mangin — later to become famous at Soissons — was charged with a counterattack to break the momentum of the German penetration. With five fresh French divisions he carried out his mission, in an heroic enterprise of which little has been heard. The losses on the French side were appalling but the situation was saved.

About noon of the first day of the battle, when the loss of ground by the division on our right was growing serious, General Bullard, accompanied by General Summerall, motored back to Corps Headquarters to reach some definite understanding regarding the business of withdrawals. Not having been present at this interview, I can only recall what General Bullard told me later in the afternoon. It seems the corps commander was not then fully informed as to the loss of ground already sustained. Also he seemed inclined to think that the French division commander on our right had acted within the authority of his orders. While the corps staff was looking for their copy of the instructions from Marshal Foch, and from the commander of the group of armies, to which General Bullard had referred, General Debeney, commander of the First French Army, in which we were serving, arrived.[2] An officer of his staff had telephoned back to him from the front an approximately correct report of the situation, and the General was much exercised over the loss of ground sustained. When informed of the discussion then going on, he promptly and emphatically declared that the American division was the only one carrying out his orders. Further, he directed that the specific orders of the commander of one front-line regiment in each of the French divisions should be submitted to him that evening, that he might see whether they understood that not another foot of ground must be relinquished.

General Bullard seized this auspicious moment to request authority to do something which we had been struggling to accomplish since the previous January. A French division had three infantry regiments, while an American division had four. Whenever the First Division was employed under French control, we had been compelled to dispose its troops, not in the manner intended by our organization, but after the fashion prevailing in a three-regiment French unit. Usually, one of our regiments was held out as a corps reserve, which left us with a mangled formation, making it difficult to fight the division, and also to effect the current reliefs. Striking while the iron was hot, General Bullard received authority to deploy his unit after the American fashion.

The termination of the last German assault, launched June 9th, found the First Division stretched along eight kilometers of front, extending from Ménil-St. Georges, near Montdidier, northward to the Château Grivesnes. The last is famous as the scene of a final desperate effort by French Chasseurs to block the advance of the Germans through the gap in the line created by the disruptions of the Fifth British Army. The fighting had much resembled the scene portrayed in the famous picture of village fighting in the Franco-Prussian War, and *L'Illustration,* the leading French pictorial, reproduced a very thrilling painting of this later-day incident.

With the passing of the German threat, orders were received to reduce our artillery fire in an effort to quiet the sector. The enemy quickly responded by similar moderation, and we settled down to enjoy the beautiful spring days in comparative tranquillity. All four infantry regiments were now in line, each in column of battalions — one in the front line, one in support, and the third resting in reserve well to the rear. Each battalion commander was required to plan and carry out a raid during his ten days of front-line service. The division commander purposely waived any desire to examine the plans, and merely required a timely notification of the hour and place. The purpose of this arrangement was to develop initiative in battalion commanders, and to experience them in requesting artillery cooperation or support. Left to their own resources, they rapidly improved in technique and leadership, and some very dashing and successful raids resulted. The most profitable, from the viewpoint of prisoners, was carried out by a small detachment of Major Theodore Roosevelt's battalion. It was cleverly planned and quickly executed, and some thirty-five prisoners were captured with but small loss to our troops, except that the officer leading the raid — an old Regular Army Sergeant — was killed in hand-to-hand fighting with the Germans.

The evenings rapidly grew longer, the sun not going down until after nine o'clock, and the division staff inaugurated a daily baseball game immediately after dinner. Played in the courtyard, with an indoor baseball, exciting and amusing contests resulted. After some difficulty, we prevailed upon our French associates to join in the sport, but, with one exception, they made poor progress, mainly not being able to hit the ball, and, if they did, being too slow in getting under way toward first base.

These little interludes had a surprisingly good effect on morale. The orderlies would gather in the windows of the château and cheer the opposing sides — not refraining from typical baseball badinage. When a high fly coincided with the bursting of a German shell in the air over the château, not even one of Babe Ruth's home runs could have produced more thrills. While General Bullard did not play himself, he was always an interested spectator. We were due for a staff conference at nine-thirty each evening, and it became exceedingly difficult to draw the players away from the game in time for the meeting. Old General, the Count de Tartigny, frequently walked in his garden, watching the game. The complete sacrifice of dignity on the part of the players, and the freedom of comment by the soldiers, evidently puzzled the old aristocrat and created in his mind a decided doubt as to the state of discipline in the division.

About this time, June 30th, General Pershing arrived to make the first personal bestowals of Distinguished Service Crosses in the AEF. The men to receive this honor had won it months before in the Toul sector. A reserve battalion of the Eighteenth Infantry was to parade in the cover of a deep ravine near Paillard, and the men to be decorated were to be formed in front of the troops. I was sent ahead to see that the arrangements were carried out as desired by General Bullard, and that all would be ready when General Pershing appeared on the field. Lieutenant Holmes, of the Twenty-sixth Infantry, was the ranking soldier to be decorated. He had that morning participated in the raid carried out by Major Roosevelt's men, to which I have referred, and he arrived at the rendezvous for the ceremony covered with mud and his clothes besprinkled with blood from a German he had killed in the raid. Some clean clothes for him were hurriedly obtained, and all was made ready, the troops formed in line, the band on the qui vive, and the·principal actors of the occasion decidedly nervous. Just at this moment two French planes became engaged with two German Fokkers immediately overhead. A thrilling fight ensued, and one German plane plunged down in flames, crashing in the edge of the woods a hundred yards from the troops, who cheered the victory of their French allies. A few seconds later, the remaining Germans got "on the tail" of one of the Frenchmen, who fell in a spinning nose dive, or vrille, headed directly for the battalion. When he seemed not more than fifty feet above the ground he came out of his dive, which had evidently been a stratagem, and skimmed off close to the earth. The German, observing this maneuver, swooped down in a hawklike dive with his machine gun firing, but our French friend escaped unharmed. Shortly afterwards, General Pershing arrived and presented the medals.

Settling down to the life of a now quiet sector, all commanders dirccted their attention toward improving the living conditions for the men, polishing up their training in the light of our battle experience, and getting the animals in first-class shape. The horses had been badly run down, but the excellent grazing in Picardy had made it possible to do much to fatten them up again. The horse lines were usually established under the cover of woods, and the division and brigade commanders, as well as the staff, inspected these daily in an effort to inspire competition between the units. General Summerall, commanding the Artillery Brigade, made a special point of this, and his animals were metamorphosed by the much-needed rest, plenty of forage, and continuous grooming. As a further incentive he planned a series of horse shows to be held on the Fourth of July, which gradually expanded into contests between all the batteries in their firing positions, as to which could make the finest showing. Everything about the guns was repainted and highly polished, caissons were scraped and recamouflaged, flowers were planted around the gun pits, and the whole command became quite enthusiastic.

A large raid had been planned for July 8th, and we had secured 7500 mustard-gas shells from the French for this occasion.[3] These were among the first of this dreaded type of gas which the Allies produced, and while we had become accustomed to suffering from the evil effect of those fired by the Germans, the enemy had not yet experienced this new horror. However, before we had progressed very far with the plans for this raid, orders were received, late on July 3rd, that the division would be relieved by two French divisions on the nights of the 5th and 6th, and the reconnaissance details from the latter would go over the sector on the night of the 4th. This sudden change in plans had us all hustling, but it was determined the Fourth of July should be appropriately celebrated nevertheless. At daybreak that morning four raids were attempted, but three of them did not find any of the enemy in his advanced trenches. The fourth, by rare good luck, encountered a German raiding party lined up in the firing trench, preparatory to starting for the American lines. There were about fifty Germans while the Americans numbered only fifteen or twenty, but our men were on the offensive and on top, while the Boche were standing in trenches. A regular knock-down drag-out fight resulted, and a much-desired prisoner was secured by dragging him out of the trench by the nape of the neck and prodding him into a run across No-man's-land. From this prisoner we learned that the Germans had anticipated some Fourth of July activities, and consequently had withdrawn their men from the advanced positions. At noon all the guns of the division opened fire on the German lines for ten minutes, as a form of national salute.

During the morning and afternoon a horse show was being conducted in the park by the château, and judges were visiting all the battery positions and horse lines to decide on the winners in that contest. An English colonel was one of the officials judging artillery emplacements, and he was much amused by the sporting contest going on while the guns being inspected were firing at the enemy. General Tartigny officiated as a judge at the horse show, and it was quite apparent that he was tremendously impressed by the swagger-looking outfits paraded for inspection — for it was hard to realize that these were the same carelessly dressed, muddy men and worn-down horses he had observed when we entered the sector. That night there was a dinner at Corps Headquarters in honor of the American Independence Day. Several French officers, including General Vandenburg, made speeches paying glowing tributes to the services of the division and expressing heartfelt regret that we were about to leave. I was called on to make the reply and had just enough champagne to undertake this duty in a very nonchalant spirit. While the other American officers claimed my speech was verbless, yet I ended in such a grand burst of oratory that General Vandenburg leaped to his feet and impulsively embraced me, kissing me on either cheek.

At nine-thirty that night, just as the French officers were starting their reconnaissance of the positions to be occupied by their troops, we turned on the last feature of our Fourth of July program, firing all of the 7500 mustard gas shells into the German lines. This was the Boche's first taste of his own medicine, and caused a tremendous rumpus, various colored flares being sent up all along his front. During the previous five or six days we had averaged about 300 German shells arriving in the sector a day, but as a result of our activities on the Fourth they fired 17,000 at us, but only inflicted four slight casualties. In contrast to this, on the following day their fire was reduced to about 300 shells, yet we had one officer killed, another wounded, four men killed, and seventeen wounded.

The next two days were a busy period as our units were successively drawn out of the line and replaced by French organizations. Finally three quarters of the garrison were French and General Bullard, at an hour ordered by the corps commander, turned over the command of the sector to the two French division commanders. The instructions required an American officer of the division staff to remain at our old Headquarters for twenty-four hours longer, and I was designated for this duty. It seemed very lonely in the château with all my friends gone, and their places occupied by Frenchmen. On the night of the 7th, the French division commander assigned to the château made dinner a farewell party for me. A delicious meal was served, the cook being a chef from a well-known Paris restaurant, and the conversation ran more or less on the experiences of the First Division and American relations with our Allies. Old General Tartigny was also present on this occasion, and remarked to me his regret that we were leaving the shelter of his roof. At one end of the large state dining room hung a life-sized painting of Louis XIV, and the "Grand Monarch" was so posed that his eye seemed to regard each person at the table. His expression appeared contemptuous, and, in replying to General Tartigny, I referred to the painting, saying, "Your King has eyed us daily at each meal and it has always seemed to me that he was somewhat cynical in his toleration of our presence." The old gentleman arose from his chair and made a very formal reply.

"Mon Colonel," he said, "I shall always remember the men of the First Division. I saw them come in the hour of France's great peril. I saw them die by the hundreds in the ruins of my other château at Villers-Tournelles. I have given orders that those ruins shall remain untouched, and after the war I will build a wall around them and erect a monument to the memory of the Americans who died defending my property and the soil of France." With tears in his eyes, he continued: "When you first came I did not understand you. Your manners and your customs were so different from ours. Direct and businesslike, you at times seemed very brusque. But I have come to know you, and now I tell you and also these French compatriots of mine that the American is nature's great gentleman." He concluded by raising his glass, and the others rose and drank a health to the First Division.

The reaction of this old Royalist was to me a very interesting thing. I had watched him for weeks, wearing much the same expression as his old King, and now there was not doubt in my mind but that, to his own surprise, he had grown to appreciate what manner of men the Americans were. He had thought that we were a crude, ruthless, commercial nation, and he had found us even more idealistic, though less voluble, than the impassioned Frenchman.

The next morning, at eight o'clock, my period of service in the Cantigny sector expired, and I motored south to Nivillers, where Division Headquarters was located in a modern château. The troops were scattered in the villages surrounding Beauvais, though some of the artillery units had not yet completed their marches. Everyone relaxed and breathed a sigh of relief that for a time at least he would be freed from the noise of exploding shells, the dampness of the dugouts, and the strain of an impending attack. Our long-continued occupancy of a battle sector had changed habits of life until it was difficult to bring one's self back to the normal routine. The vicious and continuous shelling peculiar to the Cantigny sector had forced the regimental officers to confine all of their movements to periods of darkness. Reconnaissances, visits of inspection, transportation of food and reliefs were carried out under the cover of night. Breakfast was usually served late in the evening, after which the personnel went about their active duties which generally occupied the remainder of the night. Dawn being the hour most propitious for attack, everyone was held on the alert at that time, and later would have dinner. With the coming of broad daylight most of the garrison would go to sleep, and it was not until evening that the current activities of the sector were resumed. Those who woke up hungry in the middle of the day sometimes had a light meal, but as a rule the majority of the officers and men slept through until evening. After several months of this abnormal existence, it was hard to effect a readjustment.

Beauvais immediately became a center of pleasurable activity, and, while intensive training was resumed at once, great liberty was permitted in granting passes to the men, that they might have some relaxation before undergoing any more hardships. Regimental bands were sent down to play in the quaint little "Place," and the men filled the chairs of the sidewalk cafés, and luxuriated in this new freedom. The public bathhouse did a thriving business, and the old lady who ran it quickly sold all her packages of bath perfumes and pink soap.

I recall an incident concerning myself, which occurred at this bathhouse earlier in the spring. About two weeks after my ankle had been fractured, General Bullard motored with me down to Beauvais for a bath. I had not had my clothes off since the accident and was feeling pretty seedy. With the assistance of the General and a too-short pair of French crutches, I made my way to a bathroom. The proprietress furnished me with a bag of highly colored perfume to put in the water. General Bullard thoughtfully assisted me to undress and helped me into the tub. He then went about arranging for his own bath in another portion of the building. After I had finished mine, I wanted to get word to him to help me out of the tub, and pounded on the door with a crutch. The old lady came at my call and told me through the door that General Bullard had just started on his bath, having been delayed in obtaining a vacant room, and before I could object, she opened the door, came in, and insisted on helping me out of the tub and into my clothes. I suffered considerable embarrassment in trying to balance on one leg while going through the drying process in the presence of this imperturbable old dame.

At Division Headquarters in the Château Nivillers, we were busily engaged in burnishing up the training of the troops for what we knew would be an arduous summer campaign. I had three young assistants, without military experience prior to the war, and these were temporarily assigned to regiments to get in more intimate touch with the actual conditions among the troops. The careers of these young men were very interesting and worth recounting. All of them under twenty-four and new to the Army, they had been assigned to me the previous January. With no training whatsoever as to staff duties, they had everything to learn, while I had little or no time in which to teach them. But under "Monsieur Stern Necessity" they developed into amazingly capable staff officers, and were an interesting example of the rapidity with which an American can adapt himself to the performance of an intricate and difficult task.

Chauncey Belknap had obtained a commission through the Plattsburgh Training Camp.[4] He was a Princeton graduate and had prepared for the profession of law. I used him as a general utility man to make inspections, to oversee entrainments and bus movements, to guide troops back in the darkness on their relief from battle, and for a variety of other similar duties. A complicated and important message center — new to American practice, but which was the vital center of all communication throughout the Division — was first organized in our Army by Belknap of the First Division. Gathering his ideas from English and French practice, he quickly evolved a very reliable service. Being a little too conspicuous in this position, he was soon spotted by General Conner, Chief of the Operations Division of the AEF, and shortly before we left the Picardy sector, he was relieved from duty with the division and ordered to Chaumont.[5] There at one time he had charge of all troop movements in France, and carried out this tremendous job in a highly efficient manner.

Jimmie Edgar of New York was another member of this group. He performed much the same duties as Belknap, and distinguished himself by the indefatigable and courageous fashion in which he accepted his responsibilities. During a portion of our stay in Picardy, he was made responsible for our liaison with the French division on our right, and usually made daily visits to the left regiment and brigade of that division. Highly concerned over their orders, previously referred to by me, for the withdrawal of their advanced troops in case of attack, he accepted this situation as a reflection on him because of his relation with that division, and had numerous heated discussions with the French brigade commander in his endeavor to secure a change. That the latter officer, about twenty-five years Edgar's senior in age and service, should have tolerated this young boy's suggestions was quite a compliment to him. Edgar remained with the division to the end and was the principal actor in a number of highly exciting and sometimes amusing incidents. At St. Mihiel he was charged with maintaining contact with the tanks and in this duty had to spend much of his time during the attack in advance of the front-line troops. His knowledge of the practical issues involved in the moving and fighting of a division, as a result of his many and varied experiences, was truly remarkable.

The third member of this triumvirate was Benjamin Caffey, Jr., a Salt Lake boy who had gotten his inspiration at a civilian training camp in the summer of 1916.[6] I succeeded in keeping him with me throughout most of the war, and from knowing virtually nothing of the military game in the summer of 1917, he, on at least one occasion during the Meuse-Argonne battle, prepared the draft, which was accepted unchanged, for the field order directing the next day's operations of the Army when it had a strength of nearly a million men. I carried him with me to the First Army when I became its Chief of Operations, and on to the Eighth Corps when I was transferred there as Chief of Staff. The assistance of this young man relieved me of all concern regarding a thousand and one details in undertaking a new job in a newly organized unit. His practical knowledge of battle conditions made it possible to send him to divisions engaged in battle and obtain, in a minimum of time, a very accurate forecast of just what they would be able to do and in what they would probably fail. Regular officers of many years' service, and without his experience, would have been utterly unable to size up the confused battle situations as did this young fellow. In the early part of the Meuse-Argonne battle, he filled my old job in the First Division, and finally returned to the United States as Assistant Chief of Staff of the Thirty-sixth Division.

On the night of the 12th of July, four days after I had left the Cantigny sector, orders arrived relieving me from duty with the division and ordering me to proceed without delay to Chaumont for service in the Operations Section of the General Staff of General Headquarters. My plans had all been laid to get command of a regiment in the division, and this not only denied me that duty, but removed me from the front. At the same time came orders relieving General Bullard and advancing him to command of the newly organized Third Corps, consisting of the First and Second divisions. Hurriedly packing my few effects and saying goodbye to my friends, I prepared to start by automobile at six o'clock the next morning.

About midnight, after I had retired, Colonel Hamilton Smith, commanding the Twenty-sixth Infantry, came in from his regiment to tell me goodbye. He sat on the side of the bed and talked over our recent experiences for about an hour and then wished me luck and Godspeed. While he was talking, orders were received for the First Division to move the next day to the southeast. We had expected to remain in the region of Beauvais for several weeks, so this was a great surprise. Smith left immediately, and less than a week later was killed leading his regiment in the great battle of Soissons, the turning point of the war.

No one knew the portent of these new orders, and when I took my departure the next morning, all the staff were speculating as to the immediate future. The division was thought to be too tired and exhausted for employment in battle, so I left feeling that they would probably be moved to and fro from one reserve position to another for the next three or four weeks.

It was hard to preserve one's composure in saying goodbye to these men with whom I had been so intimately associated for over a year in France. We had been pioneers and our trials and tribulations had served to bind us very close to one another. I can see them now — gathered in the broad doorway of the château. The friendly jests and affectionate farewells, as I got into the Cadillac, made a deep impression on my mind, and I drove off hardly daring to wonder when and where would be our next meeting. Six days later they dashed into the great counterattack which precipitated the retreat of the German Army, and within seventy-two hours every field officer of the infantry, excepting three colonels, had fallen. Smith and all four of the Lieutenant Colonels were killed, and every battalion commander was a casualty, dead or wounded; 3800 prisoners and 68 field guns were the spoils of the First Division, and the Soissons–Château-Thierry Road had been crossed by its troops.

Thus ended my association with this great combat organization. Bigger problems were to come — but never again that feeling of comradeship which grows out of the intimate relationship among those in immediate contact with the fighting troops. Whatever else was to happen to me — in that war or in the future — could be but a minor incident in my career. It was my great good fortune to start with these men in the first weeks of the struggle, and to see them through its first year. The huge combat armies of the AEF were to be born soon afterwards, and an uninterrupted confusion of movement and fighting was to continue through hurried months to the sudden Armistice.

CHAPTER IX

Chaumont

THE TRIP from Beauvais to Chaumont by automobile required thirteen hours, which included a brief stop for lunch in Paris. During the early stages long supply trains and columns of artillery interfered somewhat with our progress; but once south of Paris there was nothing to delay us and the roads had not been damaged by war traffic. We skimmed along through Provins and Troyes and had reached the little village of Juzencourt, ten miles from our destination, about eight o'clock in the evening, when our last spare tire blew out. I telephoned from the Mairie to the Motor Transport Park in Chaumont, requesting assistance. Fortunately, the officer answering the telephone was a veteran of the First Division, who had been incapacitated for field service by a wound in February. Otherwise, they probably would have told me to spend the night where I was.

While waiting for the repair car I entered into dinner negotiations with a nice old French lady. In a very short time she prepared an appetizing meal of an omelet, lettuce salad, coffee, and confiture. Her dining room opened out on a little walled-in garden, where she conducted me after the meal and begged for information regarding the probable duration of the war. Somehow this old lady made an indelible impression on my mind and gave me an insight of the peasant's point of view, of which I had previously been unaware. She made a definite engagement for me to return and offered as an inducement the promise of a special repast. I left with her my customary emergency rations — some bars of coarse sweet chocolate, a box of figs, and several packages of cigarettes.

About nine o'clock we started on our way and soon reached Chaumont. General Fox Conner, Chief of Operations of the AEF, gave me a room in his house, which he shared with General Leroy Eltinge, Deputy Chief of Staff of the AEF.[1] The following morning at breakfast, I met the members of the mess, who, with the exception of General Eltinge, were all on duty in the Operations Section of the General Staff, and most of them old friends of mine — Colonel Hugh A. Drum, a few days later appointed Chief of Staff of the First Army; Colonel Upton Birnie; [2] Colonel Walter Grant, later Deputy Chief of Staff of the First Army; [3] Colonel Samuel Gleaves, in charge of troop movements of the AEF; [4] Colonel John Murphy; Major Xenophon Price, the officer in charge of the famous secret battle-order map showing day by day the location of all the Allied and German divisions, and now on exhibition in the Smithsonian Institution; [5] Major Albert Kuegle, the Secretary of the Operations Section.[6] They composed a very agreeable group, all intimately in touch with the affairs of the AEF, and deeply concerned with its difficulties and achievements. A sense of humor was an essential qualification to each member; otherwise his peace of mind would be seriously disturbed three times a day. Guests were frequent and usually officers or civilians of considerable importance. From them came the latest news from the States, or England, or Italy, and it was interesting to get the diverse points of view, each prejudiced according to the individual's special environment. Ambassador and Mrs. Page, from Rome, urged the immediate dispatch to Italy of large numbers of American troops; the visitor from London desired to transfer the entire AEF to the British front; and the man from the States seemed to speak a different language from ours.

I found myself in a strange atmosphere. These new associates had been working for a year on the plans and organization for an army of several million men. Questions of ocean tonnage, ports of debarkation, construction of docks and great depots in the SOS — these filled their mind every day. The methods of training divisions newly arrived in France, the problem of securing French 75's and British heavy guns, the manufacture of tanks, and our complicated relations with the French and English were ordinary topics of conversation and discussion. To me this was a different world from that in which I had lived during the past year. In the First Division we had struggled with the concrete proposition of feeding, clothing, training, marching, and fighting the men. Their health and morale was a daily issue; their dead and wounded a daily tragedy. For six months, saving the period of the hurried move to Picardy, we had been continuously in the line in immediate contact with the enemy. Our minds had been unconcerned with boats and ports and warehouses. Huge projects for the future made no appeal to us. We wanted trained replacements to fill the thinning ranks, more ammunition and horses; less frequent visits from critical staff officers in limousines would have met our approval. Each man was living in his own little world, ignorant to a surprising degree of all that occurred elsewhere.

On my first morning in Chaumont, General Conner instructed me to gather all possible information regarding the St. Mihiel salient and to work on a plan for its reduction. The main Headquarters were located in a huge caserne or barracks, and it took me quite a while to find my way about and learn the ropes. However, before getting well started on this new job, an order came for me to proceed with General Harold Fiske, head of the training section of the General Staff, and Colonel Stuart Heintzelman, Chief of Staff of the Fourth Army Corps, as a member of a Board to investigate the circumstances of a raid conducted the previous day by the Seventy-seventh Division, which was having its preliminary trench-warfare training in the Baccarat sector.[7,8]

The following morning we motored through Neufchâteau and Colombey-les-Belles to Lunéville, and then due east to the sector in the northern foothills of the Vosges Mountains. At Division Headquarters we learned that a Captain Barrett had planned a silent daylight raid on a portion of the front where our trenches, the enemy's trenches, and No-man's-land lay in a forest with heavy underbrush. The exact number of men concerned in this operation has escaped my memory, but the party led by Captain Barrett slipped through the woods and out a passage through the enemy's wire entanglements. They then turned to their left, with the idea of eventually retiring through another gap yet to be cut. Unfortunately, the enemy was aware of the maneuver and surprised the detachment with a heavy fire. Captain Barrett and a number of men were killed and an equal number captured, a total of about twenty, I believe. The remainder made their escape, but could only give a vague idea of what had occurred, due to the confusion and the underbrush.

We motored up to Brigade Headquarters and obtained that commander's statement, and from there proceeded on to Regimental Headquarters and finally to Battalion Headquarters. Leaving our automobile at this last point, we walked forward through the trenches to the point in the front line from which the raiding party had debouched. It was possible to make a short reconnaissance in No-man's-land, which was a tangled thicket, heavily timbered. We were able to see parts of the enemy's wire but nothing of his trenches. From talks with various members of Captain Barrett's company, who were still on duty in this section, we gained a very fair idea of what had occurred and, returning to our car, motored back to Lunéville for dinner.

This detail had been most distasteful to me, because for the past year I had been in the position of resenting the frequent appearance of boards and inspectors from GHQ, to examine into what we had done and to discover what we might have failed to do. As a rule in those days it was very difficult to carry out any operation exactly according to Hoyle, because of the limited amount of training and complete lack of experience on the part of the men and the young officers, and the frequent lack of materiel and other means which, theoretically, were supposed to be available. Difficulties and embarrassments were to be expected; the problem was to carry your operation to a successful conclusion despite them. Now I found myself in the role of an inspector or probable faultfinder. Throughout the day we had all three refrained from expressing to one another any opinion as to the responsibility for this small disaster, but during dinner the question arose as to what else was to be done. Colonel Heintzelman explained that he must leave that same night for the Fourth Corps Headquarters in order to conduct a training exercise the following morning for a newly arrived division. General Fiske then decided he would accompany Colonel Heintzelman to Corps Headquarters and continue on to Chaumont that night, as he had important business awaiting him. As the junior member of the Board, I was told to go back to the sector the next morning and complete the investigation. This rather put the "finding" up to me, but I demurred, stating that I knew of nothing else to investigate which could possibly change the opinion I had already formed. They then called on me to state my conclusion, which was to the effect that a telegram should be sent to the Seventy-seventh Division Commander by the Chief of Staff of the AEF, congratulating him on the offensive spirit displayed in attempting this raid, and expressing the hope that the unfortunate result would not deter the division from undertaking further offensive operations. To my delight they agreed with me, so we started home immediately after dinner and the following morning a telegram was dispatched by General McAndrew, Chief of Staff, in accordance with our recommendation. Whether justified or not, the outcome of this incident gave me considerable personal satisfaction through a feeling that I was doing something to encourage those who were struggling to learn the intricacies of trench warfare.

A day or two later General Conner handed me the record of a meeting on July 24th between Marshal Foch and the Allied commanders, in which it was agreed that an operation should be immediately carried out by the English and French to reduce the Montdidier salient and thus clear the railroad at that point, and a similar operation should be executed by an American army in the latter part of the summer to smash the St. Mihiel salient and free the Nancy-Paris Railroad. Orders had just been issued establishing the Headquarters of the First Army with Colonel Hugh A. Drum as Chief of Staff, and he had collected his assistants and left for the scene of the fighting north of the Marne, where new American divisions were entering into battle for the first time.

The entire aspect of the war had changed. The great counteroffensive on July 18th at Soissons had swung the tide of battle in favor of the Allies, and the profound depression which had been accumulating since March 21st was in a day dissipated and replaced by a wild enthusiasm throughout France and especially directed toward the American troops who had so unexpectedly assumed the leading role in the Marne operation. Only one who has witnessed the despair and experienced the desperate resolution when defeat is anticipated, can fully realize the reversal of feeling flowing from the sudden vision of a not too distant victory. The stock of confidence in America, which had been quoted far below par, was in a day sold at a premium. Wherever American troops appeared, they were cheered and acclaimed by the French populace, truly after the fashion so frequently and erroneously described in the American press prior to this time. I am recording this passing phase of public opinion in order to present the contrast which quickly followed.

With more definite data available, I started on the preparation of detailed plans for the reduction of the St. Mihiel salient. At first, but six American divisions were to be employed. The object of the operation was merely to free the east and west railroad, which did not lie within the enemy's lines but was dominated by his artillery. With the limited number of troops then considered available, it was only possible to direct an attack against the south face of the salient a little to the east of St. Mihiel. The ground was rugged and the enemy's positions occupied dominating and heavily wooded heights extending east from St. Mihiel toward the plain of the Woëvre. As I finished this particular plan, General Conner notified me that the number of divisions which would be available had been increased to ten. This more or less completely changed the layout and I worked out a new plan. As I completed the latter, the number of available divisions was increased to fourteen, and consequently a much more elaborate operation became possible, and was planned accordingly. The most difficult phases of this work consisted in developing tentative plans for the concentration of this large force, making the calculations for the number and caliber of the heavy guns and of the tanks and special Engineer and pioneer troops to be borrowed from the French.

As this last plan was about completed, the situation so developed that sixteen American and six French divisions became available for the operation, which now contemplated the complete reduction of the salient by heavy attacks on both flanks and the advance of our lines to the outskirts of the famous fortifications of Metz. The changes had been so frequent and the demands so pressing that I forgot the number of operations planned until I found them bound in one document in the files of the War Department four years later.

At this stage of the affair the papers were dispatched to the newly formed First Army Headquarters, which had hurriedly moved from the Marne front to Neufchâteau, where General Pershing had gone in person to take immediate charge of the concentration of troops and direct the arrangements for the operation.

As our soldiers began to gather in large numbers in the region around Neufchâteau, they had much to say regarding America's plans, and, unfortunately, due to their geographical location, made alarmingly accurate guesses as to the next move. These reports spread broadside over France and finally were reprinted in a German paper; and the Intelligence Section learned of a visit by Von Hindenburg to Metz.[9] I was, therefore, put to work on plans for an operation in the Belfort gap just north of the Swiss frontier, where we were at that moment staging a fake show to draw the enemy's attention from St. Mihiel. It was felt for a time that it might possibly become necessary to give up the St. Mihiel operation and, therefore, the Belfort plan was to be prepared as a possible, though undesirable, substitute.

My state of mind at this period is impossible to describe. I seemed to be getting farther and farther away from the fight, and it was particularly hard to work on a plan and then not be permitted to attend its execution. In this situation, General Lejeune of the Marine Corps, who then commanded the Second Division, with his Chief of Staff, Colonel Preston Brown, arrived in my office to arrange for me to command the Twenty-third Infantry in the St. Mihiel fight.[10,11] Not being my own master, I could only refer them to General Conner, and implore them to make a strong plea for me. They left me to see him with the proposal that if I would be allowed to join the regiment four days before the attack, they would release me immediately after the fight. In about twenty minutes they returned with General Conner, and he instructed me to pack up and leave within the hour. It seemed too good to be true, but in the next sentence he explained that I would not go to the Twenty-third Infantry but would report as Assistant to the Chief of Staff of the First Army at Neufchâteau,

General Pershing having directed my temporary detachment from GHQ.

Without taking time to pack up my clothes, contenting myself merely with a trench coat and the necessary toilet articles, I left at once for Neufchâteau, where I arrived in the middle of the afternoon of August 20th. Colonel Drum immediately asked me to check up the plans which his staff had made for the concentration of the five hundred thousand (500,000) men to be employed in the St. Mihiel operation. This I did that evening and found nothing of any moment to suggest. He then directed me to work with Colonel Walter Grant on the battle order for the St. Mihiel attack. The latter officer, a very dear friend of mine, and one of the most efficient people in the Army, needed little assistance and in a few hours we had the first draft completed. There were a number of minor matters to which Colonel Drum had directed my attention, but I recall he told me to draw up a set of combat instructions for the First Army. With the assistance of a capable stenographer, my own experience in the First Division, the dictums of GHQ and — honesty compels me to admit — copies of Ludendorff's most recent tactical instructions for the German Army, I dictated an eight-page order, outlining the tactics to be employed in the various phases of operations, which involved a break through carefully fortified positions, followed by fighting in the open.[12] There was so much to do and so little time in which to do it that, in this particular instance, I never saw the completed order until 1920, and it was a matter of considerable satisfaction to find, contrary to the usual reaction, that the statements in the finished product impressed me more favorably than at the time they were dictated.

My next assignment was to arrange for the transfer of the front to be occupied by our army in the St. Mihiel operation to our control. This required a visit by me to the Headquarters of the Eighth French Army southwest of Lunéville, which controlled one half of the line in which we were interested, and to the Headquarters of the Second French Army at Laheycourt, northwest of Bar-le-Duc, which held the western half of our front to be. Through long experience while with the First Division, I had learned something of how to get results in dealing with French officials. They were very punctilious in their attitude, but sometimes the most courteous delays proved exceedingly irritating. Time was golden to us and to me personally, and, therefore, red tape was apt to be somewhat infuriating. About this stage of my career in France, I developed the practice of utilizing a collection of military phrases commonly employed by a certain type of French officer, who had graduated from the Ecole de Guerre and occupied most of the important staff positions in the French Army. My old friend "en principe," of disastrous consequences during early Gondrecourt days, was the leader in this collection. "C'est bien entendu" was a close second, and there were many more which I have now forgotten. It was rather amusing to see how readily the employment of one or more of these stock expressions would win for me special regard and favorable action, and I employed them freely on this hurried trip.

On returning to Neufchâteau I found the Headquarters of the Army was moving to Ligny-en-Barrois, a large town a few miles south of Bar-le-Duc. Most of the supply and administrative services of Army Headquarters remained at Neufchâteau where they could function just as effectively as at the more advanced location of the main Headquarters. The work now had become particularly grueling; changes were frequent and the recently organized Corps Headquarters were so new to their duties that orders had to be abnormally lengthy and precise in detail. My working hours ran from eight in the morning until two or three o'clock the following morning, with no chance for physical relaxation. To secure some exercise I selected a billet on the outskirts of the town, a mile from my office. This insured at least two miles of walking every day. My room was located in a small and gloomy château, from the windows of which there was a view of a walled-in garden of damp and unhealthy aspect. The owner, a former Mayor of Ligny, was a curious individual of uncertain age, who carefully avoided meeting me. He was so stoop-shouldered as to appear deformed and I gathered from his wife, a rather sprightly and agreeable old lady, that he was a confirmed hypochondriac. One servant came in during the day, and they seemed to be living in extremely economical style. Madame usually endeavored to see me as I left in the morning, and had many questions to ask about what the American Army planned to do. Throughout the hours of darkness a continuous column of our troops flowed by the door each day, all marching north. This excited her curiosity, which grew with the numbers of the passing thousands.

As the time for the battle drew near, the work became more pressing and extremely exacting. Army Headquarters had been but recently organized and most of the officers, clerks, and men had had little or no experience in active operations. The desire had been to secure officers for this duty who had already served with some of our divisions which had been engaged with the enemy, but, as was to be expected, the commanders of these divisions vigorously opposed the relief of their best men, particularly as most of the units were then involved in active operations in connection with the reduction of the Marne salient. This unfamiliarity with the practical details of initiating a modern trench-warfare battle, coupled with the squeaking of the machinery in a new organization, made the task an especially heavy one. Furthermore, this was not a simple case of an army undertaking an offensive operation, but it was the combination of the birth of an army, the procurement of materiel and detachments for its services from virtually every point in France not occupied by the enemy, and the plunging of this huge infant into the greatest battle in which American troops had over engaged. While learning the name and capability of the confidential stenographer, one was simultaneously engaged in employing him in the preparation of the final orders for the battle. Equally unknown and a stranger to his surroundings was the orderly who carried confidential messages to and fro, and located this and that officer at your request. The motorcycle and automobile couriers, hurriedly collected, were pushed night and day in the delivery of orders to units stationed anywhere from the English Channel to the Swiss frontier. I recall at least one instance of a motorcycle courier falling asleep on his machine, wrecking it and himself in consequence.

The number of officers on duty in the Headquarters at this time was in the neighborhood of five hundred (500) which was gradually decreased as the personnel became more familiar with their respective duties, and the initial concentration of the army was completed.

Major George C. Marshall

Captain Marshall; Colonel Voris; Lieutenant Hugo (great-grandson of Victor Hugo); Major Drain; Madame Jouatte, in whose house Captain Marshall was billeted at Gondrecourt; a French refugee and her little girl, 1917

Colonel Marshall conversing with Major General Henry T. Allen, Eighth
Corps Commander

Assembly of First Division Officers waiting to hear General Pershing before Montdidier in Picardy Great German Offensive, March 21–April 3, 1918. Colonel Marshall is standing addressing the officers

Colonel Campbell King, Chief of Staff First Division; General Hines;
Colonel Marshall at Beauvais, June 1918, just after Cantigny

Cartoon History of the First Division: Officers

Troops in a chapel at Vaux, Ardennes, November 5, 1918, just before
Meuse-Argonne

HEADQUARTERS, 8TH INFANTRY BRIGADE,
AMERICAN EXPEDITIONARY FORCES,
France, 15, Nov., 1918.

From: Brigadier General E. E. Booth.

To: The Adjutant General, American E.F.

Subject: Confidential Report and Recommendations.

1. In compliance with letter from G.H.Q., A.E.F., dated Nov. 12, 1918,
I have the honor to recommend the following officers for promotion to the
grade of Brigadier General:

X X X   X   X   X   X   X   X   X

(b) Colonel George C. Marshall, General Staff, A.C. of S. (G-3),
1st Army.

I have known Colonel Marshall for more than 15 years. I
served with him at Fort Leavenworth where he was an instructor
in the GENERAL SERVICE and STAFF COLLEGE, in the Phillipine
Islands where he was on duty with troops and on the staff of
the Eastern Department. I know of his services as G-3 of 1st
Division and as G-3 of the 1st Army. Colonel Marshall was an
exceptionally capable company commander. As a staff officer
he has in my opinion few equals. He demonstrated exceptional
qualities in leadership while acting as Chief of Staff of a
reinforced brigade during a very intensive maneuver campaign
in the Phillipine Islands in 1912. All officers connected
with that maneuver recognized in him one of the best qualified
men for a high command or a high staff position in the army.
He was entrusted with work of importance and responsibility
while on staff duty in the Eastern Department which he discharged with credit to himself and the service. Colonel
Marshall is an officer of excellent judgement, clear comprehension
and courage of his convictions. I think that he stands out
among his brother officers as exceptionally well qualified
for promotion to the grade of General Officer and for the
exercise of high command.

Confidential Copy to Colonel Marshall

E.E.B

Recommendation from General Booth to the Adjutant General AEF concerning promotion of Colonel Marshall to General Officer

Staff Officers, Eighth Army Corps, Montigny-sur-Aube, January 11, 1919

Le Maréchal Pétain et le Général Pershing   Metz 29.4.19.

Marshal Pétain and General Pershing, with Colonel Marshall in background, at Metz, April 29, 1919

Photograph inscribed and presented to Colonel Marshall by Marshal Foch

3.

*The Lord Chamberlain is
commanded by Their Majesties to invite*

Colonel George C. Marshall

*to an Afternoon Party in the Garden of
Buckingham Palace on Wednesday the 16th July, 1919
from 4 to 6:30 p.m. (Weather Permitting)*

Morning Dress

Invitation to Buckingham Palace garden party

Photograph taken at garden party and inscribed by Colonel Marshall:
"General Pershing and Churchill"   "Mrs. Churchill and my left leg"

General Pershing in London Victory Parade, July 19, 1919

General Pershing and Colonel Marshall inspecting battlefields, August 1919

Inspecting Montfaucon, August 1919

Inspecting St. Mihiel Field, August 1919

En route home after World War, September 1919

Leviathan docking at Hoboken, September 8, 1919, with General Pershing, General Fox Conner, Colonel Marshall, Colonel Quekemeyer

In my own case, for example, I was not formally assigned to the army, but merely attached to assist the Chief of Staff in getting the operation under way. Colonel Grant, previously referred to, was similarly attached; and we took over one job after another as the occasion demanded, and both were charged with the preparation of orders for the St. Mihiel attack and the follow-through of the battle. A little later we both received permanent assignments to the army and were relieved from all connection with GHQ — much to our delight. Colonel Grant was one of those unusually capable men with initiative and a highly developed sense of responsibility, who at the same time enjoyed the relaxation of a little frivolous badinage to lessen the strain. The more serious the situation, the more absurdities we usually indulged in, for our own private amusement, and even after our duties separated us we usually employed the telephone for a short time each day to exchange the latest story and offer a few words of cheer and encouragement. While this may seem incongruous in connection with the conduct of a battle, yet it played an important part in promoting optimism, and I find it has left me with many delightful recollections.

Finishing work one morning at four o'clock, I decided to sleep until ten, and, as luck would have it, turned a corner on my way to the office and met General Pershing. While I felt justified in the lateness of the hour at which I was going to work, yet I did not care to undertake any explanations, as excuses are poor business at best. He inquired as to what I was doing, referring, I believe, to my work, but I thought he had other things in mind and admitted, unfortunately, that I was just going to the office. He asked me what I thought about the problem of getting the infantry through the wire entanglements. This was the all-important question then under consideration and had not been decided. I replied that it presented quite a dilemma but there was no doubt in my mind that we would soon arrive at a satisfactory solution. The British had promised us heavy tanks capable of crushing the wire, and at the last moment had notified General Pershing that these could not be furnished. It was impracticable to undertake a long period of artillery fire for the purpose of destroying the wire, as this would have required more than a day of continuous firing preliminary to the attack and would have sacrificed the element of surprise so essential to the success of the operation without a heavy sacrifice in lives. Ultimately, General Pershing had the courage to take a chance and try something that had never before been attempted in the war, i.e., the cutting of gaps in the wire by the infantry, assisted by small groups of Engineers, as they advanced. The French thought the General would wreck his troops on the first entanglement. That he did not, we are all aware, but the actual circumstances attending this phase of the operation were unique and will be related at the proper time.

CHAPTER X

St. Mihiel

THE STEADY DRIVE of office work in preparation for the battle was broken by the necessity of making frequent visits to the army corps and divisions. About this time General Drum and I motored over through Toul to Saizerais, where we talked with General Liggett, commanding the First Corps, and his Chief of Staff, Malin Craig.[1,2] The various pros and cons of the preliminary orders for the battle were discussed, and a great deal was said on the subject of secrecy. It was growing increasingly difficult to conceal General Pershing's intentions. Everyone was enthusiastic and each felt that his individual part was of momentous importance and, therefore, an exception to the rules or regulations, with the result that, despite drastic orders to the contrary, the traffic on the roads in the daytime had grown to such proportions as to insure its observation by the enemy. Every officer desired to make a personal reconnaissance of the ground over which he was to operate, and there were frequent violations of the orders against promiscuous reconnaissances in the daytime.

The inexperience of the hundreds of staff officers, previously referred to, involved us in many complications. Instructions directing the concealment of all dumps of supplies and ammunitions which were being established in the area were followed up by inspectors, and one of these enthusiasts required the officer at the largest ammunition dump in the area, La Courtine, north of Toul, to cover it with paulins, notwithstanding the fact that only white paulins were available, with the result that a short time after the target was thus accentuated, a German aeroplane dropped a bomb which blew up the entire affair, representing weeks of labor and thousands of tons of ammunition. This particular dump lay within the control of our Fourth Corps, of which Tommy [Stuart] Heintzelman was Chief of Staff, and during the half hour following the explosion, his own Leavenworth friends at Army and other Corps Headquarters kept the telephones busy congratulating him on his private pyrotechnic display. Their jocularity rather cooled him down in the midst of a serious catastrophe.

After completing our visit at Saizerais, General Drum and I motored over to see General Heintzelman at Fourth Corps Headquarters in Toul. We did not reach the city until after dark and were informed that General Heintzelman was not in his office. The fact that no one could tell us where he was excited our suspicions and we made quite a search for him, but without success. It developed later that at the time he was in a private office across the street from Corps Headquarters. This arrangement had been forced on him in order to obtain an opportunity for work, as the number of visiting commanders and staff officers with pressing questions to be answered was so great that he could not attend to his duties as Chief of Staff. Unfortunately, those on duty did not recognize the fact that the Chief of Staff of the Army was to be considered an exception to the rule, so our trip to Toul was fruitless, and General Heintzelman had to motor fifty miles over to Ligny-en-Barrois, in order to talk over certain matters with General Drum.

On August 30th, Marshal Foch arrived in Ligny and went into immediate conference with General Pershing. I knew of his presence, but for some days remained ignorant of the momentous purpose of his visit, which was the first proposal for the Meuse-Argonne battle, with the possibility of abandoning the St. Mihiel operation. It also included another effort to split the newly formed American army. On September 2nd, a final conference was held between the Marshal and General Pershing, at which it was formally decided to carry out the Meuse-Argonne operation on September 25th, and definitely determined to limit the extent of the St. Mihiel operation. The last clause of the agreement was of decided interest to me, as it necessitated the alteration of the plan of battle, with corresponding changes in the orders for the attack. For a week I remained ignorant of the reasons for the change, although aware that something of major importance was in the wind; but I was too hard driven with my own problems to feel disposed to ask any questions regarding extraneous matters.

As a result of this final decision regarding the St. Mihiel, Colonel Grant and I were notified that we would devote ourselves exclusively to the coordination of the plans for the battle, the revision of the orders, and the preparations concerned. The subdivision of the Operations Section of the General Staff, which would ordinarily have had charge of this work, was withdrawn from connection with it. We established an office in a back room of the Operations Section, looking out on a pleasant little court. With the assistance of two clerks, we became completely engrossed in our duties. It was a peculiarly delightful partnership — each one aspiring to assist the other, with no thought of dominating the procedure, and with no difficulty whatever in arriving at common decisions. Colonel Robert McCleave, Assistant Chief of Staff and Chief of Operations of the army, was absorbed in the manifold problems concerned with the concentration of troops, routine administration, and, as I later learned, the preparation of the battle order for the Meuse-Argonne.[3] Here we were — a brand-new staff of a brand-new army, three times the size of a normal army, just entering the line for the first time and approaching its first operation, and already immersed in the preparations for a much larger operation, quickly to follow on another front.

Our office was continuously flooded with a stream of officers, mostly from the divisions gathering for the conflict. They usually urged some minor change in their orders which they considered entirely reasonable, without thought of how each alteration complicated the interlocking of the parts in the huge machine. The freedom of action and ample elbow room enjoyed by the small, scattered units of our old Regular Army had been conducive to a state of mind in its officers which made them slow to realize the rigidity of arrangements imposed by the massing of immense numbers of troops. It was quite evident that the longer an officer continued in France the more readily he understood the impossibility of making changes in basic plans for the benefit or advantage of a particular unit. Not that changes were not frequent, but they came from above and *not* from below. An interview between General Pershing and Marshal Foch might result in some seemingly insignificant amendment to the general plan, but it usually resulted in a wide disturbance in the lower echelons. An inch at the top became a mile at the bottom; and a division which had just marched up a hill might find itself reversed and ordered back to its starting point. These changes are unavoidable in making combinations among large armies, though they arouse the ire of the humble soldier, particularly the American with his characteristics of independent thought and action.

The critical decision to be taken at this time was the character of the artillery preparation to precede the advance of the infantry. Heretofore, when a strongly entrenched and fortified position, protected by numerous broad belts of wire entanglements, was to be attacked, very elaborate arrangements were made to destroy the wire so that the infantry might pass these successive obstacles without check or delay. Machine guns were always arranged to sweep the zones covered by the wire entanglements, and if the foot soldier was forced to pause in these dangerous localities the casualties were usually prohibitive. Prior to the German offensives, the French and British had adopted the plan of preceding the actual advance with several days — sometimes a week — of massed artillery fire, largely directed at the barbwire. A departure from this had been made at Cambrai, where the heavy British tanks had been able to tear great gaps through the wire, but, as I have already mentioned, Sir Douglas Haig, at the last moment, had informed General Pershing that he could not spare any heavy tanks for our use. The Germans in their spring offensives had solved this problem by concealing in their most advanced positions a mass of Minenwerfer (bomb-throwers) of heavy caliber, and with these were able to destroy the wire in five or six hours of fire. We did not possess sufficient heavy-caliber Stokes mortars (our equivalent to the Minenwerfer) for this purpose. Furthermore, even if these engines of destruction had been available in sufficient numbers it was not possible in the brief time at our disposal to make the necessary installations, unknown to the enemy. Prior to our arrival on this front, the French had withdrawn their lines almost a kilometer in rear of No-man's land and the Germans had not made a corresponding advance of theirs. It would have been necessary to have located the trench mortars in this abandoned zone, because of their short range, which would have required its reoccupation, and this in turn would have been plain notice to the enemy of our intentions. To place a battery of these mortars in an exposed position in such fashion that it would not show on the photographs continuously being taken from the enemy's aeroplanes would have been a long and delicate piece of work, and to have carried this out along the entire front would have required weeks, even supposing we had not had the problem of reoccupying the former forward positions.

To destroy wire by artillery fire is at best a tedious process. It first requires a series of single shots at each point of proposed rupture, each shot being observed and recorded before the next is fired. This is for the purpose of carefully registering the fire before the battle. Following this, it was estimated that five hundred shots from a 75 were necessary to cut a gap five meters wide and ten meters long. Unless the preliminary registration fire is distributed over a period of at least a month, the enemy is almost certain to draw correct conclusions, and the moment the fire of destruction was directed at the wire, the Germans would have instantly been aware of the imminence of an attack. At least a whole day would be required to cut the minimum number of gaps considered necessary. Registration fire on the previous day would also have been necessary. The large amount of ammunition required for such a fire of destruction or demolition was not available, as it could not have been brought up in time.

The three propositions which received most serious consideration were, first, to precede the infantry advance by eighteen (18) hours of artillery fire, hoping in this time to accomplish sufficient disruption of the wire to insure a reasonably free passage for the foot troops. The next proposal was to precede the active operation by about five (5) hours of artillery fire, merely for the purpose of demoralizing the defenders and inspiring our own troops. The third proposition was to launch the infantry attack without any prior artillery preparation. Both Grant and myself were strongly opposed to the last-named proposal, and for a time it appeared that this was to be the decision. We felt that the risk involved was far too great to be justified for an army undertaking its first operation, particularly in view of the strong pressure exerted by our Allies to utilize our divisions in their armies and to prevent us from organizing a separate army of our own. Any failure on our part, however small, was bound to be the basis for renewed efforts to achieve their ends. This proposal was a departure from all previous practice in the assault of elaborately fortified positions. Time and again the infantry of the Allies had broken itself on the enemy's wire, in spite of preparations to secure its passage. Heavy American losses resulting from this departure would have inevitably resulted in General Pershing's relief from command; he had too many prominent officials, civil and military, in the ranks of our Allies, who resented the unyielding, though diplomatic, attitude he had assumed regarding the formation of an American army. So strongly did Grant and myself feel on this subject that we addressed a joint official letter to the Chief of Staff for the consideration of General Pershing, appealing to him not to undertake the attack without artillery preparation; and I recall that this communication closed with the statement that to do this would be to take a gambler's chance. We recommended eighteen hours of artillery fire and General Pershing decided on five. Whether it was his sound judgment, or the accident of circumstance, I do not know, but his decision exactly met the situation, as will be explained later.

In preparing the special instructions, or annexes, to the battle order which covered the orders for the Engineer troops, supply services, signal communications, intelligence service, control of traffic on the roads, the handling of prospective prisoners, and what not — in preparing these to be mimeographed after they had been submitted by the respective Chiefs of Services, we only had two hours available, and were forced to adopt much the practice of the make-up editor of a big-city paper. Being the first of such instructions prepared, they were not standard in form nor did they cover the same general range, so it was necessary to amend and rearrange, provide headings, and attend to many little details preparatory to the final reproduction. Working at high speed on such important matters, which involved all sorts of consequences, was a very trying business, but fortunately we accomplished our task without mishap.

The battle was scheduled for the early morning of September 12th, and on the afternoon of the 8th or morning of the 9th, General Drum sent for me. Arriving at his office, I found Colonel Grant and Colonel Monroe C. Kerth also present.[4] General Drum announced that on September 25th the First Army would launch an attack from the Meuse to the western edge of the Argonne Forest; that the plans for the actual attack were under preparation in the G-3 (Operations) Section; that I would have charge of the movement of the troops from the St. Mihiel to the Meuse-Argonne front; that Colonel Grant would arrange for taking over the new front from the Second French Army; and that Colonel Kerth would arrange for the billeting of the divisions as they arrived, and would also coordinate matters between the Operations Section, Colonel Grant, and myself. General Drum read a list of the divisions which would be in the first line in the attack, giving me their order from right to left, and also the designation of the artillery brigades to accompany them, where their own organic brigades were still in the south of France completing their training. He called off the list of the divisions to be placed in corps reserve and in army reserve. I wrote this down in a page in my notebook, which I found a few weeks prior to dictating this paragraph. With this data I immediately returned to my office to consult the map. About ten minutes' consideration made it apparent that to reach the new front in time to deploy for a battle on September 25th, would require many of these troops to get under way on the evening of the first day of the St. Mihiel battle, notwithstanding the fact that the advance in that fight was expected to continue for at least two days. This appalling proposition rather disturbed my equilibrium and I went out on the canal to have a walk while thinking it over.

Now I knew the purpose of Marshal Foch's visit on August 30th, and the meaning of the mysterious withdrawal of the Subdivision of the Operations Section, which ordinarily would have handled the work of the St. Mihiel then being carried out by Colonel Grant and myself. I remember thinking during this walk that I could not recall an incident in history where the fighting of one battle had been preceded by the plans for a later battle to be fought by the same army on a different front, and involving the issuing of orders for the movement of troops already destined to participate in the first battle, directing their transfer to the new field of action. There seemed no precedent for such a course, and, therefore, no established method for carrying it out. The harder I thought the more confused I became, and I finally sat down beside one of the typical old French fishermen who forever line the banks of the canals and apparently never get a bite. In the calm of his presence I composed my mind and, after a half hour of meditation, returned to the office still without any solution of the problem, but in a more philosophical mood. There I found Walter Grant wearing a smile in keen enjoyment of my perturbation and of his luck in being assigned to the tail end of the dilemma. I must deliver the troops before he could take over the new front.

The preceding hour, and the period of futile fumbling which immediately followed, stand out in my mind as the most trying mental ordeal experienced by me during the war. The development of the American Expeditionary Forces was marked by a series of personal tragedies suffered by officers assigned important tasks and who, with the limited means or facilities at their disposal, and the short time usually available, were unable to produce the desired result. In many instances, given the same man and task, but more peace and quiet and an abundance of time, the result would probably have been satisfactory. But war is a ruthless taskmaster, demanding success regardless of confusion, shortness of time, and paucity of tools. Exact justice for the individual and a careful consideration of his rights is quite impossible. One man sacrifices his life on the battlefield and another sacrifices his reputation elsewhere, both in the same cause. The hurly-burly of the conflict does not permit commanders to draw fine distinctions; to succeed, they must demand results, close their ears to excuses, and drive subordinates beyond what would ordinarily be considered the limit of human capacity. Wars are won by the side that accomplishes the impossible. Battles are decided in favor of the troops whose bravery, fortitude, and, especially, whose endurance, surpasses that of the enemy's; the army with the higher breaking point wins the decision.

Being averse to making an inglorious sacrifice, and fully recognizing the gravity of my dilemma, I called a stenographer and started

the dictation of the preliminary order for the Meuse-Argonne concentration, realizing that it must reach the various army corps immediately, if the corps commanders were to be given time to make the
necessary rearrangements prior to the jump-off of the St. Mihiel.
With a map spread out on the table and the line-up of divisions for
the battle in my hand, I started with the proposition that the only way
to begin is to commence. In less than an hour I had evolved a method
for the procedure and had completed the order, which not only covered the preliminary movement of troops, but involved the regrouping of the organizations remaining on the St. Mihiel front at the close
of that battle, and outlined instructions for the defensive organization of the positions which they were expected to capture. My sense of
relief at having made a definite move toward the accomplishment of
the task was considerably tempered by the impression that the completed order was far from satisfactory. However, as no better solution
occurred to me, I finally decided to submit it to the Chief of Staff, but
avoided making a personal delivery. On my arrival at the office the
next morning I found a request from General Drum for me to report
to him immediately and I crossed the street to the main Headquarters
building with a feeling of reluctance. Drum was hard at work and
kept me waiting ten or fifteen minutes before explaining that General
Pershing wished to speak to me regarding some other matter on
which I had been engaged. As we went into the Commander in
Chief's office, Drum remarked, "That order for the Meuse-Argonne
concentration you sent over last night is a dandy. The General
thought it was a fine piece of work."

I have gone into the details of this seemingly small matter at length,
because it was the hardest nut I had to crack in France. My first reaction was one of extreme dissatisfaction, but my final conclusion was
that this order represented my best contribution to the war. It was the
only official paper I preserved for my personal records and brought
home from France. The essential portions of it are quoted below:

Subject: Release and readjustment of units following reduction of St.
Mihiel Salient.

1. The following information will serve as a guide to Army Corps
Commanders during the course of the pending operation, so that they

may be prepared to act promptly and without embarrassment upon the receipt of formal orders directing the changes outlined herein.

2. *PLAN OF READJUSTMENT.*

As soon as the advance has terminated, and assuming that a threat of a *heavy* hostile counter-attack does not exist, Corps Commanders will commence the reduction of the number of divisions in line and the regrouping of the divisions so released. The mechanics of this reduction must be foreseen and must be carried out promptly in order to permit the release of the various units indicated hereinafter, by the dates set, for duty in other regions.

The portions of the Army front now occupied by the 82nd Division will probably be taken over by the 8th French Army, releasing that division. The portion of the front from HAUDIMONT north will probably be taken over by the French. The 1st and 5th Corps, with their corps troops, will be relieved from duty on the front by D plus 4 and D plus 5 days, respectively, and the 4th U.S. and 2nd Colonial Corps will extend to the right and left, respectively, taking over the front of the 1st and 5th Corps.

3. *UNITS TO BE RELIEVED.*

ORGANIZATION	ESTIMATE DATE FOR RELIEF.		RELIEVING ORGANIZATIONS
	To Start	To be completed (NIGHTS)	
58th F.A.Brig.	D plus 2/3	D plus 3/4 (a)	None.
55th F.A.Brig.	D plus 2/3	D plus 3/4 (a)	None.
82d Div.	D plus 2/3	D plus 3/4 (b)	French division
1st Corps, Hq. and Troops.	D plus 3/4	D plus 4/5 (b)	4th Corps, Hq. and Troops.
1 Division from present 4th Corps (3rd if possible).	D plus 3/4	D plus 4/5 (a) or (b)	None.
5th Corps, Hq. and Troops.	D plus 4/5	D plus 5/6 (b)	2d Colonial Corps.

Note: (a) To move by marching.
(b) To move by bus and marching.

In addition to the foregoing a number of French artillery units, tank units, etc., must be relieved during this same period. Data on these units will be furnished later.

4. *EVENTUAL DISPOSITIONS FOR DEFENSE OF FRONT.*

(a) *CORPS LIMITS*

4th Corps

Eastern: Same as Army. (Probably present eastern limit of 90th Division).

Western: LACHAUSSEE (inclusive) — Southern tip ETANG de LACHAUSSEE — ETANG BELIAN (inclusive) — ETANG de VIGNEULLES (inclusive) — south west along trail in BOIS de VIGNEULLES — BOIS de la BELLE OZIERE (inclusive) — ETANG la PERCHE (exclusive) — HAUTE CHAURRIERE et GERECHAMP (inclusive) — north western tip of ETANG de GIRONDEL — FREMEREVILLE   (inclusive) — VIGNOT — (inclusive).

(Note: Joint use with 2d C.A.C. of Vignot — GIRONVILLE APREMONT road).

Southern: NANCY — TOUL road — Canal from TOUL to COMMERCY (TOUL, ECROUVES, FOUG and COMMERCY, all exclusive).

2nd Colonial Corps

Eastern: Western limit of 4th Corps.

Western: Probably HAUDIMONT (inclusive) — road to SOMMEDIEUE (road and village inclusive) — DIEUE (inclusive) — SENONCOURT (inclusive) — SOUILLY (exclusive) — road to CHAUMONT sur AIRE (road and village exclusive). Possibly present western army limit.

Southern: Route CHAUMONT sur AIRE — PERREFITTE — VILLOTTE devant ST. MIHIEL — MENIL aux BOIS — VADONVILLE — COMMERCY (road inclusive and all towns bordering road exclusive).

(b) *DISTRIBUTION OF DIVISIONS*

The following is a tentative outline of the desired distribution of divisions. It should be realized so far as the conditions resulting from the battle permit.

(1) *4th U. S. CORPS*

1st Line Divisions — (right to left) — 90th, 78th, 89th and 42nd.

Reserve Divisions — 2nd or 5th, region of DOMEVRE.

(2) *2d COLONIAL CORPS*

First Line Divisions — (right to left) — 26th French, 2d Cavalry a Pied, 26th U.S., 15th French.

Reserve divisions — 39th French, region of St. Mihiel — TROYON.

(3) *ARMY RESERVES.*
2d or 5th Division, region of ROYAUMEIX — ANSAUVILLE.
1st Division, region of GIRONVILLE — MECRIN.*

During the next two days preceding the opening of the St. Mihiel attack, my attention was divided between arrangements made concerning that battle and plans for the movement of the troops to the next. Fortunately, most of the staff work for the former operation was completed so far as concerned Army Headquarters. Colonel Ernest Dawley joined me at this time to assist in working out the purely artillery phases of the coming concentration.[5] He prepared a list of the separate artillery brigades and regiments, mostly French, which we would have to handle individually in carrying out the concentration — approximately three (3) separate brigades and about sixty-eight (68) independent regiments, not integral parts of a division.

On the afternoon of the 10th, I motored over to the Fourth Corps Headquarters to have a talk with General Heintzelman. For the past two months I had carried in my automobile a bolt of cloth from which to have a uniform made. As there was a good tailor at Nancy, I made a detour to leave with him the cloth and have my measure taken. The uniform I was wearing was rapidly disintegrating, but there had been no opportunity since the previous December to refresh my wardrobe. Incidentally, this uniform reached me in the midst of the Meuse-Argonne and was such a misfit that I never could wear it.

From Nancy I continued on to Fourth Corps Headquarters and there met General McAndrew, Chief of Staff of the American Expeditionary Forces, who asked me to accompany him to the First Corps Headquarters. Sending my own automobile back to Ligny, I joined General McAndrew and we paid a brief visit to General Liggett, and then started back to Army Headquarters. Darkness overtook us at Toul and as we could make but slow progress on the congested roads for the next fifty miles, we did not arrive in Ligny until near midnight. On this ride General McAndrew made some very interesting ob-

---

* No reference was made to the six divisions in corps and army reserve, as these normally would not advance during the attack, and therefore, could readily be put in march from their positions in reserve toward the new front. Most of the villages referred to for the purpose of designating new boundaries were located in ground yet to be wrested from the enemy's control.

servations on the character and qualifications of the American officers then in France. He was filled with admiration for their aggressive spirit, but deplored the tendency of the individual to ignore all other interests but his own, which constantly resulted in serious complications in carrying out the great combinations then in progress. The general moralized on the characteristic independence of our people and matched its advantages with the difficulties frequently developed by such traits in a huge organization, such as the AEF. He also talked at length about certain older officers of the Regular Army, who were then on duty in the AEF, and who had not yet been sufficiently tried out to justify their relief, but who, it was feared by him, were continually slowing down the machinery. He regarded them as victims of the lifelong routine of our little, dispersed Regular Army, whose problems had been purely local and frequently personal. The high standard of ideals and personal honor engendered in these men by practice and traditions made it particularly hard to relieve them ruthlessly in advance of their clearly evident failure.

As the hour for the battle approached, the tension became increasingly great. At the time I wondered what General Pershing's private thoughts were. He had created a distinctive American combat army, despite almost overwhelming difficulties, and in opposition to the pressing desires of all the great Allied leaders and most of their statesmen. As yet untried in the role of commander of a great combat army, accepting battle under most unfavorable circumstances — his reputation was decidedly in jeopardy. Any degree of failure or difficulty, even if approximately normal to the average successful engagement, was bound to be seized upon by all those who wished themselves to employ his fresh divisions of magnificent young men. If, when our men reached the barbwire entanglements, they suffered many losses, even though they made a successful passage, there would come the chorus of "I told you so" 's from all those who in the previous three years of the war had not done it in just that way. About fifty thousand (50,000) casualities was the percentage normally to be expected and hospitalization was prepared accordingly. Nevertheless, if we suffered that many casualties during the brief period involved, the American people, not accustomed, as were our Allies, to such huge payments in human life, would have seized upon the criticism of any Allied official as a basis for condemning our own Commander in Chief. Apropos of this, I have learned, since the war, that the statement of almost any junior foreign officer on duty in our training camps in the United States was accepted at this time like the "law of the Medes and the Persians." To the home folk he was the "prophet not without honor save in his own country."

On the eve of the battle we had no work to attend to and ample time for thoughtful contemplation. Everybody on duty in France in rear of the army, who had sufficient "pull" or excuse, arrived to see the show, and already we found ourselves in the state of mind of the veteran who listens with amusement, and sometimes with acute annoyance, to the comments or suggestions of these self-constituted advisers or critics. There is usually so much difference between the practice and the theory that the fellow in rear never can understand why you did it as you did, and the "doer" is apt to be too impatient to make a satisfactory explanation.

Grant and I wished to see the opening of the fight, but our duties at that hour would not permit, so we retired early and slept through most of the artillery preparation of four hours, which constituted the opening chorus. It takes a long time for reports from the front lines to percolate through the various headquarters to the rear, so we did not expect anything interesting until at least an hour after the infantry had commenced its advance, and the fact that a heavy rain fell throughout the night made it improbable that the aeroplanes could operate with any success during the early morning hours.

The infantry went forward at five-thirty and I do not think that any reports of moment reached us before six o'clock. However, with the clearing of the weather, the heavy fog which covered the plain of the Woëvre lifted and a bright sun illuminated the field of operations. Soon thereafter, reports came in to us from the Air Service, which indicated the complete success of the first stages of the operation. One aviator sent in word that an entire German company was waiting in a trench at a certain point to surrender, and somewhat similar indications were received from various points in the field. By ten o'clock success was assured so far as the main attack against the south face of the salient was concerned, but the scattered French divisions around the point of the salient at St. Mihiel had not been able to advance, nor had much progress been made by the single American division and one small French division attacking the western face of the salient south of Verdun. About noon the Secretary of War, Mr. Baker, came in to have us explain on the map the progress of the fight at that time.

As the day wore on, it became evident that only a halfhearted resistance had been made by the Germans against our attack from the south and that many prisoners had been captured. We also learned that the enemy had apparently started the withdrawal of his heavy artillery about two hours prior to the opening of the bombardment and the fire of our guns had caught these artillery columns on the road, causing great confusion and disorganization. This was a piece of rare good luck, which has since been twisted by our friendly critics, depreciating the achievement of the First Army at St. Mihiel, into a statement that the German garrison was actually withdrawing at the time of our attack, and, therefore, the reduction of the salient was assured without any particular effort by our troops. As a matter of fact, it developed that the German divisions on this front had informed their higher command of the evident intention of the Americans to attack and this information had been unsympathetically received. Therefore, when the attack actually fell as predicted, the officers with these troops were much incensed over the dilemma in which the higher command had left them and put up, as a consequence, a halfhearted defense.

About five o'clock in the evening, General Pershing received a report from a member of his personal staff, who had gone in the front line with the troops attacking south of Verdun, that caused the General to personally telephone an order that a regiment in this division (Twenty-sixth) would be directed on Vigneulles, in the heart of the salient, immediately and must reach there by five o'clock in the morning. He had gained a correct conception of the state of affairs within the salient and realized that if a junction could be formed between the left wing of the main attack from the south (First Division) and the troops attacking from the northwest, tremendous captures in prisoners would be realized. Later events proved he was also correct in his assumption that the enemy was withdrawing in the northwest, and would not make an effective resistance. The regiment previously referred to reached Vigneulles before five o'clock on the morning of September 13th, and its patrols gained contact with the patrols of the First Division in that neighborhood at about that hour. The French troops operating against the point of the salient were able in the late evening and during the night to move forward without encountering any serious opposition, and by noon of the next day it was apparent that we had captured in the neighborhood of 15,000 prisoners and over 400 guns. The southern attack had gained such momentum on the afternoon of the first day that the orders were changed sufficiently to permit the troops to proceed beyond the objectives assigned for that day.

By noon of the 13th, the First Army had established a rough line across the base of the salient after experiencing about five thousand (5000) casualties, instead of the fifty thousand (50,000) we were prepared to handle. Few of the division reserves had been employed, and of course none of the corps or army reserves (six divisions in all). Had not the operation been definitely limited in order to permit troops participating in it to be withdrawn immediately and marched to the Meuse-Argonne in time for that battle, there is no doubt in my mind but that we could have reached the outskirts of Metz by the late afternoon of the 13th, and quite probably could have captured the city on the 14th, as the enemy was incapable of bringing up reserves in sufficient number and formation to offer an adequate resistance.

That night we were called upon to express an opinion as to whether the advance should be resumed. Grant and I drew up a joint statement vigorously opposing any idea of such action. The attack had lost its momentum; the enemy had been given a breathing spell to reform his scattered units and bring up reserves; and we had stopped the advance clear of the Hindenburg Line and out of range of the heavy artillery of the permanent fortifications of Metz. At least twelve hours must have elapsed before a new decision at Army Headquarters could have been translated into coordinated action by the front-line units. Furthermore, the renewal of the advance would have rendered impossible the completion of the concentration for the Meuse-Argonne by the date set. General Pershing adhered to the original plan for the battle and proceeded to stabilize the front and withdraw as rapidly as possible the troops intended for the Meuse-Argonne.

In the aftermath of the battle we gradually learned the details of how the infantry crossed the barbwire entanglements. It seems that the special pioneer detachments and groups of Engineers, armed with long Bangalore torpedoes and wire cutters, who accompanied the first waves of the infantry and were to cut the passages through the entanglements, started on the execution of their difficult task, but the doughboys, impatient at the delay and possibly ignorant of the difficulty, walked over the wire. Practically no gaps were cut out until later in the day to open formal passages for artillery, trains, and reinforcements. So remarkable was this incident considered that few outside of those who were eyewitnesses would believe it. Marshal Pétain was convinced of the facts in the case and he sent down to the First Army, two days after the battle, about eight hundred (800) French officers and noncommissioned officers to see for themselves how the American troops had succeeded in crossing this hitherto-considered-impassable obstacle, without first having it cut by tanks or destroyed by artillery fire. A French officer in this party told me afterwards that the evidence on the ground convinced him that our infantry had walked over the wire, but he thought perhaps they were assisted in this remarkable performance by the size of their feet.

Once the success of the battle seemed assured in the afternoon of the first day, my attention became directed to the preliminary movements of the concentration for the Meuse-Argonne. It was essential that night to commence the withdrawal of certain heavy army artillery organizations and it was evident that considerable difficulty would be experienced in threading them through the tremendous traffic which always flows in rear of a battle, congesting every road for many miles. By noon of the 13th, though the advance still continued, I was wholly absorbed in the concentration for the next battle, and had already built up informally a little organization of contact for handling the matter, between myself and each of the army corps concerned.

CHAPTER XI

Opening of the Meuse-Argonne

THE REAR ZONE of the First Army was an interesting locality in the aftermath of the St. Mihiel battle. German prisoners poured in by the thousands, the first that many of our troops had seen. Notable officials — civil and military — arrived to view the field. Marshal Pétain accompanied General Pershing into the town of St. Mihiel immediately after its evacuation by the enemy. Mr. Baker, the Secretary of War, was an interested spectator at many points. Clemenceau arrived, followed shortly after by the President and Madame Poincaré, whom General Pershing personally escorted to renew acquaintance with their home in Sampigny. The Allied attachés were busily engaged in seeing everything we had done and, particularly, that which we should not have done as we did do. Every officer who could get away from his job in the SOS, and at the various schools and instruction centers, was on hand to see for himself how the battle had been won, and incidentally to collect a variety of souvenirs. I noticed some of their automobiles literally filled with German equipment, helmets, machine rifles, and antitank guns. It was interesting to get their point of view, as this was the first large battle most of them had ever seen and it had been carried out much more closely according to program than is usually the case. There were no reverses on any portion of the field, which is something unique in warfare. A veteran of a single battle like the St. Mihiel is prone to draw some erroneous conclusions. Those of the First Division, familiar with the vicissitudes of Cantigny and the terrific fighting at Soissons, felt that they had only participated in a maneuver, while the members of a previously

inexperienced division considered themselves the victors in a pro-
digious struggle.

Army Headquarters soon became immersed in the preliminaries
for the Meuse-Argonne, to which my efforts were directed to the
exclusion of everything else. Army reserve divisions were put in
march for the new front and the heavy artillery was withdrawn from
the battle and headed west and thence northward around the tip of
the former salient. The concentration involved the movement of approximately five hundred thousand (500,000) men and over two thousand (2,000) guns, not to mention nine hundred thousand (900,000)
tons of supplies and ammunition. The bulk of the troops and guns
had to be withdrawn from the south face of the salient, moved westward to the general vicinity of Bar-le-Duc, and then turned northward into the zone of the Second French Army, which was to control
the Meuse-Argonne front until four days before the battle. In general, but three roads were available for this movement. When one
realizes that the seventy-two (72) guns of a division occupy fifteen (15)
kilometers of road space, an idea can be gained of the problem
involved in the movement of two thousand (2000).

The transfer of a division was usually carried out by the employment of nine hundred (900) trucks for the foot troops, and by marching the artillery, motor supply trains, and other vehicular transportation. The trucks or buses could usually make the full distance in
the Meuse-Argonne concentration in a single night, but it required
three to six days for the horse-drawn transport. One serious problem
lay in the difficulty of coordinating the movements of trucks or tractors, animal-drawn vehicles, and foot troops, all having a different
rate of speed. So far as practicable, motor transport was held to the
southernmost road until the line of march turned northward near
Bar-de-Duc. All movements were confined to the hours of darkness,
and to carry out the project it was necessary that every road be filled
solid throughout the night. The appointment of commanders for
entire columns was impracticable, as it was impossible in the darkness
to exercise direct control over miles of congested road. The fact that
we had many French artillery regiments complicated matters by intro-
ducing another language into the enterprise. Two Americans could

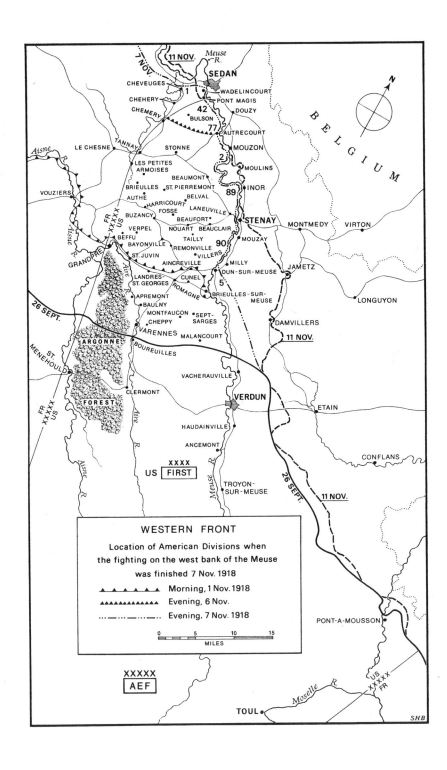

WESTERN FRONT

Location of American Divisions when
the fighting on the west bank of the Meuse
was finished 7 Nov. 1918

▲▲▲▲▲▲▲▲ Morning, 1 Nov. 1918

▲▲▲▲▲▲▲▲▲▲▲▲ Evening, 6 Nov.

·····—··—··—·· Evening, 7 Nov. 1918

0	5	10	15
MILES

stir up a pretty violent argument over an interference between their respective columns in the darkness, and the addition of a Frenchman to the discussion made it highly explosive. Our Military Police, who had to be depended upon to exercise local control along the route, were quite new to their duties. The younger men either hesitated to exercise their authority in dealing with commissioned officers — particularly with irascible Generals — or were too arbitrary in discharging their duties. I often wonder how in the world the concentration was ever put through in the face of so many complications.

To coordinate the movements of concentration it was arranged that we should deliver the troops and trains into the zone of the Second French Army to the north of Bar-le-Duc, and that that Headquarters should carry them on northward to the front into the preliminary positions for the battle indicated by General Pershing. It early became apparent that I was getting into difficulties in routing our troops north of Bar-le-Duc, because of French divisions being passed through the same area from the Vosges Mountains destined for the Fourth French Army west of the Argonne Forest. The movement of long motor-ammunition trains also interfered with the uninterrupted march of the troops, as the former were largely French trains under French control. To meet this situation a conference was arranged between Commandant Doumenc, Chief of the Military Automobile Service of the entire French Army, and myself in Ligny. Major Doumenc's position or service was an entirely new development evolved during the World War, largely by him personally. He controlled the movements of the hundreds of French truck trains, sometimes as many as a thousand trucks in a single train. The entire road system in rear of the front was organized so that the routing of these columns could be carried out with facility, somewhat after the fashion of a railroad service, except that schedules and routes were of necessity changed from day to day. Major Doumenc studied my troop movement schedules, which were based on march orders already issued, some of the movements being then in progress. We then undertook to coordinate my schedules with the French movements which must pass through the American zone. For the first time I became aware of the extent of the coming battle, which was to be a convergent attack along the principal portions of the western front from Belgium to Verdun.

With remarkably little difficulty and no disagreement, we hit upon the necessary compromises and arranged the policy of procedure to be followed throughout the remainder of the concentration. One of Doumenc's assistants, a Captain Gorju, was to report to me daily for the purpose of coordinating the American and French movements for the following day. My previous experience in dealing with the French staff was of inestimable value to me at this time, for I seemed to have learned how to get what we wanted with a minimum of friction. Both Doumenc and Gorju were very direct in their manner and always appeared to put all their cards on the table; certainly that was my own practice. It was my fixed policy to make every minor concession without question, which usually resulted in settling the more important matters to our advantage. I recall that an older Army officer, new to France, happened to be in my office during one of these conferences, and he expressed surprise at the numerous concessions I had made. To him it seemed most unwise to submit to numerous amendments and changes to an order or schedule which had been laboriously prepared. There was not time for me to explain that in movements of the magnitude of those in which we were then engaged, the initial order is merely a base of departure, subject to many amendments or modifications as the various complications of the numerous organizations concerned become apparent.

The first problem in ordering the transfer of the smaller artillery units, such as regiments, was to locate them on the battlefield and secure their withdrawal to a point from which it was safe and feasible to start their march parallel to the front. The staff officers of the First and Fourth Army Corps, along the south line, frequently searched all night to find French artillery units and, in a number of instances, after the organizations were located, their commanders would refuse to move, claiming that their horses had been exhausted as a result of the strenuous summer campaign and the heavy marches leading up to the St. Mihiel. In some instances, after the matter was arranged and the artillery had started to the rear, enemy shell fire would kill so many of the horses that the regiment could not reach its position in the column before daylight. This, of course, necessitated an immediate rearrangement of the march tables. One French regimental commander flatly refused to obey orders and expressed the determination to give his organization a much needed rest. I don't know just how much diplomacy was employed in securing a change of heart, but he did put his regiment in march. Many of the men had contracted the "Flu," which had a very depressing effect on these already worn-down units. The poor horse was the principal sufferer, because he can be driven until he falls, while a motor is immune to chastisement.

Walter Grant volunteered to help me and worked up a complicated order for putting two full brigades and eight separate regiments of artillery on one road and routing them through to the Second French Army. As he completed this job word came for him to report to General Drum, as Deputy Chief of Staff of the army, which left Colonel Dawley and myself alone to wrestle with the problem. In addition to a generous knowledge of things artillery, Dawley had a streak of dry humor which lightened our task. He also was blessed with a very elastic disposition, which was frequently stretched but never broke. Our only previous contact in the Army had been one day in the Philippines when I was Chief of Staff of a reduced division which had landed at Batangas in the role of an enemy and was engaged in an effort to march to Manila, a hundred miles away. Dawley was then a Lieutenant, serving on the other side, and was brought in to me as a prisoner by an irate officer whom he had attempted to ride down with his horse. I assigned him to the guardianship of a battery of artillery, which he had to follow on foot for two days, without blankets or mess kit, or any convenience of field equipment.

As the movement of troops was gotten well under way, I motored ninety miles over to the Moselle in order to arrange for the transfer of the Eighty-second Division from the extreme right of the First Army, to a position in reserve on the extreme left, in the vicinity of the southern portion of the Argonne Forest. The horses of the artillery were in poor shape, and it was questionable as to how rapidly they could make the long march involved. Furthermore, the rapidity with which the division could be relieved by our old friends, the Sixty-ninth French Division, was undecided. I reached Division Headquarters at Marbache, just south of Pont-à-Mousson, and there went over the draft of the order I had prepared with the division commander and his Chief of Staff. They found it practicable of execution, so I signed the draft and left it with them to be carried out.

On the return journey I visited Malin Craig at First Corps Headquarters, and Heintzelman at the Fourth Corps, near Toul. From the latter point to Ligny was fifty miles, which had to be covered in the darkness. The entire length of road was a solid mass of transportation, mostly motor-drawn. There was no light of any kind, except occasionally from the exhaust flames of the large tractors hauling heavy guns. It was surprising how few collisions occurred, though the roadside was fairly well littered with broken trucks, automobiles — particularly Dodge cars — and motorcycles. I saw one aviation truck, from which a long hangar beam projected, sideswipe two machine-gun mules, incapacitating both and injuring the driver. Near Void there was a jam resulting from one busload of soldiers being driven into the river and the following truck wedged on the bridge. At this same point the following night another busload of soldiers crashed through the railroad gate and was struck by an engine, several of the men being killed and a number injured. It was always a miracle to me how the motorcycle dispatch riders ever made any of their night trips during this concentration, without being smashed up.

I reached my office at Ligny about midnight, where I learned that the Headquarters of the army was not to move forward that night to Souilly, southwest of Verdun, as had been previously intended, so I retired to my billet to get some sleep. At three in the morning I was awakened by loud pounding on my door, and two officers came in. One of them, much excited, came over to the bed and by the light of a flash lamp showed me a copy of the order I had left at Marbache, and demanded to know whether a certain date was not in error. Though I had been awakened out of a sound sleep, it was immediately apparent to me that the date was in error, as plainly indicated by the following sentence. I confirmed his view, and, instead of his flying into a further rage, he expressed great delight, and, turning to the other officer, said, "I told you so."

It seemed that shortly after I left Marbache, this question had come up, and as the officer concerned was the commander of the division trains to which the date referred, he was called into the conference by the division Chief of Staff. The latter officer insisted that the date was right, and the commander of the trains was equally insistent that it was plainly wrong, but, notwithstanding his conviction, the Chief of Staff directed him to motor seventy miles that night to Army Headquarters. On his arrival in Ligny he could not find me, but was informed by the other officers of the staff, who had never seen the order before, that it was right and he was wrong. He then undertook to locate me and was twice conducted out in the country where my billet was supposed to be, and each time gave up the search, thinking it unlikely that I should be quartered so far out of town. Finally, after being assured by Major Allen Potts of Richmond, Virginia, who was the Headquarters Commandant, that I did live out in the country, they located the château but could not get any response for some time to their poundings on the door. Colonel Gulick, who was the other officer quartered in the house, heard the racket and talked to them out of his window, which was over the front door. He assured them that I had gone to Souilly, and then he retired. They resumed siege operations and finally Gulick let them in. None of them knew where my room was, so they searched the house and at last located me. The officer in question happened to be an old beau of my wife's, whom I had not seen for fifteen years and whom I have not since met. He was so delighted when I confirmed his view that he forgot to be angry with me for having caused him all the trouble.

The following morning at seven o'clock I was sitting in a chair in my underclothes, preparing to draw on my breeches, when the bedroom door flew open and the lady of the house rushed in, threw herself on her knees in front of me, in a paroxysm of hysterical crying. My orderly started to leave the room, but I called him back and hurriedly pulled on some clothes and endeavored to pacify the old lady. It seemed she had heard the continued pounding on the door of the château the night before and had fled from the house when the officers gained an entrance. She thought both Colonel Gulick and I had left, as had been previously intended, and assumed that the intruders were highwaymen. Hiding herself in a nearby woods without even a dressing robe to cover her nightgown, she remained there until daylight and then returned to the house accompanied by two old artisans of the neighborhood. I asked her what about her husband, and she replied that he was sick and crochety anyway, so she just left him. It required about a half an hour to restore her equanimity and I left the house, never to see her again.

Shortly after the successful termination of the St. Mihiel drive, I received a copy of a letter from the Chief of Staff of the Army to General Pershing, commending my work and recommending my promotion from the grade of Lieutenant Colonel to Colonel. A short time previous to this, General Pershing had received authority from the War Department to accomplish promotions himself up to and to include the grade of Colonel. Drum informed me that the General had taken favorable action on the recommendation and I would probably receive my appointment in a few days. However, about an hour later a friend of mine at Chaumont telephoned that my promotion had just come through from the States, dated August 5th, the result of a recommendation from General Fox Conner, which the Commander in Chief had cabled home while I was at GHQ. Walter Grant was similarly rewarded, and that night the mess opened some champagne and gave us a little celebration party.

Being in need of dental work and finding that an Army dentist had set up an impromptu establishment in Ligny, I seized this opportunity and arranged for him to fix me up one night after the G-3 office closed. While filling a tooth he endeavored to pump me as to the meaning of the tremendous concentration of troops to the north of Bar-le-Duc, and I rather feared to be too uncommunicative, lest he register his disappointment in my mouth. While we were thus engaged, a German aviator dropped a bomb into the courtyard of the Intelligence Section of Headquarters, close by, and the explosion almost resulted in the loss of my tongue, as the dentist was a trifle gun-shy and I was none too calm.

In preparation for the coming battle, Army Headquarters was transferred north to Souilly on September 21st. This insignificant little village is located on the great highway between Bar-le-Duc and Verdun, "The Sacred Way," which had been the sole supply route for the French armies in their famous defense of the latter city. The roadway had been broadened and traffic was directed over it with railroad precision. Day and night a constant stream of trucks and motors thundered through the single street of Souilly.

We were located in the offices which had been occupied during my visit the previous year by General Guillaumat and his staff and, previously by General Pétain during the Verdun fighting of 1916. The vital arteries of communication in the army centered on this village, which was to be our home until the Armistice. As the concentration had been completed so far as the issuing of orders was concerned, Colonel McCleave gave me a desk in his private office and I undertook to carry out such special jobs as he or General Drum might have for me, with the continuing obligation to handle all movements of divisions in or out of the battle.

The Operations Section of the General Staff, or G-3, as it is commonly known, then headed by Colonel McCleave, consisted of about thirty officers, and there were attached to it some eight or ten liaison officers. It was subdivided into a Report Section, a Map Section, a Planning Section, and a Troop Movement Section. Here were prepared the plans or orders concerned with the moving and fighting of the troops. The G-2 Section (Colonel Willey Howell), collected information concerning the enemy, reproduced maps, etc.[1] The G-1 Section (Colonel Alvin B. Barber, and later Colonel Leon B. Kromer), had to do with the coordination of policies pertaining to the individual, the regulation of traffic, control of the Military Police, the assigning of shelter, and similar questions.[2,3] The G-4 Section (Colonel John L. DeWitt), coordinated all matters concerning supply and construction.[4]

Drum, McCleave, DeWitt, Kromer, Grant, and myself, with the Secretary of the General Staff, Major McGuire, had our mess in a gloomy room of a dingy little house. The French and English observers, Colonel Forte and Major Geiger, lived with us. Everyone was so busy during this period that meals were hurried and unsatisfactory affairs. The small mess room did not afford accommodations for the many visitors from GHQ and Corps Headquarters, but we had to feed them just the same, and frequently could not find a place for ourselves at the table.

Souilly was a depressing little village at best, and the almost constant inclemency of the weather during the Meuse-Argonne did not add to its attractiveness. General Pershing wisely decided to live on his special train, which was parked on a siding in a nearby woods. My billet was a small room filled to overflowing with a collection of broken furniture, which had apparently been accumulated by successive occupants during the previous three years, but as I spent only a few hours in it each day, and those in sleep, the discomforts were not apparent.

Engrossed in supervising the final movements of the concentration, I did not study the order for the battle until the night before the attack. The opening advance was to be carried out by nine divisions, deployed along that portion of the front extending from the Meuse River near Verdun, where I had followed the fighting of the Foreign Legion the previous summer, westward 38 kilometers through the Argonne Forest. Three army corps were to be employed, each with three divisions in line and one in reserve. In rear of the latter, the army held three divisions in general reserve. Twenty-seven hundred (2700) guns were to sound the opening chorus, and every permanent aviation field and a number of hastily improvised ones were filled to overflowing with ships ready to secure control of the air. About 189 small French tanks, 142 manned by American personnel, were to assist the infantry in its initial breakthrough.

To the west of the Argonne Forest the Fourth French Army was to carry out a somewhat similar operation, but on a smaller scale, the two armies thus cooperating to pinch out the Argonne Forest without attempting to drive home a main attack in that difficult region. Still farther west another French army was to attack near the point of the great salient of the Western Front. To the north the English were to drive eastward, and just south of the coast in the vicinity of Ypres, the Belgian Army was to resume the offensive. It was to be a great convergent attack, the greatest battle the world has yet seen, and to the

American Army was assigned the mission of smashing the vital pivot of the enemy's lines.

The German successive defensive positions all converged as they reached the Meuse, until the distance between No-man's-land and his third withdrawal position at this point was only eighteen kilometers, while further west, near Laon for instance, the distance between these same two lines was approximately sixty kilometers. In other words, in advancing eighteen kilometers on the First Army front, we would have to pass the same number of positions and must expect to encounter the same amount of resistance that would be experienced in advancing sixty kilometers on the other portion of the front referred to. Furthermore, the enemy's main line of communication for the supply of his armies from Picardy to Verdun lay closer to our portion of the front than anywhere else. Once this was out, the Germans would be unable to supply more than a million of their troops lying to the west of us. A desperate defense of this vital artery could, therefore, be counted upon.

The battlefield of the First Army became much extended during the fighting as we initiated operations to the east of the Meuse River, but a false conception of it has grown up in the lay mind due to the name given the operation. Most Americans believe that our army made its splendid effort in the Argonne Forest, when, as a matter of fact, the great assault was driven home five miles to the east of the Forest. There was heavy fighting in the Argonne, but it was not comparable to the powerful steamroller attacks which were driven through the more open country between the forest and the river. It would have been the height of folly to have massed our troops in difficult wooded terrain, so only a sufficient number were deployed in that section to keep the enemy closely engaged and to follow up with persistence his withdrawals brought about by deep penetrations on other portions of the field. Sedan and Mézières were the joint objectives assigned to the First American and the Fourth French armies. They lay immediately south of the Belgian frontier, the latter 55 kilometers to the north of No-man's-land, and the American troops arrived on the heights dominating Sedan the day before the

German Government made its direct appeal to Marshal Foch for an armistice.

There were a number of important conferences at Army Headquarters with corps commanders and their Chiefs of Staff, during the days immediately preceding the battle, and on the afternoon of the 24th, I represented Colonel McCleave, who was temporarily absent, at a conference of the Chief of Staff and four G's of the Army, which General Pershing called in his office. The Commander in Chief questioned each of us as to the status of the various phases of the plans and concluded the meeting by remarking that apparently all that could be done had been done. On the 25th, I was engaged most of the day in visiting a number of the Corps and Division Headquarters to make certain that various eleventh-hour modifications in the movement of troops had been properly understood.

At two-thirty o'clock the next morning, the artillery opened its deafening cannonade for three hours of preparatory fire and at five-thirty the infantry advanced across No-man's-land and penetrated the enemy's positions. The problem of passing the wire entanglements was the same as at St. Mihiel, except that the men understood that it had been done and, therefore, could be done again. The first phase of the fighting was confusing in the extreme. Of the divisions engaged, three had never before been in contact with the enemy, five had not had the opportunity to complete their training, and three were forced to employ artillery brigades of other divisions, their own brigades not having yet reached the front. The troops had to pass over a devastated zone about four kilometers in width, practically every foot of which had been blasted by artillery fire incident to the Verdun battle. There was a mass of barbwire; the terrain was rugged and dotted with wooded areas, some of considerable extent which had been rendered almost impassable by the trees felled by shell fire. It presented a difficult field of operation for veteran divisions, and our hastily trained units experienced many complications in coordinating their maneuvers, especially in maintaining contact and communication between the various elements. Reports were confused accordingly, but it was early evident that the First Army had broken through the enemy's advanced positions, and by the afternoon of the 26th, we knew that

the Fourth Division had penetrated several kilometers beyond Montfaucon, though this stronghold itself had not yet been captured by
the division assigned to that task. As Montfaucon had been referred
to by General Pétain earlier in the month as the probable limit of our
advance before the winter, the immediate success of the army was
very gratifying. By nightfall of the first day we appeared to have
broken completely through the German defenses on two portions of
the front, but most of the divisions, engaged in their first fight, were
not yet qualified to exploit this tremendous advantage, which would
have required great celerity and careful coordination of movement.
There was an abundance of courage available but too little technique
to secure its most advantageous employment.

The enemy had fully expected us to resume our drive on the St.
Mihiel front, with a possible extension of this effort to the east of
Verdun. He, therefore, concentrated his reserves in that region and
was placed at a great disadvantage when surprised by the onslaught in
the Meuse-Argonne. At this time General Pershing gave hourly evidence of those rare qualities that make successful leaders of great
armies. He continually demanded fresh efforts on the part of the
divisions engaged, and was intolerant of the pessimistic reports,
always incident to the confused situation in any fight and the more
numerous in this particular battle because of the inexperience of the
majority of those concerned. He inspired the weak-hearted with
confidence and made all of the higher commanders realize that excuses were taboo and that the attack must be driven home.

About noon of the 27th came the fall of Montfaucon, and the
victorious troops pushed beyond and joined forces with the Fourth
Division in its previously exposed situation deep in the enemy's position. As casualties and extreme fatigue wore down the organizations,
and the strain of the battle produced a form of nervous exhaustion,
General Pershing increased his demands on subordinates and forced
the fighting throughout every daylight hour. He directed the division
commanders to move their personal headquarters forward, in closer
contact with the fighting line, and exerted the strongest personal
pressure upon all with whom he came in touch, to overcome the
difficulties of weather and terrain, to cast aside the depressions of

fatigue and casualties, and to instill into the troops the determination to force the fight along every foot of the front.

The vexing problem at this stage of the battle was the establishment of suitable roadways across the devastated zone. There were only three through routes across this 38-kilometer strip, and, of these, two appeared on the prewar maps but had been obliterated from the ground. The third was the "Route Nationale" from Clermont-en-Argonne north through Varennes, but, unfortunately, a few months before, the Italians, believing the enemy was attacking, had fired a mine which created a veritable chasm at the most difficult point, and all motor-driven vehicles and some horse-drawn had to be towed around this crater by tractors. The two routes farther east had to be rebuilt after the jump-off. Unfortunately for us, having just taken over this front, and our Engineer troops not arriving from the St. Mihiel battle until the day before the Meuse-Argonne, it had been absolutely impracticable to make complete arrangements in advance, as was always customary in such situations, for the rapid reconstitution of these roads. Stone in large quantities had been shipped forward in anticipation of the demand, but it requires some time to unload railroad cars and transport the material to the desired points, especially if priority in movement must be accorded to animal-drawn supply columns and the artillery. Despite the almost insurmountable difficulties of this situation, the light 75's had all crossed the devastated zone in support of their infantry by the afternoon of the 27th. A heavy rain at this time washed out much of the reconstruction, and one too ambitious commander of tractor-drawn heavy artillery tore out most of the balance on one of these routes.

During the unraveling of the congestion of traffic across the former No-man's-land, vehicular columns were often banked up for ten or more kilometers in depth, sometimes headed in both directions. This worked the greatest hardship on the wounded, as there were long and what must have been agonizing delays in the movement of the ambulances to the rear during the nights of the 26th and 27th. Division supply officers were hard put to move rations and ammunition forward from the division railheads south of No-man's-land, where the army made its deliveries to them. To a novice, the rear of the battle zone gave the impression of disorganization and a breakdown in the supply system. Such difficulties are always incident to fighting which has not been prepared for in the methodical fashion of stage operations, and becomes increasingly complicated where the face of the earth has been previously ravaged in an unprecedented manner. Those concerned with the fighting of the army and of the various army corps treated the situation merely as something which must be overcome, and that speedily, and had no thought that we had tied ourselves up. However, the ever-present visitors, naval, staff, civilian, and foreign, who in few cases were able to cross the devastated zone because it usually had to be done on foot or horseback, retired from the field and the area of the First Army, to spread reports all over France and England to the effect that we had failed and proven incompetent to coordinate so large an undertaking.

At the moment the army was accomplishing a miracle of achievement, these broadcasters furnished all the fuel possible to the flames of the Allied effort to subdivide our army and utilize its divisions after their own fashion. An immediate reaction came from London, and an American officer of some importance arrived at Souilly to ascertain the degree of our failure. Another arrived from one of the Allied Army Headquarters to press for the transfer of a number of our divisions to the foreign army to which he was then attached. The propaganda built out of this incident grew by leaps and bounds. Its poisonous touch reached even the President of the United States, and like a snowball it continued to gather weight and size after the Armistice, apparently with the object of depreciating the American effort in order to weaken Mr. Wilson's powerful position at the opening of the Peace Conference in Paris. Admiral Sims and Senator Glass, of Virginia, became involved in an altercation over this episode, which was finally carried to the Capitol, though they both apparently thought that the issue lay at Tours, the Headquarters of the Services of Supply in central France, rather than where it actually existed along the former No-man's-land between the Meuse and the Argonne. The SOS furnished the army with the necessary supplies, and the army, in turn, placed these according to custom, at the railhead of each division. It was within the division that the trouble lay, and, even so, sufficient food and ammunition went forward, though it did not always percolate down to the most advanced skirmish line, due to the inexperience of regimental supply officers.

The fighting grew increasingly vicious as German reserves were rushed to the First Army front and poured into the battle. On the third and fourth days a tremendous effort was demanded of our divisions, particularly of the Twenty-eighth, Thirty-fifth, and Ninety-first, which extended eastward from that edge of the Argonne across the Valley of the Aire and on to the high ground beyond. The two latter divisions by a herculean effort penetrated as far as the Exermont ravine, ——— kilometers from No-man's-land and the plateau to the east, but a heavy concentration of enfilading fire directed by the enemy from dominating ridges on the flanks of this penetration, combined with determined counterattacks, required the Thirty-fifth Division to withdraw its lines about a kilometer from this unfavorable terrain, and the Ninety-first to readjust its front accordingly.

On the afternoon of the 30th, Colonel McCleave returned from a conference with General Pershing and the Chief of Staff of the army, and told me to move the First Division from its position in reserve, in rear of the center of the front, over to the left corps, the First, and to arrange for it to relieve the Thirty-fifth Division that same night; the artillery and trains of the First Division were not to be permitted to cross No-man's-land until the next day or the day following, in order to avoid blocking the movement of ammunition, rations, and wounded on the sole road at the disposal of the First Corps. In reply to my statement that it would be impossible for the First Division to execute this flank movement and reach the battleground of the Thirty-fifth Division in time to accomplish the relief that night, Colonel McCleave told me that the matter was extremely urgent and would permit of no delay. I immediately went to the office of the Chief of Staff and explained to General Drum that it was a physical impossibility for the First Division to complete the relief of the Thirty-fifth Division that night. It was finally agreed that one regiment of the First should be put through in motor buses, all traffic being cleared off the First Corps's road during this movement. The Seventy-ninth and Thirty-seventh divisions, respectively, were also to be relieved;

the Third and Thirty-second divisions to take their places. This required the movement into the battle of approximately 60,000 troops and the withdrawal from the field of about 45,000. In the existing situation of the three routes across No-man's-land, the difficulties involved in this transfer were exceedingly great, as it was most important that the flow of supplies to the fighting troops should not be interrupted. I find the following pencil memoranda in my notebook of this interview:

> 1st Div. to vicinity of Neuvilly where they debuss. 3rd to 1st Corps (refers to transfer of division from the right corps to the left corps). To begin relief of 35th Div. Artillery discretion Corps Commander (refers to question of passing artillery across "no-man's-land").

> 3rd Div. relieved from 3rd to 5th Corps (refers to transfer of 3rd Division from right corps to center corps for the purpose of relieving the 37th Division). Infantry and wagon small arms (ammunition) and two days' rations, to relieve 79th Div. tonight. Later as situation regards traffic clears up, vehicular columns to go forward. (Refers to passage of "no-man's-land" by horse and motor drawn carriages).

> 79th and 35th Divs. to be sent by bus and marching to 4th Corps (St. Mihiel front) for sector (duty in front line) and training. Upon arrival of 79th or 35th, the 5th Div. will be relieved (for duty on St. Mihiel front).

> 29th Div. (Army reserve division in rear of center) by marching to Nixeville.

> 42nd Div. relieved from 4th Corps (St. Mihiel front) night of 30th to move to vicinity of Nixeville as Army Reserve, by bus and marching.*

With the foregoing instructions, I returned to the G-3 Section and in about twenty minutes arranged with Colonel DeWitt, G-4, for 125 automobile trucks or buses, as they were called, to report to the 26th Infantry of the First Division within two hours and the division commander was given instructions to embuss this regiment and rush it over to the First Corps, the latter Headquarters being notified to make arrangements for its prompt movement across No-man's-land. Formal orders for the movements of the other divisions concerned were hastily prepared and issued, involving in all approximately 140,000 troops. As a matter of possible interest, to show how such movements were directed, there is given below a copy of the order for the transfer of the Forty-second Division.

* The items in parenthesis are explanatory and were not included in the written notes.

SOF-CFJr
HEADQUARTERS FIRST ARMY
AMERICAN EXPEDITIONARY FORCES, FRANCE.
G-3
SPECIAL ORDERS }   *Secret*   29 Sept. 1918.
No. 314.   }

1. The 42d Division will be relieved from duty with the 4th Corps on the afternoon of October 1st and will proceed by bus and marching to region of SOUILLY, in Army Reserve. Upon its release from the 4th Corps it will be attached to the 5th Corps.

2. (a) *Foot Troops.*

The foot troops will embuss in the region of RAMBUCOURT, commencing at 17.00 hours, October 1st, and will proceed via GIRONVILLE-COMMERCY to the region of SOUILLY. Rolling kitchens will be carried in trucks of the Divisional Motor Transport. Divisional Motor Transport will follow busses.

(b) *Artillery.*

The Artillery Brigade will march via HEUDICOURT — LAMORVILLE — BOUQUEMONT — RAMBLUZIN.

1st march, night of October 1/2 — head of column to BOUQUE-MONT.

2nd march, night of October 2/3 — region of SOUILLY.

(c) The Horse Transport of the Division will march via APRE-MONT — ST. MIHIEL — COUROUVRE — BENOIT VAUX.

1st march, night of October 1/2 — head of column to LAHEYMEIX.

2nd march, night of October 2/3 — region of SOUILLY.

(d) The Division Commander will arrange with the Commanding General, 2nd Colonial Corps (P.C. at St. Mihiel) for the movement of his Artillery and Horse Transport through the zone of the 2nd Colonial Corps.

3. The marches of the Artillery and Horse Transports directed in the foregoing paragraph will be carried out between 17.00 hours and 6.00 hours except that the first march of the Artillery from HEUDICOURT will not start until dusk.

4. The Division is assigned the following zone in the region of SOUILLY:

SOUILLY — RAMBLUZIN — RECOURT — BENOIT   VAUX — NEUVILLE — BOIS   LANDLUT — BEAUZEE — BULAINVILLE — ST. ANDRE (all inclusive).

Many of the villages within this zone are occupied. The Division Commander will dispose of the available space.

5. POST OF COMMAND of 42d Division will close in the zone of

the 4th Corps at 8.00 hours on October 2d, and will open at the same
hour and same date at BENOIT VAUX.

    6. Information as to railhead will be furnished later by G-4, 1st Army.

    By command of General PERSHING:

H. A. DRUM,
Chief of Staff

OFFICIAL:

    STEPHEN O. FUQUA,

    Lt. Col., G.S., Asst. G-3.

The troops being relieved from the battle were withdrawn for several reasons. It had been their first experience in fighting, and they had
been required to operate in exceedingly difficult terrain, with a resulting disorganization in regiments and brigades. Furthermore, they had
not only suffered numerous casualties, but had become greatly
fatigued, due in a measure, I believe, to the novel and terrific experience they had undergone. There was probably more of a nervous
exhaustion than physical, particularly as there was virtually not a veteran of major warfare in the regiments to assure the rank and file that
their experience was typical of a battlefield. It is never possible in
peacetime training to reproduce the seemingly chaotic conditions of a
fight, and the novice is, therefore, greatly encouraged by the veteran's
matter-of-fact acceptance of the situation.

These troops had put up a splendid fight. The doughboys and
battalion officers displayed really magnificent courage in forcing the
fighting against a highly trained and long-experienced enemy. The
principal difficulty was the lack of understanding by the junior officers of regrouping their units at every opportunity. This only comes
with long experience in time of peace, or several battles in time of
war. We had had a somewhat similar experience with the First Division in its earlier engagements, but, fortunately, had a reasonable
opportunity in which to train the officers. Everywhere on the
battlefield individuals were paying the price of long years of national
unpreparedness. They paid with their lives and their limbs for the
bullheaded obstinacy with which our people had opposed any rational
system of training in time of peace, and with which the Congress had
reflected this attitude. That the Army succeeded was owing to the
splendid aggressive spirit and freshness of our men, and to the relent-

less determination of their Commander in Chief. If General Pershing had waited until his troops were properly trained, the war would have carried on into 1919, while casualties by the thousands and tens of thousands mounted up, and billions were expended.

On the morning of the 1st, General Drum and I went forward to the Headquarters of the center corps, the Fifth, and with General Cameron, the corps commander, took horses and rode forward across No-man's-land through Malincourt, to inspect the traffic situation in particular and other matters in general.[5] At the neck of the bottle in Esnes, the remnants of a once-picturesque little village and the point where the congestion of traffic was greatest, I recognized some old friends of the First Division in the column of horse-drawn and motor-driven transport, standing on the trail awaiting an opportunity to move forward. Without thinking, I inquired what the deuce they were doing on the Fifth Corps road, the division having been moved over to the First Corps to the west. Unfortunately, Drum overheard my query and was much exercised to find this violation of orders. As they were already on the road and there was no way of turning out to go back, I might well have kept silent and saved my former associates an embarrassing situation. It was not hard for me to guess what had occurred. Not having been permitted to follow the division forward on the First Corps road and, being determined to back up their outfit, they had slipped in on the one route of the Fifth Corps, where they blocked up traffic quite seriously, particularly when they turned westward beyond Malincourt, to cross over into their proper zone.

We swung around into the area of the Third Corps on the right of the battlefield and there met troops of the Seventy-ninth Division marching out after their relief by the Third. The drawn, strained expression on the faces of the men and their silence were very noticeable and gave evidence of the character of the ordeal from which they were just withdrawing. Everywhere the Engineers and pioneer labor troops were engaged in a desperate effort to improve the roads, or, rather, to construct new roads through a maze of shell craters. They, too, showed evidences of fatigue, particularly the officers, who were called upon to drive the men to unduly long hours of labor without opportunity for glory. Many portions of the routes we followed were littered with overturned trucks and motor cars which had been lifted off the road after being stuck or broken, and dumped into the ditches.

On our return to Fifth Corps Headquarters at dark, General Drum and I motored over to the First Corps to see Malin Craig, the Chief of Staff, in regard to the plans for the following day. There we learned of the relief of the Thirty-fifth Division by the First, which was then being completed. About half past ten we started back to Souilly, first motoring twenty kilometers east toward Verdun in order to reach the "Sacred Way." During this drive we became engaged in a discussion as to the existing situation and future plans, which was not interrupted until I noticed that we seemed to be going steadily downhill and guessed that we were entering the Valley of the Meuse at Verdun. A brief investigation in the dark confirmed my suspicions, so we turned back to seek the roak fork leading into the "Sacred Way." We renewed our discussion and became much engrossed, until again I had a suspicion we were not on the right road, which proved to be correct, as I found we had almost arrived back at the Headquarters of the First Corps. Reversing our course a second time, we gave careful instructions to the chauffeur and again renewed the discussion, only to find ourselves once more descending into the Valley of the Meuse on the outskirts of Verdun. By this time it was 1 A.M. I changed my seat so as to sit beside the chauffeur, who finally located the Verdun–Bar-le-Duc road, and got us back to Souilly about an hour and a half later.

While the fighting continued uninterruptedly during the following three days, the army was gathering itself for a renewed general assault on the morning of the 4th, utilizing the three fresh divisions to give a new impulse to the advance. On the morning of the 4th the storm broke afresh but without marked success, except on the front of the First Division, which drove a deep salient into the enemy's lines, and more or less completely emasculated the Fifty-second German Division. One of the enemy's regimental commanders, captured at this time, made a very impressive statement regarding the feat of arms of the First Division. This salient, which continually deepened, provided maneuvering ground for deploying the Eighty-second Division parallel to the enemy's line to assault the rear of the Argonne Forest.

Meanwhile, the Seventy-seventh Division, heavily engaged in the thickets of the Argonne, had developed the incident of the famous "Lost Battalion," commanded by the late Colonel Whittlesey. This unit had made a more successful advance than the neighboring organizations, which permitted the enemy to infiltrate until they had it virtually surrounded. It was comparatively easy for the Germans in that difficult terrain to stand off with machine-gun fire any efforts to relieve this battalion, and it was not until the Eighty-second Division by its assault, previously referred to, threatened to cut off all the Germans in the forest, and forced their immediate retreat, that a successful effort was carried out to join forces with Colonel Whittlesey's command. This occurred on October 7th, and on the same day the Army launched an ambitious attack extending the battle to the east of the Meuse.

The new operation was initiated for the purpose of driving the enemy from the heights east of the river and thus preventing the artillery located there from firing on the rear of our divisions much more advanced to the west of the river. It had not been ordered earlier because divisions were not available for the purpose, but by this time the Twenty-sixth Division had been brought over from the St. Mihiel front and the Thirty-third Division, which had been pinched out of the original battle by the narrowing of the front due to the westward trend of the Meuse, was available for employment in this new field. Large captures in prisoners were made on the 7th and 8th, particularly from an Austrian division which was located just east of the river and which put up only a halfhearted defense.

The incident of this Austrian division is interesting. The division had been in the line at the opening of the battle, and the Germans, believing that our attack would be promptly extended to the other banks of the Meuse, and doubtful of the fighting qualities of their ally, had withdrawn the division, replacing it with a high-grade German unit. As we did not attack in this quarter, they finally returned the Austrian division to the line, in order to employ the German division at a more critical portion of the field. The relief had just been completed when our assault was launched, with the disastrous results previously anticipated by the enemy.

On looking over the preceding portion of this chapter, I find that it enters more into a general description of the battle than was intended. The purpose in preparing these notes was to register my personal impressions of the operation, rather than to describe the successive phases. It is difficult, however, to provide the necessary background for a series of impressions without furnishing an outline of the principal events. In what follows I shall endeavor to picture the battle as it appeared to me at the time, elaborating on the more or less important incidents with which I was concerned.

As usual, the personal element proved to be an important consideration, in spite of the magnitude of the task and the thousands of individuals involved. At the higher headquarters one feared to make even the most casual remark regarding friends or acquaintances involved in the struggle, lest he blast a career or project the wrong man into the limelight. In the rush and confusion of America's participation in the war, particularly in this greatest of our battles, every leader was keen to locate and attach to himself any officer who was thought to be especially efficient in the performance of his duties. The difficulty was to locate the man. Our higher leaders were usually Regular officers who had had little opportunity to form an estimate of the qualifications of those not in the Regular establishment prior to 1910. Of the older officers, less than twenty-five hundred reached France, and of these the best known were promptly tied to special jobs, of necessity largely connected with staff duty. It was, therefore, almost a hit-or-miss proposition to locate, on the spur of the moment, a man with the desired qualifications among the hundred thousand officers who went to France, and after the individual was located, too frequently he was found engaged in some duty which did not permit of his relief.

It has been charged that in this war the square peg was usually driven into the round hole; in other words, that the military authorities did not give sufficient consideration to a man's previous training or experience in assigning him to duty. This may at times have been true in the case of positions similar to those in civil life, but it must be remembered that there were no such definite criteria to go by in selecting officers for duties directly connected with the conduct of battle, and this hastily organized battle in particular.

The First Army at this time required men in the key positions, of the dashing, optimistic and resourceful type, quick to estimate, with relentless determination, and who possessed in addition a fund of sound common sense, which operated to prevent gross errors due to rapidity of decision and action. The man of the conservative type, who laboriously builds up a machine until it functions perfectly, who does not instantly impress strange subordinates with his powers of leadership, had little opportunity to demonstrate his ability; the issue had passed before he could master the situation. Men of this type were the victims of our policy of unpreparedness. They usually prove to be the soundest and greatest leaders, like Kitchener for example, in a methodically developed organization or system, but the budding reputations were sacrificed with distressing frequency in the hurly-burly of unprepared America at war.[6]

Daily in the Meuse-Argonne, officers were assigned to command of regiments, brigades, divisions, or other important positions to replace casualties, some of which were not due to the enemy. Frequently they took over their duties in a situation which might be characterized as a bad mess; their officers and troops were scattered about on the terrain, under the fire of the enemy; deficiencies and special difficulties had to be ascertained. Yet there was rarely time for a pause in which to size up the officers and the troops, check over the supplies and materiel, and make a calm survey of the situation. Action was demanded and often within the first hour. A renewed attack was usually required the following morning. It should be obvious that the successful handling of such situations required a very special type of man, a type that frequently is in difficulties in a peace regime. The more conservative individual who had had combat experience under less strenuous circumstances was indeed fortunate, for he was in an important measure prepared for the seemingly chaotic scramblings of the battlefield.

As the first phase of the battle developed into a period of extremely bitter fighting, with the inevitable confusion and the weather dressing the scene in rain and mud, there was a pretty continuous stream of officers, friends, or acquaintances of mine, who called to see me on their way to and from the front. Those whose organizations had temporarily been withdrawn from the battle for rest, recruitment, and reorganization gave very interesting and instructive descriptions of their experiences. Naturally, very few of these officers could discuss the operations of their units in a frankly impersonal manner. One division commander was an exception to the rule and discussed quite frankly the mistakes committed by his troops. I had previously familiarized myself with what had happened and thought I understood the reasons. He confirmed my views, but, more important than that, he impressed me with his absolute honesty by his unwillingness to cover up the shortcomings of his command, in the fear that it might lead to his relief. All he desired was an opportunity to profit by the lessons of the recent experience. As a matter of fact, I happened to hear the question of his relief discussed, and in my small way I most energetically protested. This particular General commanded his division in action most successfully a few weeks later.

There were those who had been relieved from their commands who came in to tell me of the injustice which had been done them. It was hard to talk to men of this class, because in most instances I was convinced by what they told me that their relief was justified. To discuss with an old friend the smash-up of his career is tragic and depressing at best, and more particularly when he feels that he has been treated unfairly and an honorable record forever besmirched. In decided contrast were those who stopped by on their way to the front, selected to replace commanders of units engaged in the battle. Enthusiastic in anticipation of the opportunity before them, but a little fearful of following in the footsteps of their deposed predecessors, they pressed for tips or advice on how to succeed under the conditions of this battle. If a man had not laboriously prepared himself for his duties, there was little of profit that could be said at that late hour, but I am inclined to think that I helped a few by briefly reciting the more-or-less specific errors which seemed to be prevalent. One could form a fair estimate of the chances for success of these men by their manner during the discussion. While all asked questions, some rarely waited for a reply, occupying the time in dogmatically outlining their own views and opinions. Those who later were successful on the battlefield usually "pumped" me with the relentless persistence of a lawyer cross-examining a reluctant witness.

About this time Robert Bacon, former Ambassador to France, and then serving as American Liaison Officer with Sir Douglas Haig, came in to see me.[7] He was enthusiastic over the recent successes of the British and anxious to have General Pershing attach some of our big divisions of fresh young men to the English Army. I think he had just been notified on his arrival at Souilly of his promotion to the grade of Lieutenant Colonel. Anyway, he told me about it and I replaced his gold Major leaves with the silver Lieutenant Colonel insignia, which I had kept in my dispatch case.

The late Willard Straight was a frequent visitor at my office, a charming and highly intelligent man, who had a most interesting and successful career behind him and was intensely anxious to add to it a record of participation in the battle.[8] Assigned as a Major on the General Staff to the office of Army Headquarters, which exercised general supervision over administrative matters pertaining to personnel, he was desirous of securing a transfer to the Operations Branch of the General Staff, where he would be more directly connected with the actual fighting. He was always begging me for copies of the daily battle orders which were prepared in the Operations Section and issued to the Army Corps commanders. These, being highly confidential, were not supposed to be scattered about, but Straight was so persuasive that from time to time I gave him copies of the current field orders. He would take these back to Ligny-en-Barrois, where the second echelon of Army Headquarters was located, and study them in preparation for duty of the character he desired.

CHAPTER XII

The Crisis of the Battle

T HE FIGHTING during the middle of October marked the crisis of the battle, the enemy in his last prepared defensive position struggling desperately to withstand our assaults until the inclemency of the weather would force us to suspend major operations until the following spring. The short days and the frequent rains of this season in Northern France made it increasingly difficult to maintain an army in the open. The transportation of ammunition and supplies was rendered difficult over the water-soaked ground; the long cold nights were depressing to the troops, who were seldom dry and constantly under fire; and the normally leaden skies of the few daylight hours offered little to cheer the spirits of the men. Life became a succession of dangers, discomforts, and hungers, with a continuous pressure being exerted on the individual to do more than he felt himself or his organization capable of accomplishing.

In this situation the real leaders of the Army stood forth in bold contrast to those of ordinary clay. Men who had sustained a reputation for soldierly qualities, under less trying conditions, proved too weak for the ordeal and became pessimistic calamity howlers. Their organizations were quickly infected with the same spirit and grew ineffective unless a more suitable commander was given charge. It was apparent that the combination of tired muscles, physical discomforts, and heavy casualties weakened the backbone of many. Officers of high rank who were not in perfect physical condition usually lost the will to conquer and took an exceedingly gloomy view of the situation. However, when the Commander in Chief arrived, they "bucked up" for the period of his visit, only to relapse into further depths of despondency after his departure.

Throughout this crisis General Pershing carried himself with an air of relentless determination to push the operation to a decisive victory. His presence inspired confidence and his bearing convinced those with whom he came in contact that the weak-hearted would be eliminated and half measures would not be tolerated. A flood of advice and criticism was projected at him from every direction. A group of expatriated Americans in Paris did their best to broadcast tidings of American failure and mismanagement, and found convenient avenues of dissemination among certain of our Allies, civil and military, who feared American prestige on the battlefield and desired to break up our army and employ our young men in their own. The propaganda initiated during this period grew like the proverbial snowball, which sometimes does not melt away until long after the spring has come. A pessimistic view of the operation was also shared by officers of some rank in our own army, honest in their convictions, but shortsighted or ill-advised as to the general situation. I imagine that we were in much the same situation as Grant's army in the Wilderness campaign.

At this time the First Army faced the enemy along ninety miles of front, one third of which was the scene of continued assaults. The normal frontage of an active army in this war rarely exceeded twenty miles, but there had not been time, nor were the staffs available, to subdivide the First Army. Now, on October 12th, General Pershing issued an order turning over the eastern or quieter portion of the line to General Bullard, who was advanced to the command of the Second Army thus created. General Liggett was given command of the western portion of the front, which continued to function as the First Army. General Pershing himself assumed control of the Group of American Armies. There were several other changes, the most important of which were the promotions of General Summerall and General Hines to the command of Army Corps. A few days later I was formally relieved of my assignment to GHQ, and made Assistant Chief of Staff for Operations of the First Army.

In connection with this change in my status. I recall that General

Drum sent for me and, without any preliminaries, merely announced in effect, that "You are now the G-3 of the First Army. General Pershing has agreed to Marshal Foch's request to send two of our divisions to reinforce the Belgian Army. The Thirty-seventh and Ninety-first have been selected. See that they are entrained by tomorrow night. Let me have your recommendations tonight for the further operations of the army."

Changes came so rapidly in those days that one spent little time in cogitation over what had happened; reflecting in the past tense found no place in one's mind, and I returned to my office to make immediate arrangements for the transfer of the two divisions mentioned, which was then quite a problem, as one brigade of the Ninety-first had just been relieved from the battle and was a long distance from the possible entraining points, and the men were exhausted from the privations, hardships, and dangers of three continuous weeks of fighting. The division staff officers told me the brigade could not make the necessary march, that the men had to sleep, had to be fed, and had to get rid of their filthy garments, get a bath and a new issue of clothing. However, they did make the march and boarded the trains the night of the 18th.

I sent for my orderly to move my belongings to the billet of the former G-3, where a telephone was already installed beside the bed. The following day I discovered an unoccupied room in the home of the curate of the church, where we had recently moved our mess. This new billet seemed luxurious for Souilly, and several days passed before I learned that it had been Marshal Pétain's room during the famous defense of Verdun, and on at least one occasion, it had been occupied by Clemenceau. Through oversight, it had not been assigned to some higher-ranking officer of our Army Headquarters, so I continued to enjoy its comforts until the end of the battle. Many of my friends, passing through Souilly, would come to me seeking a place to sleep, and often I would reach this room long after midnight to find three or four recumbent figures sleeping on the floor. As they were tired and I was tired, I never woke them up and they usually left in the morning before I woke up. Several times I recognized men whom I had not seen for years, evidently friends of friends of mine, who had followed the latter into the room, and they would usually disappear without my ever having any conversation with them. I found Joe Baer, a Colonel in the Inspector General's Department, occupying half of my bed on more than one occasion.[1] It was a strange life, though I never paused long enough to think so at the time.

The fighting in the latter half of October consisted of a series of seemingly detached operations, but all were directed with the object of securing a favorable line of departure for a general assault as soon as enough experienced divisions could be collected for that purpose. About October 20th, I was directed to prepare the plans for an advance to be made all along the line west of the Meuse, scheduled for October 28th. The preliminary battle instructions, really the rough draft of the battle order, were issued on October 22nd. Meanwhile heavy assaults were being directed against the enemy on the other side of the Meuse, northeast of Verdun. In the preparations for the attack of October 28th, we were able to take advantage of our previous experience, and all the arrangements were much facilitated by the fact that each of the army corps had, through this same experience, acquired facility in carrying out their portions of the undertaking. The First Division, which had suffered about nine thousand casualties between the first and eleventh of October, was being hurriedly groomed for a return to the fight. The Second Division, after its splendid assault on Montblanc in the center of the Fourth French Army west of the Argonne, was moving east to join us. The Seventy-seventh and Fifth divisions had been withdrawn from the front lines for a few days to freshen up in preparation for a prompt return. The Eightieth had been out of the line two weeks and was ready — though the Division Headquarters for a time didn't see it quite that way — to return to the struggle. The Eighty-ninth and Ninetieth, two splendid divisions from the middle and south west, had come over from the St. Mihiel front and were already in the line working into favorable positions for the scheduled assault. Most of the French artillery, Engineer, pioneer, and other technical units, had been withdrawn by Marshal Foch, and were replaced by newly arrived organizations from the United States. Like Kipling's ship, the army had found itself, and was crouching for the final spring. American girls served the telephones at Army Headquarters, and there were fewer and fewer evidences of a foreign nature in our midst.

During this period we had some difficulty in directing the operations of the Seventeenth French Army Corps on the high ground beyond Verdun, which was employing a mixed French and American force, there being a majority of the latter. The French commander and his staff endeavored to handle the American units after the same fashion as their own. Small and complicated maneuvers, with frequent pauses, was the method pursued, which was not well adapted to the temperament and characteristics of the American soldiers. Our men gave better results when employed in a "steamroller" operation, that is, when launched in an attack with distant objectives and held continuously to their task without rest or reorganization until unfit for further fighting. Their morale suffered from delays under fire, their spirits were best maintained by continued aggressive action, even though the men themselves were approaching the point of complete exhaustion. They bitterly resented casualties suffered while being held in position, without doing any damage to the enemy. Even though rapidity of action might give few opportunities for preparation or minor reorganization, the results obtained were generally greater when such a course was followed. The French corps commander General Claudel, however, could not see it that way. I paid several visits to him and talked as frankly as my knowledge of French would permit, but he evidently regarded me as too young and inexperienced. This view was probably influenced somewhat by the fact that his Chief of Staff was the same Colonel Kastler who had been Chief of Staff of the Moroccan Division in the fight in this same neighborhood in August 1917, and who had personally conducted me, then a Captain, to a vantage point from which to view the opening of my first battle.

Kastler and I were good friends, even if our views differed. He was a splendid officer, fine-looking, with four years of brilliant service to his credit, not to mention campaigns in Morocco. One day he came into my office and exclaimed, "I hope I never serve again in the American Army. You do nothing but change, change your orders all the time." This struck me as being very funny, as the shoe was now certainly on the other foot. I replied, "My dear Colonel, we Americans are mere novices at this business of changing. Since you and I watched the attack of the Foreign Legion fourteen months ago, I have served in five French army corps, and they seemed to do nothing else but change their orders as fast as they were issued. 'C'est la guerre.' " He laughed and agreed.

On October 26th came the decision to delay the general attack planned for the 28th until November 1st. The change was caused by the inability of the Fourth French Army to prepare to make a similar assault at an earlier date, and the conception of the operation contemplated the simultaneous convergence of these two armies on Sedan and Mézières. This gave us something of a respite, during which an opportunity was found to polish up all preparations to an extent we had never before enjoyed. For the first time we were about to engage in a grand operation on a front which we already occupied. Our own special service troops were manning practically all the installations: railroad and dumps, telegraph and telephone lines, and water plants, etc. Individual divisions were moving in and out, but the higher organizations had been in place for approximately a month. It was a great contrast to the opening of the battle, when both staffs and troops all arrived on the scene for deployment at the eleventh hour.

During this period a considerable portion of my time was occupied in visiting Army Corps Headquarters and divisions along the front, something I had not hitherto had much time to do because of the long delays imposed in getting through the dense traffic, which demanded too much time away from Headquarters. On one trip I went up in the northern end of the Argonne Forest to get a view from the bluffs of the Grand Pré–Juvigny valley where the Seventy-eighth and Eighty-second divisions were engaged. In Châtel-Chéhéry I visited the spot where Colonel Jimmy Shannon had been killed earlier in the month.[2] He had belonged to GHQ, but sought a temporary command during the battle and was given a regiment in the Twenty-eighth Division. Notwithstanding the fact that his command was already engaged and so deployed that it was impossible for him to come in intimate contact with the various units, within two or three days Shannon had impressed his personality on the entire organization and his death was genuinely mourned by all. We had been friends for years in the old Army, and he was always my ideal of a Christian gentleman. Very religious, but most unobtrusively so, a jolly companion, an unusually fine athlete, gentle with his horses, and a perfect model of a husband and a father. I don't recall any tragedy of the war that so distressed me as the news of his death. It seemed so unnecessary that this particularly fine man should have been selected to make the great sacrifice, while others much less worthy were to survive; but after I sensed the effect of his death on the Army in general, it seemed to me that in no other way could his rare qualities and shining example have been so forcibly impressed on a large number of people.

On another of these trips along the line I recall crossing over the present site of the great cemetery at Romagne, where at one time forty thousand of our dead were buried. I visited this cemetery with General Pershing on Decoration Day in 1919, and the contrast between the peaceful field of white crosses on that day and the littered battlefield of the previous October, with its shell craters, foxholes, discarded arms and equipment, and the sticks or rifles thrust into the ground and surmounted by helmets to mark the temporary graves of those who had fallen, caused perplexing thoughts regarding the bickerings of the Peace Conference then in session in Paris.

My old First Division associate, Campbell King, now a Brigadier General, was established in Romagne as Chief of Staff of the army corps under General Hines, who had graduated successively from the Sixteenth Infantry, First Brigade, and the Fourth Division, to the command of this corps, numbering about 150,000 men. Their troops were to form the right wing of the coming assault and later were to turn eastward and make a brilliant crossing of the Meuse, penetrating deep into the plain of the Woëvre in the direction of Montmédy, near the Luxembourg frontier.

Shortly after my appointment as Chief of Operations of the First Army, I secured the transfer of Captain Caffey from the First Division to me. He had become a veteran staff officer, intimately familiar with the practical methods necessary in moving large bodies of troops and handling them on the battlefield. His presence was a great comfort to me, familiar as he was with my methods and experienced in numerous engagements. Colonel Dawley continued to help me in artillery matters and was occupied most of his time in moving French regiments out of the battle and replacing them with newly arrived American organizations. Another problem that occupied him was keeping accurate track of the status of the horses in the artillery brigades. Our losses in animals had been tremendous. I believe there were more than forty thousand casualties after the opening of the St. Mihiel, principally in the artillery regiments, from exhaustion, shell fire, and gas. It became necessary in some cases to tow the guns and caissons of artillery regiments out of action with trucks, there not being enough horses left for this purpose. Our men knew little about the care of draft animals and it took them a long time to learn.

As everyone had become better accustomed to his duties in the Operations Section, it became possible to materially reduce the number of officers, and I released ten or fifteen for assignment to other places. This voluntary action on my part brought about an investigation by General Drum, with a view to making reductions throughout Army Headquarters, which at that time numbered nearly 600 officers and 2000 men. Apropos of this investigation, there was a fire on October 28th, which burned down the offices of the Chief Signal Officer and a portion of the Headquarters of the Chief of Artillery.[3] I remained in my office to utilize this opportunity for work without the annoyance of constant visitors. After the fire had been gotten under control, Colonel Dawley returned from the scene and, in response to my inquiry as to the result of the fire, replied that one artillery officer had been found who they thought had left for the United States several weeks ago. This appealed to me as a very humorous reference to the size of the Artillery Staff, and I made the mistake of telling the joke at the next staff meeting, where everyone laughed except the Chief of Artillery.

By the evening of October 31st, the troops had all been moved into position preparatory for the grand assault scheduled for five-thirty the following morning, which had Sedan as its most distant objective. There were a number of captains and lieutenants in the Operations Section who bitterly bemoaned the fact that they were being denied the opportunity of taking part in the active fighting, so I took this occasion to give them a stomachful of battle, while trying out an experiment in communications. Selecting Captain Lydig Hoyt, Lieutenants Ragnier, Bandini, and one other officer whose name I have forgotten, I sent them over to the Chief Signal Officer to be instructed in the handling of carrier pigeons, and later in the day had them instructed in the preparation of messages and map references to be written on tissue paper and placed in the little tubes carried by these birds. They were then assembled in my office, and I read to them a letter of instructions which they were to carry to the commanders of the divisions to which they were to report that evening. In brief, the division commanders were directed to see that these officers accompanied the assault troops and were at all times at least as far advanced as the commander of the leading assault battalion. The officers themselves were each given an orderly to carry six pigeons and were directed to release a message at 7 A.M., 9 A.M., noon, and 3 P.M. on November 1st, and at 9 A.M. and 1 P.M., on November 2nd, giving the exact point which the leading troops of their respective divisions had reached at the designated hours, including such brief references to the status of the fighting as could be put in such a message. After the last bird had been released, they were to make their way back, as best they could, to Army Headquarters.

On the morning of November 1st, a terrific barrage of artillery and machine-gun fire was directed against the German lines west of the Meuse and at five-thirty the infantry advanced. Instead of a proper complement of about five hundred tanks, to protect the doughboys against excessive losses in such an advance, we were only able to muster 18, and these were all employed against the little village of Landres-et-St. Georges. Here was a commentary on the price of unpreparedness to be paid inevitably in human life. With America the master steel-maker of the world, American infantrymen were denied the support and protection of these land battleships.

The advance was initiated with unprecedented power and dash and with perfect cohesion on almost every portion of the front. The veteran Second Division, with the big westerners of the Eighty-ninth, formed the center of the thrust and carried the line forward with unparalleled rapidity, overwhelming all resistance attempted by the enemy. On a battle front of approximately 18 miles the troops of the First Army swept forward in an assault which on the first day overran the German infantry lines, broke through his artillery positions, and continued on, gathering momentum until the troops reached the heights overlooking Sedan five days later.

Between 7:30 and 8:00 A.M. the arrival at Army Headquarters of the pigeons released at seven o'clock by the young men from the Operations Section had been reported to me by telephone and their messages delivered in my office. We thus had an accurate statement of the location of the most advanced troops of the Seventy-seventh, Eightieth, Second, Eighty-ninth, and Fifth divisions at the same hour, written by men who were eyewitnesses of what they described. A sketch with map coordinates was also included in each message. Reversing the usual procedure, I telegraphed this information forward to each Army Corps Headquarters, and they in turn communicated it to the respective Division Headquarters. In most cases this information reached the divisions before reports had reached them from their own troops.

Everything was going splendidly except on the front of the Seventy-seventh Division, where Lieutenant Bandini reported by his pigeon that the advance had ceased in front of Champigneulles a little farm village five kilometers north of east of Grandpré. The Corps Headquarters concerned attached little importance at the time to this one unfavorable item, but when the nine o'clock birds arrived with a statement from our representative on the front of the Seventy-seventh Division, that there had been no further advance, little firing, and few casualties, then the seriousness of this one failure became an urgent matter for the commander of that army corps. The pigeon messages from other sections of the front indicated a tremendous success, and by late afternoon it was apparent that the army had broken through the enemy's last organized position, having reached the heights east of Buzancy, a penetration of nine kilometers. Every pigeon released by the officers of the Operations Section reached the army loft at Souilly, and gave us earlier information of the progress of the attack than was obtained by the Army Corps and Division Headquarters closer to the front. The situation remained unchanged on the front of the Seventy-seventh Division, but the gains of our troops farther east gave us ground on the flank of the enemy from which attacks could be launched during the night and the next morning to straighten out the line.

During daylight of November 2nd the advance continued, the left of the line gaining nine kilometers, which carried it abreast of the center, where more difficult country had been encountered. On the 3rd everything swept forward, and the Infantry Brigade of the Second Division drove ahead after dark for an additional gain of five kilometers, following a single road through the Forêt de Dieulet, reaching the high ground overlooking the village of Beaumont, and surprising German officers in their billets and at least one organization at roll call. This last affair presents one of the anomalies of history, for German troops in 1870 marched through this same forest and surprised a French Division in bivouac around Beaumont, in the opening phase of the Battle of Sedan, and later that same day an American officer, General Philip Sheridan, rode through the forest to inspect the scene of the French fiasco of the morning.[4]

General Sheridan, in his *Memoirs,* gives a detailed description of his movements after the Battle of Gravelotte, which makes strange reading to an American officer of the World War. Starting from Pont-à-Mousson, the approximate right of the First American Army, Sheridan accompanied the German troops on their famous marches which led up to the capture of the Emperor Napoleon and MacMahon's entire army, September 7, 1870.[5] Throughout this movement he followed the main axis of the concentration for the Meuse-Argonne battle. Proceeding westward in the rear of our old St. Mihiel front, he billeted for the night at Commercy and then moved on to Bar-le-Duc, where he watched the Bavarians enter the town from the east and turn northward on their march toward Clermont-en-Argonne, traveling over the identical route followed by the American troops 48 years later. He billeted in Clermont and moved on northward through Varennes, which was one of the first captures of General Liggett's corps. He rested another night in Grandpré, where the Seventy-seventh and Seventy-eighth American divisions fought so gallantly. The following morning he rode north, through the Forêt de Dieulet, for the purpose I have already mentioned. He was moving north with Germans who were attacking Frenchmen. We advanced north over the same trail, driving Germans out of northern France. The last leg of his journey presents a still more striking coincidence, which will be narrated later on.

During this phase of the battle communication between Army Headquarters and the corps and divisions was difficult to manage, due to the rapidity of the advance. The roads were filled with battle traffic and even the motorcycle messengers could seldom make the trip from Army Headquarters to the more distant army corps in less than four or five hours, and frequently for one reason or another, failed to get through at all. The telephone communications were naturally poor, as it was next to impossible for the Signal Corps to erect satisfactory pole lines as rapidly as the troops went forward, and those laid on the ground were promptly cut by the traffic. To meet this situation I adopted the practice of delivering the daily field order by aeroplane, though this involved the possibility of its falling into the enemy's lines. Before the end of October, I had adopted another practice which considerably facilitated the delivery of orders, so long as the telephone connections were satisfactory. About ten o'clock each evening reports from each army corps reached me, giving the results of the day's operations up to five o'clock in the afternoon. Unfortunately, the statements of the location of the front lines were often inaccurate, but this was the best information we could obtain at the time. These reports were immediately consolidated in the Operations Section and a formal Operations Report for the army prepared. In addition a map showing the area occupied by each division in the army at five o'clock in the afternoon was also prepared and a copy of the Operations Report and of the map dispatched by motorcycle couriers at midnight to General Pershing's train, to his advanced Headquarters at Ligny-en-Barrois, to GHQ at Chaumont, to General Pétain at Provins, and to Marshal Foch at Senlis. I always remained in the office in order to personally supervise the preparation of these reports and maps and their prompt dispatch, and also to supervise the preparation of the draft of the field order to be issued to the army the following day.

I generally reached my billet in the Curé's house about 1 A.M., and the next morning returned to the office about seven-thirty to go over the draft of the field order which had been typed during the night. With four copies of this typewritten draft, triple-spaced, I would meet General Drum at his office at eight o'clock. In the meantime the Chief of Staff of each army corps would have telephoned any additional information which had developed since the submission of the corps's Operations Report. General Drum and I would then go over the drafts of the field order, making such changes as appeared advisable and to meet the army commander's desires, which had been expressed since my preparation of the draft. This interview usually lasted until eight-thirty and I would then return to the Operations Section and hurriedly correct all four copies of the draft. One of these was immediately turned over to the mimeographer, and the other three were taken by officers and telephoned simultaneously direct to the three most distant army corps, their stenographers taking down the dictation. In this way, the Corps Headquarters received at an early hour a draft of the order and could immediately commence on the preparation of the detailed corps field orders. Meanwhile, the mimeographing of the order would be completed in the Operations Section, and authenticated copies of the formal order turned over to an aviator to be dropped at each Corps Post of Command. Motorcycle couriers carried the orders to the two army corps in the vicinity of Verdun.

After I had completed the correction of the four draft copies of the order, I turned the matter over to assistants and reported back to General Drum's office for the morning conference of the heads of the various staff sections. At this time Colonel Howell, G-2 of the army, would give an outline of the situation of the enemy, and I would then be called upon for a statement as to the situation and prospective movements of our own troops. Following this there would be a general discussion, covering matters of supply, communications, artillery cooperation, and numerous other matters of daily concern at Army Headquarters. I do not recall that General Liggett ever attended any of these conferences. His directions were given us by the Chief of Staff, General Drum. It was only occasionally that I dealt with General Liggett directly, though we had many personal discussions regarding the courses of the operations, as I had been his Aide-de-Camp in the Philippines and our relationship had been very intimate.

Throughout November 4th and 5th the advance gained momentum, the eastern portion of our attacking troops was gradually swinging to the right and coming to a halt along the banks of the Meuse River, and the left wing of the army had progressed far beyond the right of the Fourth French Army. A fresh impetus was given on the night of the 4th, when the Rainbow Division was passed through the Seventy-eighth Division, and another impetus was provided a day later by shoving the old First Division forward through the ranks of the Eightieth, which were in need of relief.

While this operation was developing into a pursuit action, following up the hasty withdrawal which the enemy was covering by rear-guard fighting, the final notes between President Wilson and the German Government were being exchanged. The end of the war seemed in sight unless the Germans outmaneuvered us diplomatically and secured a temporary respite for their exhausted troops. Our heavy guns had been in position since the 4th from which they could fire on the sole line of rail communication which supplied all of the German Army from Picardy to Carignan, southeast of Sedan. If the fighting could be continued ten days longer, about a million German soldiers in front and to the west of us would either have to surrender or disperse as individuals. There were not sufficient roads to permit the retirement of the German divisions from the southern face of the great salient on the Western Front, and there was no means of supplying these troops during such a withdrawal. Our men were tired from the exhausting attacks, and continuous marches across country for the preceding five days, but everyone was driven to the limit to keep the machine moving until a complete rupture of the German forces between Verdun and the Champagne could be effected.

On the morning of the 6th, the First Division, in the center corps, launched a direct attack due northward and lunged forward six kilometers before noon, reaching the Meuse at Mouzon. On its right the Second, Eighty-ninth and Ninetieth divisions had already reached the river. To its left the Seventy-seventh and Forty-second divisions were advancing steadily northward. It was plainly evident that we had the enemy on the run and that he was withdrawing his troops to the north side of the Meuse River as rapidly as possible. In this situation I had a rather unusual interview with General Fox Conner, the Chief of Operations of the entire AEF, who came into my office at four o'clock in the afternoon to discuss future plans. After I had explained the status of affairs, he, like myself, felt that the enemy was in a critical predicament and should not be allowed any pause for reorganization. We debated the question of whether or not the troops on the left wing of the army had enough punch left in them to be driven forward throughout the ensuing night. This portion of the line was headed direct on Sedan, but Marshal Foch, on November 4th, had announced a western boundary or limit to the zone of operations of our army, which bent eastward so that it reached the Meuse River three kilometers below Sedan. In other words, we would have to swing the left wing of the army to the northeast, leaving Sedan as the goal of the Fourth French Army, which at this time was considerably in rear of the First American Army.

Our discussion lasted about half an hour, when Conner suddenly said, "It is General Pershing's desire that the troops of the First Army should capture Sedan, and he directs that orders be issued accordingly." I remarked that this was a rather important order, and calling a stenographer, I dictated the following:

November 5, 1918

Memorandum for Commanding Generals, 1st Corps, 5th Corps.

Subject: Message from Commander-in-Chief.

1. General Pershing desires that the honor of entering Sedan should fall to the First American Army. He has every confidence that the troops of the 1st Corps, assisted on their right by the 5th Corps, will enable him to realize this desire.

2. In transmitting the foregoing message, your attention is invited to the favorable opportunity now existing for pressing our advantage throughout the night. (Boundaries will not be considered binding).*

General Conner expressed approval of the form in which I had drafted this order, and told me to issue it immediately. We were on

---

* Note: Last sentence added later at Gen. Drum's direction.

very intimate personal terms, so I laughed and said, "Am I expected to believe that this is General Pershing's order, when I know damn well you came to this conclusion during our conversation?" General Conner replied, "That is the order of the Commander in Chief, which I am authorized to issue in his name. Now get it out as quickly as possible." As General Liggett, the army commander, and General Drum, his Chief of Staff, were absent from Souilly on that afternoon, I did not fancy making this drastic change in the course of the operation, which involved our entry into the zone of the Fourth French Army, without their having an opportunity of expressing an opinion, though I highly approved of pressing the Germans hard throughout the night and saw sound tactical reasons why we should not leave the enemy undisturbed on our flanks because of a theoretical line drawn on a map. The French could not possibly reach this ground immediately south of Sedan until a day later, so we must either control it or refuse our left flank, and this was no time to give the enemy any advantage.

In this predicament, I proposed a compromise by stating that I would delay issuing this order until 6 P.M., and if neither General Liggett nor General Drum had returned by that time, I would transmit it by telephone to the commanders of the army corps concerned. General Conner was not enthusiastic over my attitude, but agreed to the proposal. Every ten minutes during the following hour, I telephoned to find out if General Liggett or General Drum had returned, and finally at five minutes to six, I learned that General Drum had just reached his office. Taking a copy of the proposed order with me, I hurried over to see him and explained the situation. Without hesitation, he agreed immediately to the dispatch of the order, but caused me to add the sentence which read, "Boundaries will not be considered binding." This I had omitted through oversight, but as it would be necessary for the First Corps to cross its left boundary into the zone of the Fourth French Army in order to carry out the instructions, the amendment was obviously necessary.

I telephoned the order to the Headquarters of the First and Fifth corps about 6:10 P.M., and it developed afterwards that General Pershing, in person, had given instructions to General Dickman of the

First Corps, about five o'clock that afternoon, to advance directly on Sedan.[6] General Conner was for some time unaware of this last-mentioned incident.

Out of this affair grew one of the bitterest contentions between American troops during the war, not to mention some lively discussions with the French higher Headquarters. The Rainbow Division, on the left of the army, pushed ahead in the night on Sedan, while the Seventy-seventh Division, to its right, endeavored to keep abreast of the movement. The First Division had reached the Meuse at Mouzon. It belonged to the center corps and was ordered late that evening to move by its left flank and drive northwestward, with Sedan as the objective. Following a night march, remarkable for the fortitude and endurance displayed, the troops of the First Division cut across the front of the left corps, and swung northward toward Sedan. The southernmost regiment, under Colonel Roosevelt, had the longest march to make and it passed through the Seventy-seventh and Forty-second divisions and the most advanced troops of the right of the Fourth French Army, and gained a position beyond the Bar River six kilometers southwest of Sedan. Other troops of the First, intermingled with organizations of the Rainbow Division, reached the high bluffs looking directly down into Sedan. A platoon of the Forty-second reached the suburb of Wadelincourt, but was unable to cross the river, which was in flood, in the face of German machine-gun fire. This climax occurred on the morning of November 7th, coincident with the application of the German Government direct to Marshall Foch for an immediate armistice. One battalion of the First Division had followed General Philip Sheridan's approximate route from Beaumont, when he accompanied the entourage of the Emperor William in 1870, and this battalion came out on the identical hill, overlooking Sedan, from which General Sheridan viewed the trapped French Army in the town thus made famous, and into which the American troops were later to drive the Germans.

The reports of this confused, but highly successful, finale to this portion of the battle which reached Army Headquarters were for a time difficult to understand. A report from Rickenbacker, the leading American ace, was telephoned into the Operations Section, stating that he had dropped newspapers to American soldiers in the streets of Sedan.[7] The Headquarters of the Fourth French Army telephoned over to find out what we were doing in their zone, and they were assured that our troops would be withdrawn as soon as the French came up. As they were not satisfied with this, a succession of inquiries came from them and also from the Headquarters of the French Group of Armies of the Center, and from General Pétain's G-3. To each the same reply was given, that the American troops would be withdrawn from the French zone as soon as the French troops came up. Meanwhile the First Corps was objecting to the passage of troops of the center corps through its zone, stating that the movements of both troops and supplies were being seriously interfered with. To meet this situation, orders were issued for the withdrawal of the First Division within the limits of its own corps, and my old friends, after an attack, a forced night march, and a final skirmish, were put immediately in march en route to the southeast. The Forty-second Division and the Sixth, immediately in its rear, were also withdrawn as rapidly as the French troops came up, to take over the heights along the river in front of Sedan.

The culmination of the northward advance of the First Army was a typical American "grandstand finish." The spirit of competition was awakened in the respective divisions to such an extent that the men threw aside all thoughts of danger and fatigue in their efforts to exceed their neighbors. There were numerous cases where soldiers dropped dead from exhaustion, wonderful examples of self-sacrifice and utter devotion to duty. It requires far less of resolution to meet a machine-gun bullet than it does to drive one's body to the death. The men in the Sixth Division, which lacked thousands of draft animals, substituted themselves for the missing horses and mules and towed the machine-gun carts and other light vehicles. In six days the army had advanced 38 kilometers, and had driven every German beyond the Meuse from Sedan to Verdun. It was a wonderful and inspiring feat of arms, yet the world was so intent at this time on the exchange of messages between President Wilson and the German Government that our people at home failed to realize that American troops had achieved a splendid victory.

CHAPTER XIII

The Armistice

W HILE THE ADVANCE toward Sedan was progressing, General Hines' corps, which reached the line of the Meuse River on the second day of the attack, turned its attention to another operation. On the night of November 3rd, the first step was taken toward forcing crossings of the Meuse River near Dun and at a point five kilometers farther south. The Fifth Division, under General Ely, who had commanded the Twenty-eighth Infantry at Cantigny, was given this difficult task. In the face of an enemy entrenched on high bluffs, General Ely's men struggled for two nights in an effort to cross the Meuse River and the parallel canal. Gaining a lodgment under the bluffs on the night of the 4th, they pressed forward over the high ground on the following morning and by the evening of the 5th had effected a penetration of more than two kilometers along a front of six, in the wooded bluffs of the Côte de Meuse. There were many daring acts by individuals and by organizations in the crossing of the river and the penetration of the rugged country beyond. So rapid was the advance of the troops that the Division Headquarters west of the Meuse, and all the higher headquarters, had much difficulty in keeping track of the front line. On the afternoon of the 6th, the situation was so uncertain, because of the successful prosecution of the operation, that I sent out an aviator from the squadron assigned to the G-3 Section, to make a special reconnaissance. He returned in about an hour with the information that the American infantry had reached the eastern edge of the bluffs overlooking the plain of the Woëvre. I transmitted this forward to the Corps and Fifth Division Headquarters, and was told in reply that the infantry was several miles in rear of the position given by the aviator. The latter insisted he had seen our men lying on the ground on the bare crests of the bluff near Brandeville, eight kilometers beyond the Meuse River. First sending him out again for a second reconnaissance, I called for another aviator, showed him on the map what the dispute was, and directed him to proceed as rapidly as possible to check the issue on the ground. Both returned in a remarkably short time and reported that not only had the infantry reached the point claimed near Brandeville, but that a considerable amount of the Fifth Division artillery was firing from a position beyond that which the division thought its infantry had just reached.

The receipt of this information demanded instant action, as the heavy guns of the army and corps artillery were then firing into a portion of the area now occupied by their own troops. I endeavored to telephone instructions to the Chief of Artillery to discontinue this firing, but was told by the young lady at the switchboard that the line was busy. In accordance with custom, I demanded an instant connection on the ground that this was an urgent Operation call. She told me that she knew of no such rule, and that only for the army commander or the Chief of Staff, could such an interruption be made. I then informed her that I was the Acting Chief of Staff, at the moment, which I was, but she quibbled over this, quite evidently doubting the accuracy of my statement. I then demanded that she give me the Chief Signal Officer, Colonel Parker Hitt, which she did.[1] I told him in a few words what was wanted, and, as his office was close to the Artillery Headquarters, requested him to run over personally and see that the order was given to stop the firing. Evidently Central listened in, because she called me up in a few minutes and in a rather hysterical fashion attempted to explain why she had failed to give me prompt service. Feeling that the delay had probably cost the lives of some of our men, she had worked herself up into a very excited state of mind, and finally came over to the office to learn in person how much damage her action might have caused. This was apparently the first time any of the women centrals at Army Headquarters had been brought into such immediate contact with the direction of the battle.

The advance of the Fifth Division in the plain of the Woëvre continued with such rapidity that a portion of the Thirty-second was thrown in on their right to fill up the constantly lengthening front. By the 4th of November, a new operation was launched on the front of the Seventeenth French Corps, to cooperate with the successes gained by the Fifth Division. In this affair one French division, the Seventy-ninth and Twenty-sixth American divisions participated. By the 8th, the enemy had been thrown entirely clear of the high ground east of the Meuse and was falling back on the dense woods and the swamps of the plain of the Woëvre. The Fifth Division on a front of ten kilometers, about three times the normal frontage for a division in battle, made a maximum advance of almost eight kilometers on the following day, most of the progress being through the dense Forêt de Woëvre. On its left the Ninetieth forced a crossing of the Meuse near Mouzay, while splendid progress was being made further south. Everywhere on this portion of our front, the enemy seemed to be on the run and certainly our troops were doing everything to aid and abet his departure.

On the night of the 9th, instructions were received at Army Headquarters, repeating Marshal Foch's orders for all the troops to press the enemy as vigorously as possible. Accordingly, the Second and Eighty-ninth divisions were ordered to force a river crossing near Beaumont. The troops in the plain of the Woëvre pressed forward wherever possible, and on the right of the army, eighty kilometers southeast of Sedan, the Eighty-first Division advanced through the swamps of the plain with little artillery support, as they had horses for but few of their guns. The air was filled with wireless messages which indicated a break-up in the German Army and the trembling of the nation. The Soldiers' and Sailors' Committee, in possession of the wireless station at Metz, communicated with similar committees all along the front, at Wilhelmstrassen, the German Naval Base, and with other points in the interior. The women of Germany appealed by wireless to the women of the United States, and all sorts of rumors spread about.

My time at this moment was absorbed in preparing orders for the constantly changing battle front, and in arranging for the transfer of four of our reserve divisions to the Second Army, for a great attack which was scheduled for November 14th southeast of Metz, and the movement of other divisions, then out of the line, toward Dun-sur-Meuse, in preparation for a purely American advance eastward toward Montmédy, which we hoped to launch on the night of November 15th. In addition, a special operation had been arranged to clear the Germans from the railroad line immediately beyond the eastern exit of the Verdun-Etain Tunnel, in order to permit our Engineer troops to reconstruct the track which would be essential to the supply of the army for its further advance toward the Luxembourg frontier.

On these last days our principal concern was the movement of four divisions from the general vicinity of Bar-le-Duc over to the Second Army, in preparation for the joint French-American assault which was to be launched on the 14th, southeast of Metz. Lack of trucks to transport the foot soldiers was our dilemma, as the French had withdrawn their great truck trains which had been at our disposal earlier in the battle. I calculated that it would be an utter impossibility for the artillery of these divisions to reach the scene of the prospective operation by the 14th, and this would mean that the infantry would have to go into the battle without its artillery. This situation, I believe, was represented to Marshal Foch, but he held to the date set regardless of the fact that the animal-drawn guns would not be present to support the infantry. Colonel DeWitt, the G-4, or head of the Supply Section of the General Staff, had motored down into the SOS with authority to pick up all the trucks obtainable, and we planned to use whatever number we secured to shuttle back and forth, picking up the most advanced marching infantry and carrying it over to the Moselle.

The principal subject of conversation in our mess at this time was the possible terms of the Armistice, and what the Allies would ultimately demand of Germany. Colonel Forte, our French Attaché, and Major Geiger, the representative of the English Army, held the floor most of the time, discussing the distribution of the German colonies. It was amusing to listen, because it evidenced so clearly the habitual viewpoint of the English and French in this matter. We had no thought of colonies, but they thought of little else, and at one meal Colonel Forte told me that the United States should take Syria. I replied that from the viewpoint of an Army officer, America was opposed to any colony that had a wet or a dry season, and an abnormal number of insects. On the spur of the moment, I added that Bermuda was the only possible colony we would consider. All of the Americans at the table were flabbergasted when Geiger took me seriously as to Bermuda. He quite apparently thought that here at last was what America was after in this war, aside from dollars and cents, and he disputed violently any possibility that America had a claim on Bermuda. Geiger referred to this at almost every meal until he left six days later, and he undoubtedly carried away with him the fixed conviction that my statement was founded on official information.

General Wagstaff, the head of the British Mission at Chaumont, had dinner with us on the 10th, and as a report had been received that day that the British had captured Mons, the scene of their disastrous fight in the opening days of the war, we made the meal a formal celebration, in his honor, of this event. One of the officers from the Map Section of G-3 prepared a menu which depicted a German Humpty Dumpty crashing from the wall of Mons, from which two British soldiers regarded him with complacent triumph. A speech was demanded of Wagstaff and he doubled himself up over his chair in true British fashion, and rambled and mumbled over his appreciation of the honor done him, our tribute to the British Army, and the American contribution to the war. We all became quite sentimental and affectionately disposed toward one another, and dispatched the mess officer for more champagne.

I reached my bed about 2 A.M. on the 11th, having left two officers in the office with detailed instructions regarding the movement of the four divisions to the Second Army, which was to be initiated that morning at six-thirty o'clock, and would be dependent to a certain extent on the trucks secured by Colonel DeWitt. At two-thirty the ringing of the telephone by my bed awakened me and DeWitt's voice informed me that he was at Neufchâteau and had secured a certain number of trucks at various points in the SOS, which would reach Bar-le-Duc shortly after daylight. He added that he was almost dead with fatigue, but must continue on to Souilly and would see me in the morning. I telephoned this information to the officers on duty in the

Operations Section and then turned over and fell asleep. About 6
A.M., the telephone again awakened me, and this time Colonel Carl
Boyd's voice came over the wire to inform me that the Armistice had
been signed a few minutes before and that all fighting was to cease at
11 A.M.[2] He was General Pershing's senior Aide, and as I recognized
his voice, I could accept this as authentic. Without getting out of bed,
I telephoned to General Drum and found that he had already received the same information and had dispatched the necessary telegrams and couriers to the army corps.

I then turned my attention to the four divisions which were to
march at six-thirty. The weather was quite cool and generally inclem-
ent, and there would be no shelter for these troops when they arrived
in the Second Army area. I therefore hoped that we could hold them
where they were, but no order had been received from GHQ termi-
nating this movement. Still telephoning from the bed, I called up
General Heintzelman, the Chief of Staff of the Second Army, at Toul,
and asked him if he wanted those divisions sent on over to his army.
He replied that he didn't want them, but he was not authorized to say
that he didn't as GHQ had given no orders. I suggested that they
would have long, hard marches and no shelter, but he did not feel
authorized to take action himself. I then called up my office and told
the officer on duty there to stop the movement of two of these divisions, I think the Third and the Twenty-ninth, but to let the other two
go ahead. About ten minutes later, General Heintzelman telephoned
me again and said that he thought we might take a risk and hold up
the movement until we could hear from GHQ. When he learned that
I had already accepted the responsibility for stopping two of the
divisions, he took the risk of requesting me to hold up the other two.
Unfortunately, however, these last had gotten on the road, and it
required about two hours to head them off. With this matter attended
to, and the information that the war was to cease in about four hours
and a half, I turned over and went to sleep and did not wake up until
ten o'clock.

All the members of the mess assembled for a late breakfast at ten-
thirty, and the Englishman and the Frenchman again took the floor in
deciding what was to be done with Germany. Colonel Forte was par-

ticularly aggrieved that he could not go into Germany at the head of a regiment of Moroccans and see that the Germans were given something of the same treatment that they had accorded the French inhabitants at various times. Geiger had little to say about revenge so far as fighting was concerned, but he was very set in his mind as to colonies, and the freedom of the seas, under British supervision. In the midst of this discussion, and coming as a sort of parting thrill, there was a tremendous explosion in the garden just outside the single window, which was in the prolongation of the length of the mess table. We were blown out of our chairs and I landed on the floor sitting on the back of my chair, my head getting a fairly heavy bump against the wall. I thought I had been killed and I think each of the others had the same idea, but we picked ourselves up and found that aside from the ruin of the breakfast, no particular damage had been done. A few minutes later a young aviator hurried in to see what had happened, and he explained that he had been out in his 'plane with some small bombs, all of which he thought had been released, but it seems that one stuck to the rack and as he sailed down just over our roof to make his landing in the field beyond our garden wall, the remaining bomb jerked loose and fell just ten yards outside the window. The thick walls of the house and the fact that the window was in direct prolongation of the table, and no one was sitting at either end, saved us from a little tragedy just thirty minutes before the hour for the Armistice.

Getting word to the troops to cease fighting and advancing at eleven o'clock, was quite a problem on some portions of the lines. The Second and Eighty-ninth divisions had been engaged in a river crossing near Beaumont that night, and some of these troops made such rapid progress in the wooded hills beyond the river that the messengers did not reach them until just before twelve o'clock. They had captured prisoners after 11 A.M., and these we were promptly called upon by the Germans to release, which we did.

The right of the Eighty-ninth and the left of the Ninetieth divisions both reached the town of Stenay, the former Headquarters of the German Crown Prince, in the last hours of the fighting, and, of course, both claimed the town, particularly as everyone was looking for a dry place to sleep. After examining the map, I telephoned up instructions that a certain east-and-west street would divide the town between the two divisions so far as billeting was concerned, but the Ninetieth Division would be charged with the security of the entire place.

About five o'clock in the afternoon, we intercepted a wireless message from the German High Command, presumably Von Hindenburg's Headquarters, to the Allied High Command, Marshal Foch, stating that an American lieutenant with a platoon had entered Cervisy, a little village beyond the Armistice line north of Stenay, and had directed the German Major to vacate the town immediately because it was wanted for billets. The Germans protested against this violation of the terms of the Armistice. There was also another wireless message intercepted from the German High Command earlier in the day, stating the Americans were still fighting after eleven o'clock and requesting that they be made to desist from further hostilities. This undoubtedly referred to the incident east of Beaumont, previously explained, and it always gave me some satisfaction to feel that while we had been condemned so unmercifully for delaying our entrance into the war, the last reference to fighting was an appeal to have the Americans stopped.

The reaction in the village of Souilly on the day of the Armistice was interesting, not because of any particular excitement or demonstrations, but because of the absence of such evidences of rejoicing. At the suggestion of Major Geiger of the British Army, a band was brought in from a nearby regiment and played the national airs of the various Allies, and other patriotic music for about an hour. Aside from this and the occasional cheering of the occupants of trucks headed up and down the "Sacred Way," there was nothing to indicate that this was the Headquarters of America's largest army and that the greatest war in history had that day come to a close. One aviator gave a demonstration of stunt flying over the village, and apparently the wings on one side of the 'plane collapsed, because he fell in a crash which ended his life.

The detailed terms of the Armistice, which reached us that afternoon, required that our troops should not go beyond the line they had reached at 11 A.M., until the morning of November 17th, when a general advance toward the Rhine would be begun, its progress carefully regulated day by day, according to specific terms of the document. By the following morning, reports began to drift in that the Germans had promptly withdrawn all along the line, and there was thus left a zone in which there was no constituted authority to maintain order. Released prisoners, Russians, Italians, Rumanians, etc., were reported to be endangering the lives of the French inhabitants left in this region. We were forbidden, however, from taking any action as we could not go beyond the Armistice line. Continued reports of this nature were received, and the French mayor of a little town in the plain of the Woëvre reached our lines with the information that the Russians had gathered up the arms and ammunition left behind in the supply dumps of the Germans, and were terrorizing the women and children. I, therefore, started out to go beyond the lines and ascertain the real facts in the case.

With my chauffeur, I motored up by Montfaucon and Romagne to the pontoon bridge near Dun-sur-Meuse, and, crossing there, continued on to Stenay, and there passed through our lines into the unoccupied ground. About two kilometers beyond Stenay on the Montmedy road, I found the highway filled from side to side with long-bearded, filthy-looking Russians. Getting out of the car, I climbed a steep bank beside the road, and with my appearance they instantly formed up into a column of squads and stood rigid and motionless, looking straight to the front. I could not speak any Russian, but I had yet to find practically any large group during the war in which there was not someone who understood English, so I called out to them, using the greeting that I understood they always received from their Czar, "Good morning, my children." To my embarrassment, not a child moved or spoke, and the chauffeur indulged in some ribald laughter. I then pointed toward our own lines and motioned them forward, and the column marched by like a regiment passing in review. That night, when I returned to Stenay, I found these 1800 Russians held up at the outpost line by a distracted Lieutenant, who did not know what to do with them, as his orders forbade the passage of anyone. I there learned that these men had been captured in Hindenburg's famous battle of the Masurian Lakes in the fall of

1914, and had been worked like slaves by the Germans on the lines near Verdun ever since.[3] They were so cowed that at the least frown they jerked into a rigid posture, from which it was hard to relax them. I told the Lieutenant to pass them through the lines, as they had to be fed and could not be held starving before our outposts. Incidents of this same nature were developing all along the front of the army, and released prisoners of a variety of nationalities were striving to get food and shelter and transportation home.

Continuing on my reconnaissance, I swung around to the southeast and found scattered parties of released prisoners at various places, but none of them were disorderly. The inhabitants all seemed to have hidden — certainly they were not in evidence. Entering our lines near Jametz, I found my way blocked by a destroyed bridge, which was being repaired by the Engineers of the Fifth Division, so I had to give up the idea of continuing on around to Etain, and was forced to retrace my route. Everywhere were scenes of a disorganized German effort to delay our further advance, though it was quite evident that their Army had, at least for a time, started to melt away. On my return to Souilly, I reported the situation as I had found it, and it was then decided to send out several regiments to certain localities in this unoccupied zone and to give the commanders of these regiments authority to act in accordance with the situation as it developed.

The prison cage at Souilly quickly became a most interesting place, as the barbwire stockades enclosed a variety of our Allies, who were all crazy to start home, wherever that might be. As there were no trains available and the agreements between the various Allies had not yet been fully developed in this matter, a certain amount of delay became necessary, during which it was necessary to keep these men together, and the prison cages were the only available places. The Italians were particularly difficult to handle; they all talked at once and there were thousands of them. We had no English under such restraint, as very few of them came into our lines and the English attachés arranged immediately for the handling of their own people, who were quiet and restrained and very tired looking. The French released prisoners were, of course, turned over to their own people and promptly routed toward their homes by trucks or any other means of casual transportation. At dusk, to meet one of these little groups of returning Frenchmen, with their worldly goods in a handkerchief carried on a stick over the shoulder, tramping along the roads into our lines, talking with each other in low tones, and with a set purpose showing in their faces to get home to their families, was a very touching sight and awakened unusual emotions.

During this period the air continued to be filled with wireless messages from a variety of sources. Von Hindenburg appealed to the soldiers of the Army to march back with him in honor to the Fatherland. The German women appealed to the women of America; the Soviet Committees of the Soldiers and Sailors engaged in discussions with other committees along the front and to the rear in Germany. This wireless phase introduced an entirely new situation. Heretofore, in any national break-up or incipient revolution, the means of communication remained, as a rule, within the hands of the previously constituted authority, but in this instance it was only necessary for a group to seize a wireless station — division, corps, army, or commercial — in order to put itself in touch with other disaffected elements, who all seemingly had done likewise. The messages from Belgium indicated the dissolution of the German Army and it was touch and go whether or not this would spread along the line.

It will always remain an open question as to what would have been the result of continuing the fighting for another week. Certainly, we would have gone straight through the enemy's line, as his last remaining available division, and a tired one at that, was thrown into the battle on the front of our Third Corps on the afternoon of the 10th. But our situation might have become very difficult, as the German Army was on the verge of a break-up and very probably would have dissolved into independent groups, which would have engaged in guerrilla fighting and would have terrorized the inhabitants. And a more serious result would have probably been a revolution in Germany and the complete disorganization of the existing government. The Allies would then have had no organized group with whom to deal and would have been under the necessity of taking over practically all of Germany, which would have been a very difficult and lengthy task. Nevertheless, it seemed a pity then, and even more so now, that we did not crown the victory with the disarmament of the German troops, and thus have avoided the effect on the German populace of having their armies march home claiming that they had never been defeated. Old England was much wiser in this matter and demanded the complete surrender of the German fleet, leaving no question in anybody's mind as to the masters of the sea.

The terms of the Armistice permitted the Allies to start their advance toward the bridgeheads on the Rhine on the morning of November 17th, and any troops or war material which the Germans could not evacuate in advance of this movement would fall into our hands. Early in November, General Pershing had directed the organization of a Third Army, but this was not given effect until the 12th or 13th. General Dickman was assigned to the command of this new force, and General Malin Craig was made his Chief of Staff. He came to me on the evening of the 13th and requested that I do anything I could to help get the divisions assigned to this army in place for the march on the 17th, as his Headquarters could not be organized to handle this matter for several days. He also requested that I give him selected officers and clerks from the Operations Section to bolster up his new organization. General Fox Conner then gave me the line-up of the divisions for the march into Germany, all but one of which were to come from the First Army. I noticed that he designated the First Division to be in the second line in the advance to the Rhine, and on inquiry as to why this veteran unit was not to be permitted to lead in the triumphant march, he explained that it was too far in rear to reach the position from which the first line would move off on the morning of the 17th. After he left, I called up the Headquarters of the First, which was located north of Romagne, and asked the Chief of Staff, Colonel Fuqua, if the troops could reach a point east of Verdun by the afternoon of the 16th.[4] After consulting the map, he told me that the distance was too great and the men too tired for such a march to be undertaken. When I replied, "Is the honor of leading the advance into Germany worth the effort, or would you rather go up in the second line?" he hastily informed me that all they needed to know was where they were to be on the morning of the 17th, and I gave him instructions accordingly. I did not tell General Conner of this change in his plans and the troops were on their way into Germany before he discovered that the line-up was not as originally directed, but he generously waived my ignoring of his orders, and made no mention of the matter higher up. At one o'clock on the morning of the 17th, General Frank Parker, commanding the First Division, and Colonel Theodore Roosevelt of the Twenty-sixth Infantry stopped at my office to learn where the division was located. They had been off on a hurried trip to Paris, and when I told them that the Headquarters were east of Verdun, and the march toward Germany would commence at five-thirty, they made a hurried departure.

My last days with First Army Headquarters were occupied in deploying the troops of the Third Army for their march into Germany, and arranging for the march of the remaining troops of the First Army south to the old billeting areas around Chaumont. Altogether there were some 600,000 men involved in these movements, but we had been working with such big issues and numbers and in such rapid succession that no one ever commented on the magnitude of the undertaking, which was carried through without a hitch.

About five days before the Armistice, I was notified that orders were being issued appointing me Chief of Staff of an army corps, which was to participate in the attack southeast of Metz, but as the battle was apparently drawing to a rapid close, I was instructed to remain on my present duties until matters had cleared up. This position was supposed to be filled by a Brigadier General, and I was informed that on October 15th, General Pershing had cabled to Washington a recommendation that I be made a Brigadier General. Colonel Laurence Halstead reported to the Operations Section to take my place and served as an Assistant until my departure.[5] The task of gathering up all the loose ends in order to evacuate the First Army from its battle area was a lengthy one. The special troops and organizations, in addition to army corps and divisions, numbered about 75,000 and these were much harder to handle, because a separate order was required for practically every unit. In other words, a division of 25,000 could be moved almost as easily as a company of gas troops or a delousing unit. We were engaged in the Operations Section for almost a week in planning and getting out the orders for the various movements concerned. The divisions had to be given an order which would cover their daily marches for from two to four weeks, and as there was a great movement of French divisions from western France toward Alsace-Lorraine, many complications were encountered. The shortage in horses and the necessity of turning over a great many animals to the newly formed Third Army made it impossible for the divisions to move with their artillery. Each artillery brigade was first marched to the nearest railhead, and there all its horses, except enough to haul rations for the men, were detached and turned over to the trains of the foot troops, the artillery brigades in some instances having to wait a month before rail transportation could be obtained to move them south.

Finally, on November 19th, I left Souilly, and motored down to Chaumont to start on the organization of the Eighth Army Corps, of which I was Chief of Staff. The corps commander had not yet been appointed, but a few days later General Henry T. Allen was designated.[6] General Drum accompanied me to Chaumont, and for 150 kilometers we reflected on the events of the past two months and reminisced over incidents of the battle. He had been the Chief of Staff of an army which numbered at one time over a million men, and owing to the frequent absences of General Pershing from Army Headquarters, required by conferences with Marshals Foch and Pétain, and business at Chaumont and in the SOS, General Drum had carried a vast burden of responsibility. In a veteran army his task would have been heavy, but the complications and difficulties involved in organizing and fighting, at one and the same time, an abnormally large army beggars description.

On my arrival at Chaumont, General Conner and General Eltinge again took me into their house and mess, and I spent the next five days in collecting the officers and special troops for the Headquarters of the Eighth Army Corps. Realizing that we were to endure a dreary French winter before there would be any chance of return to the United States, I made it a point to select not only efficient officers, who were experienced in the duties they were to undertake, but also men of agreeable dispositions, who would not be likely to grow pessimistic during the coming months of waiting. Colonel Erickson, my old friend of the First Division, was appointed G-3 of the corps, and Major Catron, formerly Executive Officer of the Intelligence Section of the First Army, was made G-2.[7] Colonel Graham, G-1 of the Sixth Division, joined the Eighth Corps as G-1, or Chief of the Supply Section.[8] When it came to obtaining corps troops, I encountered a peculiar situation. There were plenty of troops available, but no means of transporting them, as the French were not giving us any rail rolling stock at this time, and all our movements had to be made by marching. Unfortunately, the distances in the case of most of the troops available were too great to consider moving them on foot to Corps Headquarters. In this situation, I decided to capitalize on some friendships, and called up Walter Grant, who was now Chief of Staff of the First Army Corps, and asked him if he still held me in high regard. He replied that his love and affection for me were undimmed, and I thereupon asked him if they had a value of 25 trucks. After a little further conversation, he generously turned over to me, for seven days, a train of 40 trucks. I telephoned to various other friends, who were in positions controlling transportation, and finally succeeded in collecting about 150 trucks, all of which I was bound to return in a specified number of days. In one case I was calling a man in Neufchâteau, and was given the wrong telephone connection and found myself talking to a stranger in Langres. He had heard most of my tale before I discovered the error, and he was such a generous fellow that he loaned me 25 trucks sight unseen. I was careful not to tell General Fox Conner about this impromptu transportation arrangement, as he had been rather laughing up his sleeve when he generously offered without question the Engineer, Signal Corps, and other corps troops which were needed, well knowing that I had no means with which to move them. About three days later his section suddenly woke up to find that I had grabbed the troops and that they were rapidly being assembled by a series of night-and-day truck movements, and I enjoyed a good laugh. While collecting these troops, the officer handling the trucks picked up the material for any hangars or Adrian barracks which he found scattered about.[9]

Colonel Joseph McKeany, who had been a Captain, Quartermaster, in the First Division, and was promoted in a day to Lieutenant Colonel, and Division Quartermaster, due to the killing of his two seniors by a bomb, had joined me as Chief Quartermaster of the corps.[10] He had served with great distinction as Deputy Chief Quartermaster of the First Army, and I felt sure that if anyone could obtain the various things we needed, McKeany was the man. When he reported to me at Chaumont, he had an automobile filled with German trophies, helmets, sabers, antitank guns, etc., and he said he thought he could trade these in for some good requisitions for supplies in the SOS, and a day or two later proved this idea was sound. He visited the commanding officer of the great Regulating Station at Is-sur-Tille, and after presenting him with all the trophies that officer desired, McKeany among other things shipped up to the Eighth Corps Headquarters two box cars containing office equipment and furniture, which gave us a more complete outfit than I ever saw any other organization have in France.

The location of the Headquarters of the Eighth Army Corps was curiously arrived at. When preparing the orders at Souilly for the march of the troops of the First Army to the south of France, I had located the Headquarters of the First and Fifth corps in the most desirable towns I knew of, and gave to an unnumbered corps, which was to be turned over to the army later, a town of which I knew nothing except that it was centrally located in the area to be controlled by that corps. I had expected to go to an army corps which was to be in the Second Army, but when I reached Chaumont, I found that I was assigned to the Eighth Corps, which was headed for the unknown village I had previously selected. A hurried trip by automobile to this village disclosed the fact that it was a little farm community, with no resources for sheltering the Headquarters of an army corps. I motored about for the remainder of the day and finally came to Montigny-sur-Aube, between Chatillon-sur-Seine and Chaumont, about 48 kilometers west of the latter city. Montigny had a twelfth-century château which had been remodeled and actually had a furnace. This made an ideal office building for the corps staff. Furthermore, on the edge of the town was a modern château, with beautiful grounds, and for the time being, unoccupied. This made a delightful home for the corps commander and a few members of his staff. There were good billets in the town, the people were friendly disposed, and there were several other châteaux in the neighborhood. I immediately returned to Chaumont and called up my successor at Souilly, Colonel Halstead, and requested him to change the order so as to locate the Eighth Corps Headquarters at Montigny. At first, he refused, saying that there was probably a good reason for the original location assigned the corps and he could not make the change without careful consideration. I assured him that I was the only reason for choosing either of the places and that no complications were involved, but as he still hesitated, I got General Drum on the phone and requested him to insure for me a comfortable winter home, which he did.

General Allen, with his Aides, arrived at Chaumont about November 26th and went on the next day to Montigny, but I remained two days longer in Chaumont, where I had the best of telephone connections to coordinate the assembly of the corps troops and supplies. By the first of December we were delightfully established at Montigny, and entered into one of the most enjoyable winters in my experience. General Allen, with his two Aides, Captain Allen and Captain Sidney Fish, Colonel Erickson, Colonel Graham, Major Catron, and myself, were established in the modern château.[11] The grounds were beautiful and even boasted of a swan we named "Mike," who sailed sedately along a little stream which ran close under our windows. There were several delightful French families in the neighboring châteaux, with whom we soon established intimate social relations. Monsieur Paul de Souzy, with his wife and a daughter, Mademoiselle Juliette,* lived at the Château Gevrolle, just three kilometers from our place. Prince ———, with his wife and daughter, had a beautiful place seven kilometers from Montigny, and there were several other charming homes within easy reach.

General Allen started immediately on assembling the best horseflesh he could obtain from our various remount stations and soon had a

* Now the wife of Captain Allen.

string of fifty fairly creditable looking animals. The high ridges of the Côte d'Or furnished fine going for the horses and we spent a great deal of time in the saddle.

By the middle of December, the three divisions assigned to the Eighth Corps had arrived in their areas, the Sixth, Seventy-seventh, and the Eighty-first, and we were immediately involved in the strenuous training program laid down by GHQ. As the troops had been on the march since November 20th and the weather was cold and raw, there was no enthusiasm over this work. Everyone wanted to relax, but there was little of comfort for the men to enjoy and to have allowed them to loaf would have undoubtedly destroyed discipline and endangered the integrity of our army, as the restless desire to get home filled all minds.

General Allen decided to have a formal dinner for our French friends on Christmas Eve, and there were gathered about the board about twenty of us for dinner that night. We had an orchestra from one of the bands and everything progressed with great formality; in fact, entirely too much of the formal and too little of the convivial. This was the first party these French people had enjoyed since the summer of 1914, and naturally they were not at their ease with us. We attempted a little dancing after dinner, but found the French ladies did not understand our steps and that we were unable to engage in the constant whirling of the French waltz. When the orchestra retired for its supper, Colonel Erickson and I, with Miss Wiborg, a relative and guest of General Allen, and Mademoiselle de Souzy, decided to organize an orchestra of our own. With the piano, trombone, saxophone, and snare drum, we mangled a few pieces, but awakened things a little. As the enthusiasm grew, we gained volunteers and finally we had an old French Count proudly manning the cymbals. From a stiff party the dinner was rapidly transformed into a rather riotous celebration and our guests, instead of leaving at eleven, remained until 2 A.M.

Diaries
Notes
Index

DIARY OF A VISIT TO ENGLAND
WITH GENERAL PERSHING

July 15–23, 1919

July 15th We left Paris at one-thirty on the morning of July 15th, after spending the evening doing the round of the various street dances following the Bastille Day parade. We arrived at Boulogne at 9 A.M., and the train pulled on the dock along side the British destroyer *Orpheus* which was to take the General over the Channel. We boarded the destroyer at nine-thirty and it put off for Dover immediately, being accompanied by another destroyer, both flying the American flag.

On our arrival in the harbor at Dover, the guns of the fort fired an appropriate salute for the General. The destroyer pulled alongside the dock, and a company of British troops, with band, was paraded. The General commanding that District and the Mayor of Dover were awaiting General Pershing. After the usual formalities — inspection of the Guard of Honor, etc., we moved on, via a gorgeous red carpet to the station proper, which was elaborately decorated and carpeted and hung in red. A luxurious special train stood waiting, and after appropriate pourparlers we departed for London.

General Sir John Headlam had been designated to accompany the General throughout his visit, and he met us at Dover with a staff of five officers and remained with us from that time until our departure from Dover on July 23rd.

A light lunch was served on the train going up, and we arrived in London at twelve-thirty, and found the same sort of a setting as at Dover. Mr. Winston Churchill, Secretary of State for War, and a number of General officers and other dignitaries were present. After the inspection of the Guard of Honor, the Generals in the party and I embarked in three of the royal carriages and drove to the Carlton Hotel, where quarters had been prepared for us by the British Government.

The members of the British Mission which had been assigned to us for the trip entertained us for luncheon, and immediately afterwards we went in turn to Buckingham Palace, St. James's Palace, and York House to register in the Visitors' Books of the King, the Prince of Wales, and Queen Alexandra.

That afternoon, I indulged in a little shopping, though I did not purchase anything for myself.

At eight-thirty, General Pershing, General Harbord, and myself went to the American Ambassador's for dinner.[1] As I recall, the following were guests: Duke of Connaught, Princess Patricia, Duke and Duchess of Sutherland, Lord Milner, Lady Middleton — and a couple of other Lords and Ladies that I don't recall. The dinner was very interesting to me, being my first experience on such an occasion. I had Lady Middleton for a dinner partner and she was quite agreeable. Her husband was at one time Secretary of State for War. When the ladies left us at the close of dinner, the Duke of Sutherland and General Storr, Governor of Jerusalem, pulled their chairs up next to mine and talked about the Bolsheviks. After dinner, I had a long conversation with Lord Milner about his participation in some of the important conferences during the war, and he took me over to the Princess Patricia, with whom I talked for about 30 minutes.

July 16th At 11 A.M., we all went to Whitehall, the War Office, where General Pershing presented some DSMs to Winston Churchill and other civilian officials of the Government. Following this, we went to the Savoy Hotel, where the General was the guest of the American Luncheon Club. About 400 were present at this affair and we had the usual speeches.

After our luncheon — and a quick change — we went to Buckingham Palace for a garden party. These garden parties served this year as courts for presentation, instead of the usual night courts. The weather was beautiful, and about 2000 had been invited. We were received at a special entrance, which saved us considerable time as carriages were lined up for more than half a mile. After passing through the Palace to the grounds in the rear, we were conducted around to a position opposite the door where the King and Queen were to appear, and there awaited them. We stood under the trees just across a walk from such royalty as were present. Behind us and some distance away were the members of the Diplomatic Corps, and on beyond them were the guests.

The King and Queen came out attended by an elaborate suite, the most notable member being the Duchess of Sutherland, who is a very young and beautiful woman. The King wore a gray topper, and the Queen a very close-fitting gray dress with the usual small hat of gray resting on top of a high headdress. They walked across to the royal gathering first and spoke to the various people assembled, among whom were the King and Queen of Portugal, Duke of Connaught, Prince Arthur of Connaught and his wife, a lot of young princelings, and the Crown Prince of Sweden and his wife. He then crossed over with the Queen and met General Pershing, conversing with him for about five minutes, after which he passed along our group and shook hands with each of us, being followed by the Queen who repeated the procedure. They usually made some colorless remark to every person. While he was shaking hands with me, the Prince of Wales appeared, very ceremoniously greeted his father and mother, and then came along and talked to us. He was quite informal as he knew a number of the staff, having stayed with them at Chaumont. The King and Queen then passed through the Diplomatic Corps and were immediately engulfed by the crowd on the lawn, all of whom were striving for an opportunity to shake hands with them — I speak of them as a "crowd"; as a matter of fact, they were the "high society" of England.

The grounds of the Palace are beautiful and very extensive. Fine old trees, lakes, broad stretches of grass make it look more like a country estate than a great city house. The very elaborate toilets of the women, brilliant uniforms of the officers, with the background of green trees and velvet lawn made a wonderful picture. Small tented marquees were dotted about from which elaborate refreshments were served. General Pershing had his tea with the King and Queen in the Royal Pavilion. The remainder of us had tea at the Diplomatic Pavilion.

I walked around quite a while with Lady Curzon who is supposed to be one of the beauties of London. She introduced me to a number of people, and pointed out all those who occupied important positions. Later, Lady Drogheda joined us. She is a very dashing sort of a person and one of the champion golf and tennis players of England. I left with her by a little private gateway in the rear of the Garden and drove around to her house where we had some Scotch and talked for about an hour or more — then she drove me to the Carlton.

That night, we were the guests of Sir Douglas Haig at a dinner at the Carlton. The speeches here given by Sir Douglas and General Pershing were very interesting as they were quite personal and informal, that of Sir Douglas being a very remarkable tribute to what the General had done and the effect of American participation in the war. After dinner, a few of us went to a ball being given by Lady Ribblesdale, the former Mrs. John Jacob Astor. We arrived at about eleven o'clock and had a very pleasant time, though I did not know very many, and it was not easy to meet people on account of the indifference of the English to formal introductions. However, I had a couple of dances with the Duchess of Sutherland, Lady Drogheda, Lady Ribblesdale, Lady Curzon — and several others whose names I do not remember. I left at about 2:30 A.M.

On this day, General Pershing was due to lunch with the King and Queen, and the rest of us were free until four-thirty in the afternoon. Three English officers on the Mission took five of us up to Windsor for lunch and to see the Castle. We motored up, arriving at about 11 A.M., and were given a special trip over the place, seeing some very interesting things that they usually do not show to strangers. We had lunch at our old friend, "The White Hart," where you and I lunched with the Russell-Murrays in 1910. To add to the pleasure of the lunch, we invited the young women who drove the cars, they being members of the Women's Army Service Corps. We found that the English officers had very kindly arranged to have most attractive chauffeurs for the cars. To our surprise, they were all of them very nice, and several of them were women of some position. After lunch we started back, and the girl driving the car that Frank Pershing and myself had drawn was so very entertaining that we both sat on the front seat of the limousine with her.[2] She took us back through Hampton Court and Richmond Park and made herself so generally entertaining that we were late in arriving for a reception at the House of Commons. However, we were in time to hear some of the speeches in honor of General Pershing and to take tea on the terrace.

That night we had a home dinner at the Carlton, from where we went direct to the great pavilion where Wilde and Moore were to fight for the lightweight championship of the world. We had a fine box from which to see the fight. General Pershing received a tremendous ovation when he came in. A little later, the Prince of Wales arrived in the royal box and the General left us to sit with him. The fight was most exciting, going 30 rounds, and the crowd was most interesting, there being a number of women present. In the box adjoining ours, and sitting next to me, was Delysia, the famous French dancer. She became quite excited over the procedure and was betting very heavily.

From the fight we went direct to Dudley House where Lady Ward was giving a ball in honor of General Pershing. Her home is beautiful and a very interesting crowd of people was present. Among the best known were the King and Queen of Portugal, the Prince of Wales and his two brothers, Princess Mary, the Princess Royal (daughter of Queen Alexandra), and a number of other minor members of the royal family. I had a fine time as I had come to know a number of people, which simplified matters. I danced more frequently with the Duchess of Sutherland and Lady Bingham than anybody else, but toward the latter part of the evening I met a Mrs. Ward, formerly Muriel Wilson, a famous beauty in London. She was a marvelous dancer. We had three on a stretch. I was principally impressed by the huge fans of ostrich feathers all the women carried, many of them in brilliant colors: Lady Ashburn's was scarlet, the Duchess of Sutherland's was an emerald green, as was her dress. Their jewels and tiaras were so massive that they did not make much appeal to me as they looked like glass. Pearls were as common as beads.

During the dance, I had the pleasure of stepping on the foot of the King of Portugal, who was sitting on the side lines, and I think I about ruined his Royal Highness. He looked quite furious — but I had no apologies for that particular person. I had supper with Lady Bingham. About three-thirty in the morning, after a number had gone home, the party became very lively. The Princess Victoria was making her first effort to learn American dances, and those she singled out for the honor of dancing with her were having the deuce of a time. I received an intimation that I should ask her to dance — and immediately went home. General Pershing stepped on her foot and left a large black spot on her slipper. She told a lady-in-waiting she was going to keep it as a souvenir. I imagine her foot would make about as good a souvenir as the slipper after he got through walking on it.

I finished up at this party with three straight dances with the Duchess of Sutherland. She is really beautiful, dances extremely well, and is quite delightful to talk to. She is at the head of the Queen's household, and occupies the first position in England after royalty.

We left the hotel at about 9:30 A.M. for Hyde Park where our American regiment was paraded. Some thirty British officers were present to be decorated with the DSM by the General. I had quite a time getting their medals sorted out as many who were supposed to have been there failed to arrive, and others who were reported as not to be present turned up at the last moment. Immediately after this ceremony the Prince of Wales arrived and reviewed the troops. I followed the General on his walk around, accompanying Winston Churchill. Just as we reached the end of the line, he turned around and remarked to me: "What a magnificent body of men never to take another drink." After the troops passed in review, the Prince made quite a talk to the assembled officers and they were then dismissed. During this period, I took Mrs. Winston Churchill and Lady Bingham up where they could hear the proceedings. Lady Bingham is a beautiful woman, an American from Louisville, Kentucky, though she told me she left there when she was five years old. I had met her at the dance the previous night, and found her one of the best dancers in London.

After the review, we motored direct to the Guildhall where General Pershing was to be presented with a Sword of Honor and with the freedom of the City of London. The ceremony here was most impressive as the Guildhall is a wonderful room. All of the various officials and underlings were in marvelous uniforms and the entire setting was dignified in the extreme. The General entered last. As the rest of us came in, we were preceded by a lot of chaps bearing some sort of batons, were announced in turn, and walked up a short flight of steps to be greeted by the Lord and Lady Mayoress. We were then seated immediately in rear of the Lord Mayor. General Pershing then came in — last — and was accorded a very ceremonious entry. The proceedings were quite elaborate and the speeches very formal. About everybody of importance — officially — in England was present.

From the Guildhall we went direct to the Mansion House. The way was lined with troops. The General rode in the famous gold coach with postilions and outriders, and the remainder of us in automobiles. On arriving at the Mansion House he appeared on the balcony and made a short and very happy speech to the assembled crowd. The banquet was the usual elaborate affair, the principal item of interest to us being the official toastmaster, a paid functionary who stands immediately in rear of the host and announces each toast and the speaker and prays silence — and a lot of other stuff like that. The Lord Mayor, Winston Churchill, General Pershing, and the American Ambassador were the speakers; the last named by the way is the most accomplished orator in London. We finished up with this banquet at about 3 P.M. and returned to the hotel. From there, General Harbord, Colonel Lloyd Griscom, and I motored 45 minutes out into the country to Esher, the country estate of Lady d'Aubrey, to see the finals of an informal tennis tournament which had been proceeding throughout the day. This home was one of the most attractive I saw. It was on a knoll, somewhat after the manner of houses in Virginia. Below the house were two tennis courts, one was placed in a sunken garden, and the other one had a setting of irregular box hedges, rose trees, and a steep hillside dotted with magnificent trees. The surroundings of these two tennis courts were most exquisite. Only about twenty people were present. The most distinguished players were Admiral Beatty, the Duchess of Sutherland, and the Crown Prince of Sweden. An orchestra was playing on the lawn and everything was most informal. I was impressed to referee the final match of the tournament, which was between the Duchess of Sutherland with Lord Hope playing against Lady Drogheda and some other chap.

We had to leave at a quarter to seven and motored directly back to London in time to attend dinner at the House of Commons, where, at 8 P.M., Winston Churchill entertained the General at a formal dinner. Here the speeches were unusually interesting, as no reporters were present, and everyone talked most freely. I sat between General Horne and General Rawlinson, two Army commanders.

The dinner was finished at about ten-thirty. General Pershing and three of us went over to the Savoy Hotel where a dance was being given the men of the American regiment. We went down to the ballroom, and the appearance of the General was greeted with tumultuous applause which rapidly developed into a mob scene. All the girls started for him to get his autograph, and in order to break up the formation we got the music started and got him up on the platform where the orchestra was. He then made a short speech and going out on the floor, took a girl and started the dance. He and his partner were followed by all the other dancers, as close to him as they could get, and the only way he could manage was for me to take another girl and keep directly behind him and elbow people out of the way. The moment the music stopped, they rushed him again, forcibly removing the girl he had — about five others trying to take her place. Under great difficulties he danced with about three, when it became impossible to continue, and we slipped out a side door.

The General and three of us then went on to Lady Guinness' for a dance. By this time, I had come to know a number of people and was able to make a prompt start toward a very enjoyable evening. The usual crowd was present, including the Prince of Wales and his brothers, the Duchess of Sutherland, Lady Bingham, the Duchess of Marlborough, Lady Lytton, Lady Curzon, the Duchess of Roxburghe. The Duchess of Marlborough is a washed-out looking person and did not dance. We finished up here at about 3 A.M.

We had to leave the hotel at eight o'clock in the morning in order to reach our rendezvous for the start of the great Victory Parade. Our horses were furnished by the English Army, and after the various Generals had made their selection I picked out a nice quiet-looking one, and found him most satisfactory. We mounted and rode about a mile to Rotten Row in Hyde Park, where we were to make our formal start in the parade. During this ride, it developed that the horse which General Brewster had selected was both fractious and vicious, and he found he would not be able to ride him in the parade. As the extra horses had been sent away, I turned over my quiet animal to him and undertook the riding of his horse. General Pershing led the parade and General Harbord, Sir John Headlam, myself, and Colonel Quekemeyer followed immediately in rear.[3] Colonel Quekemeyer's horse was rather a bad actor, though not vicious. Mine proved to be everything he ought not to be, so Quekemeyer and myself dropped back and rode immediately in rear of Harbord and Headlam. The crowd was dense along the entire line of march, and tremendously enthusiastic — all of which did not add to the peace of mind of my animal. For eight miles I had the ride of my life, and the worst phase of the trouble was that the horse tried to kick everything in reach. While I did not see it myself, I am told that he struck one little girl in the chin, and I am afraid he must have hurt her very badly, if he did not kill her. With each fresh cavorting, the crowd would indulge in very frantic cheers, which added to the excitement of the occasion. Fortunately, the horse did not pull very hard but he endeavored to go sidewise, and each time I straightened him out, he would rear. However, I eased him along for 7½ miles, until we reached the Admiralty Arch, which forms the entrance to the Mall from Trafalgar Square. In going through the small passageway of the Arch, I was forced to keep him straight, because women and children were jammed in close, and he would have killed a few if I had allowed him to turn sidewise. As a result of my straightening him out, he reared, and at the top of his pitch, lost his footing and went over backwards. However, I had been expecting this throughout the affair, and fell clear, landing on one foot, and then on my hand and hip. I was rolling before I struck and went over three times to keep out of his way. He was down so completely that I was able to get to him and get back into the saddle before he had gotten entirely up, and in that way was able to mount him. Otherwise, if he had gotten to his feet, I never could have done anything with him. As it turned out, I entered the Arch on a horse, and came out of it on a horse — and did not even lose my place in the line-up, but I lost my temper for the rest of the ride. The fall apparently broke a small bone in my hand, but it does not give me any trouble. As this occurred at the head of the Mall, I only had a brief period in which to straighten out before reaching the Royal Pavilion where the King and Queen reviewed the pageant. After passing by the reviewing point, General Pershing and General Harbord turned out of the procession, and Colonel Quekemeyer and myself with him. General Pershing proceeded to the raised dais on which the King and Queen stood with the Prince of Wales, and remained there throughout the procession. Quekemeyer and myself found a place in the Pavilion and were able to see the entire parade file by.

The Royal Pavilion was on the site of the Albert-Victoria Memorial, immediately in front of Buckingham Palace, and was luxuriously carpeted in heavy green velvet and filled with about 100 golden white-upholstered chairs. We found a seat close by the Princess Patricia, Prince Arthur of Connaught, Lord Milner, and Lord Curzon. As seats in some of the hotels were selling for about $1000, I suppose ours had a value of about $5000 or $10,000. The parade was even more stunning than that in Paris, though the setting, of course, could not be compared with that of the Parisian boulevards and avenues. Successively, Marshal Foch, Admiral Beatty, Sir Douglas Haig, and several of the other Allied commanders passed, and, turning out of the procession, joined the King and Queen.

The Duke of Connaught saw young Warren Pershing in his uniform, a "Sergeant," standing in the crowd about 200 yards from the Pavilion.[4] He sent over for him and had him brought to where the King and Queen were. They received Warren, had their photographs taken with him; he shook hands all around, and was finally kissed on both cheeks by Marshal Foch. This last rather "fazed" him. He then returned to his place in the crowd with Captain Pershing. The Prince recognized Quekemeyer and me and waved his hand to us and acknowledged our salute. Some strangers who were close

by and had viewed us with apparent contempt as humble commoners immediately drew back and gave us air space.

After the parade had finished, the General and General Harbord filed out
with the Royal Party to lunch at Buckingham Palace, and Quekemeyer and
I humbly beat our way back to the hotel, having turned our horses over to
orderlies — mine with a curse.

We had lunch with General and Mrs. Wagstaff of the English Army, at the
Carlton at three o'clock. About an hour and a half later we had tea at the
Carlton with some other friends, whose names I have forgotten.

That night, General Pershing and I and Warren went around to Mrs.
Waldorf Astor's for supper. Nora Langhorne (Mrs. Phipps) was there, as
were two or three Lords and Ladies, whose names I have forgotten. Warren
had a great time with the Astor children, and after supper we started to beat
our way through the crowd to Lord Dalhousie's on Hyde Park, from where
we were to watch the fireworks. The General, Mrs. Astor, and the children
went in the car which was to come back for the rest of us, but we became
impatient and started to walk. Nora Langhorne was in a great gale and was
very amusing. She had on a black velvet cap, like students in the Latin Quarter wear, and was trying to pass herself off as one of that class. Everybody in
the streets was singing and dancing, greeting everybody else. We met three
old ladies with their arms around each other, hats on the back of their heads,
singing at the top of their voices — and giving evidence of lots of the beer of
Old England. In taking them to task for their joviality, we became embroiled
in the mix-up in the street, during which I was separated from the rest of the
party — and never found them again. I went on up Piccadilly Circus and was
there appropriated by three girls, and after some maneuvering, and a good
deal of excitement, I decided to return to the Carlton, as I did not know
where Lord Dalhousie's place was. At the Carlton, a tremendous party was
on. I found a place at the table where Sir John Headlam was giving a dinner
to such of our officers as had remained at the hotel. Lady Drogheda, and
several others that I knew, were there, also three of our young chauffeurettes.
A riotous scene was in progress. Everybody had favors, wearing caps, playing
with balloons, and Marshal Foch was engaged in autographing all the dinner
cards. Dancing then began and continued until two-thirty. About midnight, I
was sitting on the steps that led from the main dining room into the palm
garden, to the room which you may remember, as we had tea there once or
twice with the Murrays, when Delysia suddenly appeared beside me in a very
remarkable and risqué evening gown and sang the "Marseillaise." The crowd
became much excited, as they always do on such occasions, and after so much
champagne, and applauded her vociferously. Marshal Foch congratulated
her and she impulsively and artistically kissed him about a dozen times —
then all the women tried to follow suit.

After the main party broke up we retired to the suite of rooms which had been furnished our party for offices and conducted a private dance which lasted until about 4 A.M. Two English officers gave an exhibition of a golf game, with a lump of ice in the waste basket, which was very funny. I was called upon to make a speech out of the window at the crowd — holding a pot of flowers in my arms.

After our strenuous Victory Day, we did not get up until about 10 A.M. I might explain that the English Government being our host, everything in the hotel was ours — the valet was at your service for pressing clothes, elaborate meals were served in your room, fresh flowers were kept about, and no chits were presented — even drinks were free.

At 11 A.M., General Pershing and Generals Harbord, Brewster, and Hines, Colonel Griscom, Warren Pershing, and myself motored down to Sutton Place, the country home of the Duchess of Sutherland, where Colonel Griscom and myself were to play tennis with the Duchess and some others in the afternoon.[5] It was about a 45-minute ride through very attractive country. Sutton Place is a wonderful old house filled with paintings that are famous all over the world. The Duchess had her father and mother (Lord and Lady Mansfield), her sister (Lady Betty Butler), her sister-in-law (Lady Denham) and two or three men to meet us. Just as we entered the main salon, Warren Pershing stopped me and asked me: "What's her name?" I told him, and he repeated it and asked me if he had it right. Then he started off, stopped again, and with a very troubled look inquired: "Does she speak English?" I told the Duchess this and it created much amusement. Later, I heard it going the rounds at some of the dances. Some people asked her, when they came up for a dance, if she spoke English. We had a pleasant lunch, but a heavy rain in the morning had made it impossible to play tennis, so we went into a big room, turned on the phonograph, and had a lively dance for about an hour, then we strolled around the grounds and down to the river, starting home at six o'clock. She gave me a very attractive album of photographs of the place, signing her name in it.

That night, we attended a dinner to all the Allies, given by the English Government at the Carlton Hotel. The Prince of Wales presided. Lloyd George and Winston Churchill were present, and the usual speeches were exchanged. The General and I had to run over to the Palace Theater before the dinner was over, so that he might reach a box which was held there for him before the close of the performance, and thank several wealthy men in London who had provided a gala performance that night for the men of the American regiment. He made a short speech from the box. There was the usual cheering and enthusiasm. We were to have gone on the stage to thank the company, which I rather looked forward to, but we had to hurry back to the Carlton in order that he might be present when the Prince of Wales left.

On Monday morning our official visit terminated, and while some of the party stayed at the Carlton Hotel, General Pershing and I and Frank Pershing went to General Biddle's and stayed there.[6] I was busy all that day, fixing up letters of thanks and appreciation to people who had entertained the General, and British officers who had served us, etc., and arranging for interviews with various press representatives and other people. However, I had to go with the General to St. Paul's Cathedral at eleven-thirty, where he was to officiate as the godfather for the little daughter of our Military Attaché in London. Mrs. Davis, the wife of the Ambassador, was the godmother. The setting for the ceremony was impressive. I took time to go to luncheon at the Waldorf Astors'. Warren Pershing had moved over there a few days previously in order to be with the children, and at lunch on this day, in addition to about ten grown-up people she had three young Princes of Sweden and two other kids in for Warren's benefit. Nora Langhorne was there also and she and I planned a party for the next afternoon and evening. The last I saw of Warren, he and the Astor children and the Princelings were all on the ballroom floor going through the motions of swimming. That night I dined somewhere, but I have forgotten with whom. After dinner, I went to a dance at the American Embassy, which was very exclusive and seemed to be composed largely of royalty. All the Princes and Princesses were there. I had an unusually good time on this occasion, despite the fact that at three different times a Prince had my girl when my dance came around. I had a laborious dance with the Princess Mary. If she doesn't reign any better than she dances, they are in a hard way, but she is a nice sweet-looking little Dutch girl. The Duchess of Sutherland gave me a string of dances, and Mrs. Ward and I tried everything new. Mrs. Keppel, the former friend of King Edward, was present on this occasion and at several of the other dances before this.

This was another busy morning for me. Lady Bingham had invited me to lunch with her, but at twelve o'clock I found it was impossible to go, so I had to telephone her. At about half past three General Pershing and I started off to do a round of calls. We motored up to Kingston and had tea with Sir Douglas and Lady Haig and their children. They live in a very simple house, but with attractive grounds. Sir Douglas was in Scotch tweeds and Lady Haig had just come in. He poured the tea and the conversation was very intimate and informal. After tea we went out on the lawn and sat there while the two girls, twelve and thirteen years old, played tennis. I talked to Lady Haig while Generals Pershing and Haig walked about the rose garden and had their final conversation.

From there we motored back to Whitehall, called on Winston Churchill, then went on to the Ambassador's and talked to Mr. Davis, and then on to Dudley House and called on Lady Ward. We had a long string of other places to go, but did not have time to do them. As it was, we only reached General Biddle's at eight-twenty and General Pershing was due at a dinner in his honor at Lord Curzon's at eight-thirty, and I had been due for a party with Nora Langhorne since six o'clock. The General got off for his dinner, but I had to telephone my regrets and apologies.

At ten-thirty, I went around to Lady Willoughby's for a final dance. Practically the same crowd was present there, and I had a most enjoyable evening. I was feeling in the mood to dance on indefinitely, though it was about 2 A.M. when I received another intimation from a lady-in-waiting of Princess Victoria that I should dance with her. That was the last seen of me at Lady Willoughby's.

Lady Bingham took me home in her car, and I got out at her place and stayed there about half an hour, and then went on in her car to General Biddle's.

At 9 A.M., General Pershing and General Harbord and Sir John Headlam and myself, also Warren Pershing, started by motor for Cambridge, 60 miles to the north. We reached Christ College at 11:20 A.M., where the General got into his red robe and velvet hat, preparatory to receiving the degree of Doctor of Laws. Admiral Wemyss, Admiral Sturdee, and the commanders of all the British armies were also to be given the same degree. After they were all dressed, they marched through the streets of Cambridge. General Harbord, Warren Pershing, and I accompanied the procession. We entered the Senate House where the ceremony was to take place. The floor space was filled first with those with the red robe (Doctors of Law who had previously received the degree), and then the prominent people. The gallery was filled with a crowd of fellows, most of them having served in the war. Warren and I sat directly behind General Pershing, and Warren was much exercised over "Papa's hat." When the orator of the day, Sir John, started to declaim in Latin, all the fellows in the gallery set up a great shout and from that time on the scene beggared description. Each man was called forward in turn and a long speech was made to him in Latin, characterizing and eulogizing his service. As he stepped forward, the students would raise the very devil. It amounted actually to hazing. Sometimes in the middle of a speech they would interrupt the entire proceedings, throw down balloons and other things.

On the completion of this ceremony we filed out and marched back through the streets to Christ College. In the middle of this procession, a crowd of students rushed the General, and, picking him up on their shoulders, carried him through the streets into the courtyard of Christ College.

They almost allowed him to fall, for, as Warren said, "they pretty nearly didn't have enough." The General then had to make a speech to the students, which was wildly applauded, and Warren became so excited in his efforts to see "Father" that I had to hold him up on my shoulder. We then went on to a banquet in one of the most interesting halls I have ever seen. After the usual speeches we had to leave and hurry to the special train which was awaiting us at Cambridge. We only had three minutes to spare when we reached the train. There, we relaxed and had a very pleasant trip down to Dover, having tea served on the train, with lots of good jam and cake.

At Dover, the other members of the party met us and the General was received with a Guard of Honor. The Mayor was there also. We immediately boarded the British destroyer *Orpheus* and reached Boulogne at 8 P.M. where our special train was awaiting us. After dinner on the train, we all turned in for a real sleep — and found ourselves in Paris this morning at nine o'clock.

DIARY OF A TRIP OVER THE BATTLEFIELDS
OF THE WESTERN FRONT WITH GENERAL PERSHING

August 1–12, 1919

THE GENERAL's special train left Paris at 1 A.M. on August 1st for Coblenz, arriving there at two-thirty in the afternoon. He was making his last inspection of the Army of Occupation.

General Allen, with his staff officers, met us at the train, where the usual Guard of Honor was drawn up. In the plaza of the city, a battalion of the First Division was paraded.

That afternoon, I knocked about with Montgomery, Virginia Lee's husband. We had dinner in the garden of a little German restaurant, and it was one of the best meals I have eaten. After dinner, we returned to the house where Montgomery and several others lived, and fooled around until about one in the morning.

The next morning, August 2nd, the General was to inspect some troops about the city and go to the athletic meet of the Third Division at Andernach, up the river. I elected to go with Bowditch to the race meet of the English at Cologne. We motored up to Cologne, and took so long for lunch that we were late for the races and returned to Coblenz, arriving at about five o'clock.

That night, General Allen had a formal dinner for us all, followed by a dance. In the middle of the dance, I ran across Laura Powell Tucker, who was quite the belle of the occasion. We had several dances together, but she was so pursued by various men that I had little or no opportunity to talk about Lexington. She told me she had seen you before coming over, also said she was coming to Paris, but I must admit I have not looked her up here. She is a very pretty girl and most charming — quite a contrast to her sister, whom you may remember I never thought much of.

We left Coblenz at midnight, and found ourselves at seven-thirty, on August 3rd, at Pont-à-Mousson on the Moselle River. There we left the train, the cars having been unloaded, and spent all of that day motoring about 150 miles over the battlefields of St. Mihiel and of Gravelotte and Mar la Tour. We had lunch on a high hill overlooking the plain of the Woëvre. The day was bright and clear and the view very beautiful. We reached Chambley, north of Mar la Tour, at seven o'clock in the evening, and found the train waiting for us there. After dinner on the train, we all "turned in," and woke up the next morning in Verdun.

We left the train at Verdun and did about 125 miles around the southern part of the Meuse-Argonne battlefield. We ran into Dun-sur-Meuse for lunch, to which place the train had moved, and then continued motoring all afternoon.

The General spent some time at the great cemetery at Romagne, where 22,000-odd Americans are buried. We did not return to the train at Dun-sur-Meuse until eight o'clock and had dinner at nine o'clock, going to bed immediately afterwards.

The train did not move that night, and we made a start from Dun-sur-Meuse for the northern half of the battlefield. We had lunch that day on the top of a very high hill overlooking Sedan, the northernmost point occupied by our troops in the final rush northward of that battle.

Leaving Sedan, we worked down the Meuse River and did that portion of the battlefield east of the Meuse and north of Verdun, running through Spiney, Luppy, Jametz and Damvillers. The General returned again to Romagne Cemetery, but I left the party and motored over to Breheville at the foot of the eastern heights of the Côte-de-Meuse to look up the little maid who waited on our G-3 mess at Chaumont. She and her husband were endeavoring to establish a home here. Unfortunately, she was out in the fields working, but the remainder of the village collected to tell me how she was getting on.

We had dinner on the train at Dun, at nine o'clock that night, and wound up the next morning in Châlons, east of Rheims.

From there, we did the Champagne battles in the eastern half of the Marne pocket or salient which extends down to Château-Thierry, picking up the train at the latter point late that evening.

The next morning, we started for Château-Thierry and did the western half of the battle, working up to Soissons, the scene of the great counterattack in July 1918, where our First and Second divisions made their magnificent advance.

From Soissons, we motored north and stopped at a little destroyed village where Miss Anne Morgan has organized her committee to assist the people in the devastated regions. She was absent, but about ten of her women were on hand. After showing us something of their work, they gave us tea.

I was sitting in front of a closet which had some chintz in lieu of a door. Pulling aside the chintz, I found six bottles of champagne, which very much upset these staid ladies — who had to serve champagne immediately.

From there we motored through Coucy-le-Château, a fortified village — a wonderful château on a high hill, which had been knocked to bits by the German artillery. Passing northward, we went through the Forest of St. Gobain, the stronghold at the tip of the great salient of the Western Front, held by the Germans until the very last moment before the final retreat began. In this forest we had some difficulty in traveling as the road had been mined about every 200 yards and long detours were required to get around the craters. Here were placed two of the great guns which bombarded Paris.

We reached the train at eight o'clock that evening, in St. Quentin, and started out early the next morning to do the battles in that region. All of this country had been completely devasted, and sometimes for miles there is not even a tree. Late in the evening we reached the sites of the battlefields of the Twenty-seventh and Thirtieth American divisions, who fought with the English, finally picking up our train at Le Cateau.

The next morning, we started out to do the English battlefields in this portion of the front, including their first offensive at Neuve Chapelle and Vimy Ridge. On top of the latter height we had our lunch. The weather still continued to be beautiful, although the roads were becoming somewhat dusty.

In the afternoon, we went through Lens which is the most impressive scene of utter desolation and destruction that I have visited. To see a city, a great manufacturing center and mining district, as large as San Francisco, completely leveled to the ground, gives one a better conception of the horrors of war than anything else.

We picked up the train in Lille and had a late dinner.

The following morning we started northward, going first to Messines Ridge. While standing on the lip of the great crater which had been blown by the mine exploded at the initiation of the attack by the English in May 1917, a company of 200 German prisoners appeared on the edge of the crater and descended to the large lake which has been formed there to take their weekly bath. They ran down yelling and in great enthusiasm to get into the water, and in a few moments they were diving in all around the edge of the lake.

We motored north to Ypres, and from there went out to Passchendaele Ridge, the scene of heavy fighting by the English in the summer and fall of 1917, where they suffered some 400,000 or 500,000 casualties. From Passchendaele we motored eastward to the final battlefield of our Thirty-seventh and Ninety-first divisions, fighting with the Belgian Army, in their advance toward Brussels.

After doing these fields, we continued on, arriving in Brussels at seven-thirty.

The villages in Belgium present a great contrast to those in France — they are cleaner, brighter, and more attractive in every way. The crops exceed anything I have ever observed in the way of intensive cultivation and efficient farming.

The night we arrived in Brussels, we were entertained by the Military Attaché at a formal dinner. After dinner, at about ten-thirty, the General returned to the train, not going to a hotel, as he had declined an invitation of the King to dine with him that night. The remainder of us went to the Palace Hotel in order to find some dancing partners to take to the Savoy where the Military Attaché had reserved tables. The first person I saw on the floor at the Palace was the girl Celi, that I wrote to you about before. She joined our party, along with two others, and we all went to the Savoy where we danced until 3 A.M. It was exceedingly hot, and I left them at three different times to find an open window on a landing one flight up where I could stretch out my legs, get some fresh air and a nap. Every time, after I had been asleep about ten minutes, someone, a stranger, would wake me up and ask me what I was trying to do. Then I would return to the party. General ———— was dancing furiously, and the rest of the party were all busily engaged. Celi made a great hit with all of them, being very amusing and animated as well as a beautiful dancer. We returned to the train after this, and did not get up until eleven o'clock the following morning.

The General turned out at eight-thirty in the morning, and with Warren motored down to the château of the King in the Ardennes, where he had lunch. The King had gone down by aeroplane earlier in the morning. The rest of us were taken out to lunch at the Royal Golf Club where we spent most of the afternoon, returning to the train in time to meet the General at five o'clock. I motored up to Antwerp with him to inspect the installations we have there for shipping out material from the Army of Occupation and for supplying that army with rations, etc. After motoring along the water front of the Scheldt, just at sunset — a very beautiful evening — we had dinner with the staff at a very elaborate Boche house which had been confiscated by the Belgians. The trip back to Brussels was delightful, as there was a full moon.

We reached the train at a quarter of twelve and pulled out for Paris at twelve, arriving here at nine o'clock the following morning.

DIARY OF A VISIT TO ITALY

WITH GENERAL PERSHING

August 16–22, 1919

As ALL of our official visits have their beginning in Paris, I will start there with this one on the evening of August 16th.

After a long hot spell, it rained in the late afternoon and then cleared up beautifully. I went to dinner with the Butler-Ameses at the "Coucou" by the Sacré-Coeur, where we dined out in a little open square and enjoyed the cool and fresh air. It was a beautiful evening and the surroundings were very attractive. A long-haired violinist passed by and played everything but "Hearts and Flowers." Mr. Filene, whose large store you may remember in Boston, was at a table close by with Lincoln Steffens. They came over and joined us for a bit, as the former is a close friend of Mr. Ames'. A little later, Mr. Messer or Mazelle with his daughter (Boston people) arrived and sat at our table.

The train was due to leave the Gare de Lyon at nine-thirty, and as I had only finished the lobster course at nine o'clock, I had to desert the party and hurry to the train. At the train were a number of Italian officials to pay their respects to the General. The train pulled out on time and after a rather rough night's trip we found ourselves in the morning entering the mountains on our way into Italy via Mondane. General Hines and myself were the first to breakfast and discovered that the train was standing in the station at Aix-les-Bains, where our mutual friend, Lady Bingham, was spending the month of August at the Hôtel de l'Europe. We hurriedly drew up a joint note on the page of my notebook and dispatched it, with 5 francs as an accelerant, in the hands of a French boy in the station. I doubt if she got it.

At Mondane, the frontier station, we were met by General de Lucca and three other Italian officers who had been assigned to accompany us on the trip. The Lieutenant General commanding that district, with Headquarters at Turin, was also there. All boarded the train, the last two leaving us at Turin.

At Turin, the train stopped for ten minutes. The General went into the station where he was received on the usual red carpet by a committee of officials. Champagne was served, etc., and a Guard of Honor was paraded in the station.

From Turin we went on to Genoa where the same proceedings were repeated, this time the train remaining about 15 minutes in the station. The remainder of the evening, we followed along the seacoast of the Italian Riviera. Crowds of summer visitors were at most of the stations, particularly at San Margarita, the bands playing, etc. At several points military commanders and naval commanders were at the station to pay their respects. At one point, the General was presented with a huge bouquet of flowers by the usual "small daughter" of the Mayor, who had to be kissed.

You may remember this section of the railroad as the place where the train passes in and out of tunnels. There are about 69 in all, I think. We went over it in 1910. It was raining then, but on this trip it was a beautiful summer evening and the views along the coast were very attractive.

At nine-fifteen the next morning the train pulled into Rome. It was a blistering hot day, and everybody was prepared to melt several times over, as we had a strenuous program ahead of us, covering the entire day up to ten o'clock that night, when we were due to leave for Venice.

The Minister of War, the Commander in Chief of the Armies, and a number of other officials, were at the station, which was elaborately decorated. The Guard of Honor was present and the usual ceremonies carried through. We left immediately in automobiles for a large caserne in the city where the King was awaiting the General. Upon our arrival at the latter place, we were all presented to His Majesty, and then mounted, and preceded by the King's cavalry troops, a glittering body of cuirassiers, we passed through the streets to the field on which the troops were to be reviewed. The way was lined with carabinieri in their blue uniforms with red-striped trousers, brass buttons and silver-gilt épauletted coats, cockaded hats with red and white plumes. As we entered the reviewing field, a double column of trumpeteers sounded the salute for the King. After riding around the troops, we dismounted and lined up on a raised dais where the remainder of the ceremony could be carried out without our being exposed to the heat of the sun.

All the Italians who were to be decorated were then lined up, and General Pershing presented them with the Distinguished Service Medals. Immediately following this, General Pershing was decorated by the King as a Grand Commander of the Order of Savoy, there being only four others in existence. After his decoration, some of us were lined up — and I drew my second Italian decoration. However, they made a mistake and gave me the same one I had before, but immediately after the ceremony they switched, and I was given an Officer of the Crown of Italy order.

Following this the troops passed in review. They had elements of practically every class of troops in the Italian army. The last foot troops to pass were a battalion of Bersaglieri who, according to their custom, went by at a full run, which was quite a feat on this particularly hot day. The artillery and cavalry passed at a trot.

On the departure of the King, we were whisked off to the Grand Hotel where rooms were awaiting us. Our things had already been sent there, and in ten minutes everybody was in the bathtub. After thirty minutes of this cooling operation we departed for the Quirinal Palace to lunch with the King. Here, every ten feet, was a flunkey, and I was reminded very vividly of our previous experience in walking in the Palace on an off day, when the King found you in the courtyard waiting while I was talking to the Officer of the Day.

The luncheon was a very brilliant affair. All the ministers of state and higher officers of the Army and Navy were present. I sat three removed from the right of His Majesty, between the Admiral of the fleet and the head of the King's household. While neither of them spoke English, they both spoke French and I had a very pleasant meal. After luncheon, we adjourned to some other apartment for coffee and cigars and finally took leave of His Majesty at about two o'clock.

The afternoon was spent in visiting the principal points of interest about Rome. We first drove to the Pincio Gardens, where you and I used to spend our afternoons, and while it was a very hot day the view was as beautiful as ever. We next went to St. Peter's and they took us into all the choice places to see the treasures of the church, and things of that nature. Then we motored over to Capitol Hill where we were received by the Lord Mayor of Rome and the General was given an elaborate reception. Refreshments of champagne, other cold drinks, cakes, etc., were spread in a large room which was filled with statuary. The band of the carabinieri played in the Court of Neptune. It was too hot to go into the Forum, but we were taken out on a balcony in the rear of the Capitol building, which has a view of the entire ruins. A senator who speaks English and is the great authority on the historical archaeology of Rome explained the ruins to the General.

After leaving the Capitol, we motored to the Coliseum and spent about ten minutes there. The party was to have gone on to several other points — the catacombs, the baths of Caracalla, etc., but we all struck and headed for the hotel and a bath.

Immediately after this second change we departed for the Excelsior Hotel to dine with the Minister of War. About fifty sat down to dinner here at one table. I sat between General de Lucca and the English Military Attaché. The music during the dinner was particularly fine and made all of us long for an opportunity to dance. The usual toasts were made, and the General made a particularly happy response which delighted the Italians. I had quite a time seeing that the translation into Italian was properly made for the newspaper men.

We left the dinner table at five minutes of ten and motored straight to the railway station, being accompanied by the Minister of War, General Diaz, the Admiral of the fleet, and a number of other officials. At the station, a battalion of Italian troops, with band, was drawn up, and, after much formality, we pulled out for Venice.

The next morning we had to turn out of the train at two different stops, in order that the General might accept the greetings of the military and civil officials of the cities we were passing through.

We arrived in Venice at eleven o'clock and found the usual crowd awaiting us in the station. We walked directly out of the station into a royal launch and were whisked down the Grand Canal to the Piazza San Marco, where we disembarked and were taken through the Palace of the Doges. Following this, we spent about five minutes in St. Mark's and then walked across the Piazza and along the Canal front to our old friend, the Royal Danieli Hotel, where you and I refrigerated in the winter of 1911. Here, refreshments were served in the way of champagne, cold drinks, cake, etc., by the Admiral in command of the station. This occupied about thirty minutes, when we re-embarked and were taken across other canals, reaching the station at one o'clock, the train pulling out immediately for Treviso.

General Caviglia, who commanded an Italian army and had been a close friend of the General's in Manchuria, met us at Venice and was our guide for the battlefields. We lunched on the train and arrived at Treviso at two-fifteen. Here we embarked in high-powered open Lancia automobiles and started on a trip along the front.

Our first objective was the Piave River, along which the Italian Army made its stand after the great retreat following the Caporetto disaster, and from which they launched their great offensive in October 1918, taking some 300,000 Austrian prisoners. Caviglia's army made this great attack, and it was therefore very interesting to hear his description of the operation.

We followed the Piave to the low mountain of the Montello, and had some difficulty in getting through bad roads. After doing the Montello, we motored around its base and headed for Mount Grappa, rising 6500 feet above the plains. Here began the most remarkable and exciting automobile trip I have ever taken. In ascending the mountain, the slopes of which seem almost vertical, the road climbs up one face and does not pass around. It consists of a number of hairpin turns, repeating on itself, until on one slope I estimated there were 22 loops, one above the other. Our chauffeurs were selected men, the automobiles had no mufflers, we drove at top speed — and it required quite a little time to become accustomed to the continuous series of hairbreadth escapes, because when you looked out of the car you usually looked down about 2000 feet straight. In reaching the top of the mountain, we made a distance of one kilometer horizontally while rising two kilometers vertically. The last half mile we had to walk until we stood on the pinnacle where the Italians had made their strong point to hold this at any cost as it dominated the plain, and its fall practically meant the fall of Venice. When we first arrived, we were above the clouds and it was quite cool, but later the atmosphere cleared and we had a magnificent view, not only of the mountains around us but of the entire Venetian Plain.

We motored down by another road, and while we thought we had reached the limit in exciting driving going up, we found new things to think about going down. In order to make the turns, the drivers skidded or slewed their rear wheels. However, we were becoming accustomed to luck, but when they would put on full power just as they started down an extremely steep slope, and the car would leap forward with a roar of the exhaust — it looked like all hope was gone! General Pershing said Caviglia was perpetually punching his driver and telling him to go faster. I, personally, thought we were going to hell.

Going down the mountain we passed several Austrian prison camps, and frequently mule carts with loads of hay or wood. At the foot of the mountain we turned into the plain and driving through Bassano, we headed across for Vicenza. This portion of the trip was made in the late evening and the Italian villages through which we passed were marvelously picturesque, particularly the ancient covered bridge at Bassano. A light fog had now formed, which added to the perils of the voyage, because the chauffeurs could not see more than fifty feet ahead of their cars. However, we reached our destination at ten o'clock at night to find that officers of the First Italian Cavalry Division had been waiting to entertain us at dinner since eight o'clock. Our train had moved over to this point, and after a hurried freshening up, we went to dinner. The table was spread out in a courtyard with a typical Italian setting of odd-shaped windows and balconies around us. Close by our table were two large treees in full bloom, like purple lilacs — I do not know what the name actually was. Our dinner lasted until twelve-thirty when we returned to the train. The next morning we started across the plain for the mountains and made a rapid ascent to the Asiago Plateau where the lines lay in the summer of 1918. Here again we were on the scene of fighting which was carried out under the direction of General Caviglia. After hearing his explanation of the maneuvers, we began a further ascent of the mountains, passing over the former Italian frontier into the Trentino. Our previous experience had included beautiful scenery, but what now followed surpassed anything I had yet seen. Baguio and the Benguet Trail were trivial affairs in comparison; Miyanoshita, with its high mountains and precipitous heights, in far-off

Japan, was a miniature affair in contrast with our present setting.[1] We rose to 7000 feet, the road always following the edge of almost vertical cliffs. Near the summit of our climb we went through a series of short tunnels cut in the face of the bluffs, and between tunnels a marvelous view could be had of the valley some few thousand feet below. We then descended with startling rapidity to Lake Caldanazzo, which is considered much more beautiful than Como, but is too inaccessible to be much enjoyed as a summer place. Motoring around the lake we followed the river valley down to Trento, the present headquarters of the First Italian Army.

Here we stopped at the hotel long enough to wipe off the dust, and then went to the Headquarters of the army, to be entertained at lunch by the army commander and his staff. After luncheon we followed the river valley down to Verona. This portion of the trip was very beautiful, as the mountains rose on either bank to great heights and are very rugged and picturesque. By some marvelous arrangement, Italian children, dogs, mules, etc., keep the center of the road clear, otherwise an automobile trip at the pace we traveled would be a continuous succession of disasters. The chauffeurs go through towns at 50 miles an hour. The streets are exceedingly narrow and the turns sharp. However, no accident occurred and we all arrived in Verona at six-thirty, going immediately to the train to clean up in preparation for the evening.

At eight o'clock, we were entertained at dinner by the civil and military officials at Verona. At nine-thirty, we all walked to the old Roman Coliseum which is in a remarkable state of preservation. Here, we found about 15,000 people present in the Coliseum, and as the General ascended to the royal box, the former box for the Roman Emperors, he was given quite an ovation.

Sitting in this old stone box we witnessed a performance of the Italian opera of the *Prodigal Son*. Naturally, everything was in the open; the stage settings were beautiful; about 300 made up the cast. Everyone agreed that it was not only the most beautiful and artistic setting they had ever witnessed, but it was the most delightful and tuneful opera that they had ever heard.

The orchestra was led by one of the most famous Italian conductors. The music was charming.

After the first act we descended from our box, and passing across the floor of the Coliseum, went on the stage in order that the General might congratulate the principal actors. Here we were surrounded by the entire company, and if one could overlook the violent smell of garlic, he could imagine himself back in the days of the old Romans. I slipped away from the mob scene which was being enacted around the General, and passed through the green curtains which closed the main opening at the rear of the stage and went down and inspected the ballet, of which there were about 150. It was all very interesting.

The actors would disappear through the palms at the side of the stage and would sit waiting in the seats of the Coliseum in the rear until the next occasion arose for them to appear, unless the action required them to pass out through the main entrance way. In addition to the main stage there was a secondary affair in prolongation of the former, which was a partially enclosed oriental-looking room, apparently inhabited by the harem.

After the performance we returned to the train, and turned in at about two o'clock in the morning. We retired, surrounded by a guard of carabinieri in their picturesque uniforms and plumes, who remained on duty all night.

The next morning, the train passed through Brescia at seven-thirty, making a stop of about 5 minutes. We were all in bed and were much startled by the music of the band playing the "Star-Spangled Banner," and the arrival outside our windows of a formal company of civil and military officials. I woke up to find the plumed cockade of a carabiniere at my window. One of the Italian officers with us leaped into his uniform and dashed off the train to make our apologies. However, in his hurried dressing he had forgotten his suspenders, which were hanging down below his blouse. I stood "pat" and remained in bed. The General did not wake up until the band had played the "Star-Spangled Banner" about a dozen times.

At eleven o'clock we arrived in Milan and found a large crowd at the station, the usual red carpet, officials, Guard of Honor, etc. We immediately left in automobiles for a whirlwind tour of the city, stopping at several interesting points. Our visit here terminated with a visit to the famous Caproni plant where we had a look at their system of manufacturing these giant planes. During our entire stay here the air was filled with aeroplanes. They served champagne, cocktails, and cakes to cool us off after our arduous trip. Here I met the American Consul who told me he had just received a telegram from the Butler-Ameses, who were now at their place on Como, having left Paris two nights after I did, so I sent a note to them by him, as he said he was going up to stay with them the following Sunday.

I had to hurry to the train in Milan in order to draft a letter for the General to write to the King, which was to be given to our Acting Ambassador, Mr. Jay, who had accompanied us on our trip from Rome and was to leave the train at Turin, at four o'clock that afternoon. The idea was to get the draft ready so that the General could write the letter while the train was not in motion, but he had only got the first sentence started when the train pulled out and he had to wait until the next stop. Between Milan and Turin, a run of two hours, we had lunch, and I had to hurriedly dictate the draft of a number of telegrams to officials in Italy, expressing thanks for their courtesy and hospitality. As the character of these letters may be of some interest to you, I will quote two or three of them here. The style is not very good, but as I had to dictate them on the train and they were sent without any correction — you cannot expect very elegant English:

(Draft)

Your Majesty:

Upon my departure from Italy, permit me to express my high appreciation of the honor accorded me and the Army I represent by Your Majesty's gracious reception and hospitality. The ministers of State, the local officials of the Government and the officers of the Army of Your Majesty have extended to me and to the officers of my staff courtesies and consideration which can never be forgotten.

During the past two days it has been my rare privilege to inspect the battlefields of the Piave, Mount Grappa, and the Trentino under the guidance of General Caviglia, where your Majesty's Army turned the tide of the war by their brilliant victories. This personal visit to the difficult terrain of those fields has given me a proper conception of the magnificent valor and fortitude of the Italian soldier.

I assure Your Majesty that the cordiality of my reception in Rome and the other cities through which I have passed will be greatly appreciated by the American people and will further warm their hearts and increase their close friendship for the people of Italy.

I remain, Sir,

Your obedient servant,

(Draft of Telegram)

General Diaz,
Commander in Chief of the Italian Armies.

Your Excellency: Permit me to express to you upon the completion of my visit to Italy the deep appreciation I entertain for the most cordial reception tendered me and my staff by Your Excellency and the officers of your army. Throughout our visit your commanders have extended to me and my companions the warmest hospitality. General Caviglia afforded me a wonderful opportunity to study battlefields upon which you gained your great victories and where I gained an increased respect and appreciation of the valor of your soldiers.

Believe me, Sir, with assurance of my high regard and esteem for Your Excellency,

Sincerely yours,

John J. Pershing.

(Draft of Telegram)

His Excellency,
      Mayor of Brescia, Italy.

Your Excellency: Please accept my sincere regrets for my failure to accept your courteous and cordial greeting at the station at Brescia this
morning. Due to my ignorance of your intentions and the fact that the
program in Verona did not permit me to retire until an early hour this
morning, I was denied the pleasure and honor of meeting you and your
officials. I assure you of my deep appreciation of the distinguished courtesy with which you honored me.

John J. Pershing.

(Draft of Telegram).

Lt-General Count Albricci,
      Minister of War, Rome.

Your Excellency: In departing from Italy I desire to express to you both
my personal appreciation and thanks and that of my Staff and the Army
I represent for the distinguished courtesy and delightful hospitality with
which I have been received by you and the officials of the Italian Army
during my visit to Italy. My tour of the Piave and Trentino under the
guidance of General Caviglia was not only intensely interesting and instructive but it afforded me an opportunity to form a just appreciation of
the magnificent feat of arms executed by the Italian Armies. General de
Lucca and the other officers designated by you to accompany me and my
staff have made a lasting impression upon us by the efficiency and consideration with which they have arranged our itinerary, provided for our
pleasure and guarded our comfort.

   Believe me, Sir, with expressions of my warmest regard and esteem,
Sincerely and respectfully yours,

John J. Pershing.

(Draft of Telegram).

His Excellency, —————,
      Prime Minister of Italy, Rome.

In completing my visit to Italy, I wish to assure Your Excellency of my
deep appreciation of the courtesy and cordiality with which you wel-
comed me in Rome, and with which the officials of the Italian Government greeted me and my staff throughout our journey. We have been

deeply touched by our reception, and will carry back with us to America a lasting impression of the good will and friendship of the Italian people.

Believe me, Sir,

Sincerely and respectfully yours,

John J. Pershing.

(Draft of Telegram).

His Excellency, General Citadini,
    First Aide-de-Camp to H.M. the King, Rome.

Please convey to His Majesty my deep appreciation of the distinguished courtesies and warm cordiality which have been extended to me and the members of my Staff by the officials of His Majesty's Government and Army during our visit in Italy. Please express my regret at the early completion of this visit, and assure His Majesty of my respectful esteem and high regard. I beg to remain, Your Excellency,

Respectfully and sincerely yours,

John J. Pershing.

We arrived in Turin at four o'clock and practically duplicated the procedure at Milan. Here we were taken through a model of an ancient castle where everything had been restored, including furniture, to exactly represent the period in which it was built. Again champagne, cakes, and this time ice-cream, were served. Upon our return to the train at six o'clock, Mr. Jay, the American Military Attaché, and several others left us, and we pulled out for Mondane, the frontier town, where we arrived at six-thirty. General de Lucca and his officers took their leave at this place, and at seven-thirty the train departed for Paris.

The scenery through the mountains was magnificent, and the air cool and fresh — quite a contrast to that in the Italian plain. The run through the night was rather rough, as our schedule was a fast one and the road bed not too good.

This morning, at nine o'clock we arrived in Paris, and came immediately to the office. I dictated this while it was still fresh in my mind — and now will have to go to work to clean up our last affairs before leaving here on the first for the States.

August 22, 1919

Notes

AEF	American Expeditionary Forces
DSC	Distinguished Service Cross. Second highest award for heroism. Ranks just below Medal of Honor
DSM	Distinguished Service Medal. Highest award for service other than heroism. Ranks just below DSC
FA	Field Artillery
GHQ	General Headquarters. The senior US Headquarters in any theater of war
HQ	Headquarters
NATO	North Atlantic Treaty Organization
SOS	Services of Supply
VMI	Virginia Military Institute

1. The First Months (pages 1–10)

1. James Franklin Bell was not only a combat cavalryman of no mean repute — he won the Medal of Honor in the Philippines — but also a member of the bar. He was Chief of Staff of the Army from 1906 to 1910 and then commanded in succession the Department of the Philippines, the 2nd Division, the Western Department, the Eastern Department, and the 77th Division. He was in France from December 1917 to March 1918 on special observer status. Ill health forced his return to the U.S., where he died on January 8, 1919.

2. Benjamin Alvord, Jr. (son of Brigadier General Benjamin Alvord, who distinguished himself in the Florida Indian War, the Mexican War, and the Civil War), fought in the Philippine Insurrection and served as Adjutant General of the AEF in France until, being sick, he returned to the United States in 1918. He retired as a Brigadier General in 1924 and died three years later. His grandson, Benjamin Alvord Spiller, graduated from West Point in 1941.

3. Leonard Wood entered the army as a contract surgeon. He was soon commanding troops as an infantryman and received a Medal of Honor during the Apache Campaign. He succeeded J. Franklin Bell as Army Chief of Staff in 1910. Four years later he took command in turn of the Department of the East, the 89th

Division, the Central Department, and the Sixth Corps Area. Retiring in 1921, he died six years later, aged sixty-six.

4. Fort Mason was one of the Coast Artillery forts defending San Francisco and at that time provided housing for some officers on duty in the area.

5. Governors Island in New York Harbor was the location of Headquarters Department of the East. It housed Headquarters Second Corps Area after World War I and HQ First Army after World War II. It is now used by the Coast Guard.

6. Ewing E. Booth served with the 1st Colorado Infantry in the Spanish-American War. He joined the Regular Army in 1901 and rose to Brigadier General in World War I. After the war he served in various staff and line positions until his retirement as a Major General in 1934.

7. Halstead Dorey, a veteran of the Spanish-American War, the Philippine Insurrection, and the Moro Expedition, commanded the 4th Infantry Regiment of the 3rd Division in the AEF. He was awarded the DSC and the DSM, and was wounded in action three times. He retired as a Major General commanding the Hawaiian Division in 1936 and died ten years later.

8. Charles H. Bridges, having fought at San Juan and the siege of Santiago in Cuba, then participated in the Philippine Insurrection, where he was the custodian for four months of the rebel leader Aguinaldo. He went to France as the Inspector General of the 2nd Division and later became its G-1 (Assistant Chief of Staff for Personnel) until transferred as G-1 to the VI Army Corps in July 1918. In 1928 he became The Adjutant General of the Army. After 40 years of service he retired in 1933 as a Major General and died in 1948 in Sandwich, Massachusetts.

9. John Burke Murphy, having washed out of West Point in 1899, joined the army as a private. He was soon commissioned in the Infantry and transferred to the Coast Artillery in 1901. He became a Colonel at HQ AEF being awarded the DSM. He died on active service in 1927.

10. John Joseph Pershing, born in Missouri in 1860 and commissioned in the Cavalry from West Point in 1886, was no stranger to combat. He had fought in the Sioux Indian War, Cuba, the Philippine Insurrection, and had commanded both the Moro Expedition in the Philippines and the Punitive Expedition in Mexico chasing Pancho Villa. He had been promoted directly from Captain to Brigadier General in 1906 and was to go directly from Major General to full General on October 6, 1917 as Commander in Chief of the AEF. After the war Congress named him General of the Armies, the only man to bear that title, and in July 1921 he became Chief of Staff of the Army. He retired in 1924 but remained active as an unofficial military adviser to Presidents. His influence on military matters during the interwar years was substantial. His support of Brigadier General George C. Marshall was instrumental in deciding President Roosevelt to appoint Marshall Army Chief of Staff in 1939. General Pershing died at the age of eighty-seven in 1948.

11. James Lawton Collins served in the Philippine Insurrection initially with the 8th Cavalry and later as Aide-de-Camp to General Pershing. He was General Pershing's Aide in the Mexican Punitive Expedition and accompanied him in that capacity to France. He later became the Secretary of the General Staff at GHQ AEF, leaving that position to lead a Battalion of the 7th Field Artillery in the 1st Division during the last months of the war. During World War II he commanded the Puerto Rican Department and the 5th Service Command in Columbus, Ohio. He retired as a Major General in 1946 and died in 1963, too soon to see his youngest son, Michael, go to the moon as Command Module Pilot of Apollo 11, the first moon-landing flight.

12. Prior to becoming Chief of Staff, Tasker Howard Bliss had served mainly in staff and school assignments and at the outbreak of war with Spain was the Military Attaché in Madrid. He returned to participate in that war in Cuba and Puerto Rico and was later Department Commander of the Philippines. At the end of 1917, when he had reached the mandatory retirement age of sixty-four, he was kept on active duty by order of President Wilson. In May 1918 he was appointed U.S. Military Representative to the Allied Supreme War Council and later was a delegate to the Versailles Peace Conference. Subsequently he served as Governor of the Soldiers Home until 1927 when he finally left active duty. He died three years later at seventy-six.

13. William Luther Sibert founded a distinguished army family. His two sons retired as Major Generals and two grandsons and a great-grandson have been in the army. An Engineer, General Sibert built bridges in the midwest, saw service in the Philippines and assisted with the Panama Canal (for the latter he was promoted to Brigadier General and given the Thanks of Congress on March 4, 1915). After commanding the 1st Division in France until December 1917, he returned to the United States and served as Director of the Chemical Warfare Service. He retired in 1920 and from 1923 to 1933 he was the manager of the Alabama State Docks Commission, which constructed the Ocean Terminal at Mobile. In 1928 Congress appointed him chairman of a board to investigate and report on the Boulder Dam project. He died at Bowling Green, Kentucky, in 1935, aged seventy-five.

14. Newton Diehl Baker had been Mayor of Cleveland before Wilson appointed him Secretary of War in 1916. During his tenure the United States Army was involved in the Punitive Expedition into Mexico in pursuit of Pancho Villa as well as the First World War during which the army expanded from 190,000 to almost 4 million — about half overseas. He also presided over the winding down of the war with minimum impact on the economic well-being of the country. After he left office in 1921 he was a counsel to many corporations and in 1928 joined the Institute of Pacific Relations. President Coolidge appointed him to the Permanent Court of Arbitration at the Hague and he was reconfirmed by President Roosevelt in 1935. He died on Christmas Day 1937, aged sixty-six.

15. The Staff of the 1st Division was a singularly distinguished group as the following biographical sketches of some of those officers will show.

> Frank Winston Coe, initially the Chief of Staff of the 1st Division, was promoted in August and took command of the 1st Separate Brigade, Coast Artillery, and the Railway Artillery Reserve of the AEF. In May 1918 he returned to Washington to become Chief of Coast Artillery, a position he held until his retirement as a Major General in March 1926.

> William Mackey Cruikshank, the Adjutant of the 1st Division, having served with the Field Artillery at Santiago, Cuba, soon moved on to command the 15th FA Regiment in the 2nd Division, the 3rd FA Brigade in the 3rd Division, and finally the Artillery of the IV Corps. He remained in the Army of Occupation in Germany and returned to the U.S. with one of his wartime commands, the 3rd FA Brigade of the 3rd Division. Fittingly he wound up his career as Commanding General of the Field Artillery School at Fort Sill, Oklahoma, from whence he retired as a Brigadier General in 1934.

> Campbell King entered the service as a private of the 5th Cavalry in 1897. Appointed a Second Lieutenant of Infantry in 1898, he participated in the Spanish-American War and was on the Mexican Border. After service with the

1st Division he was promoted to Brigadier General and ended the war as Chief of Staff, III Corps. Returning to the U.S., he graduated in 1920 from the Army War College for the second time (he had been in the class of 1911) and served on the War Department General Staff before retiring as a Major General in 1933.

B. Frank Cheatham entered military service with the 1st Tennessee Infantry during the Spanish-American War. He was soon commissioned in the Quartermaster Corps of the Regular Army. After wartime service with the 1st Division he attended the Army War College and in 1926 became the Quartermaster General. He retired as a Major General in 1930.

Lesley James McNair had gone to France in 1913 to observe French artillery methods. Following this he was with General Funston's expedition to Vera Cruz, Mexico, in 1914 and with the Punitive Expedition into Mexico in 1916. He was with the 1st Division in France until August 1917 when he was transferred to GHQ AEF in the training section, where he became the youngest Brigadier General to serve in France. On his return to the U.S. he reverted to his permanent grade of Major and between the wars had various assignments, mainly in the training area. With the outbreak of World War II he became the Chief of Staff and later the commander of Army Ground Forces, the command responsible for training the millions of soldiers in the U.S. As part of the deception plan of Operation Overlord, the invasion of Normandy, Lieutenant General McNair went to Europe ostensibly to command a fictitious Army Group, to convince the Germans that the Pas de Calais area would be assaulted after Normandy. On a visit to St. Lo, France, July 25, 1944, while observing front line units General McNair was killed.

Graduating third in the class of 1910 at West Point, William Carrington Sherman was commissioned in the Corps of Engineers. For a year (1912–13) he flew with the Signal Corps but returned to the Engineers and participated in the Punitive Expedition into Mexico. He came to France as an Aide-de-Camp to General Sibert, but in August 1917 became the Acting Engineer for the 1st Division. He went on detached service with both the French and British and returned to the 1st Division to become the Assistant Chief of Staff G-2 (Intelligence) and in July 1918 the Assistant Chief of Staff G-2, III Corps. In October he was assigned as Chief of Staff of the Air Service, First U.S. Army, until he returned to the US in 1919 where he became the Chief of Training for the fledgling U.S. Air Service. He served in various Air Service assignments until his untimely death in 1927 at the age of thirty-nine while an instructor at the Command and General Staff School, Fort Leavenworth.

Franklin Cummings Sibert, one of the distinguished sons of the Division Commander, rose to the rank of Lieutenant Colonel during the war. In World War II he was a Major General on the staff of General Joseph W. Stilwell and participated in the retreat from Burma. He later commanded the 6th Division and the X Corps in the Pacific Theater before retiring in 1946.

Hamilton Allen Smith, commissioned in the Infantry in 1893 from West Point and a veteran of Cuba and the Philippine Insurrection, was destined to die at Soissons at the head of his command, the 26th Infantry.

Beverly Allen Read had entered West Point with the class of 1892. He did not graduate, but after participating in the Spanish-American War as a Captain of

U.S. volunteers he was commissioned in the Cavalry in 1901. Transferring to The Judge Advocate General Department in 1909, he rose to the grade of Colonel in France. During the war he was cited twice for gallantry in action. He retired in 1922 and died six years later in the District of Columbia.

16. Frank Ross McCoy had been wounded at San Juan and fought the Moros in the Philippines. He joined GHQ AEF in June 1917 as assistant to the Chief of Staff. He commanded the 63rd Infantry Brigade in the last battles of the war. In 1929 he was named Chairman of the Commission of Inquiry and Conciliation (Bolivia and Paraguay) which settled the Gran Chaco war. He retired as a Major General in 1938 while commanding the First Army and the Second Corps Area at Governors Island, New York. In 1939 he became the President of the prestigious Foreign Policy Association and during World War II he was the President of the Military Commission which tried and convicted the German Saboteurs landed in the U.S. He died in Washington on June 4, 1954.

II. *Early Days in France (pages 11–27)*

1. Jacques Aldebert de Chambrun, known as Bertie, was a direct descendant of La-fayette and hence an honorary American citizen. He served through the war as French Aide-de-Camp to General Pershing and rose to the rank of Brigadier General. His son, René Comte de Chambrun, was active in the U.S. seeking support for the French in 1940.
2. Samuel D. Rockenbach, a VMI graduate, was temporarily on detail with the Quartermaster Corps. He soon was called to GHQ AEF, where he became the U.S. member of the Tank Committee, Supreme War Council, and was promoted to Brigadier General. He was listed at GHQ as Chief of the Tank Corps. He retired in 1933 as a Brigadier General. The author must have made a mistake in the name. General Rockenbach was still a Colonel at St. Nazaire and would not be promoted to Brigadier General for more than a year.
3. Joseph Jacques Césaire Joffre, Marshal of France and hero of the Battle of the Marne where the Germans were stopped in 1914, had been commander of all Allied Armies in France. However, in 1917, at the age of sixty-five, he gave up his command. He then became an adviser to the French government and undertook trips abroad seeking support for France.
4. George Creel had been appointed chairman of the Committee on Public Information by President Wilson. He was a distinguished journalist, having edited, among others the Kansas City *Independent* and the Denver *Post.* Following the war he wrote extensively for magazines and was the author of numerous books, ranging from *The War, The World and Wilson* in 1920 to *Russia's Race for Asia,* 1949. He died in 1953, aged seventy-seven.
5. Robert Lee Bullard had earned campaign badges for Indian service, Philippine service, Cuban pacification, and for service in Mexico in 1916. Thus he was no stranger to combat and was the logical successor to General Sibert in December 1917 as commander of the 1st Division. However, after seven months he was promoted to command III Corps and then for the last month of the war he led the Second Army as a Lieutenant General. After the war he commanded the Eastern Department, retiring in 1925. He was president of the National Security League

for many years and wrote two books on the First World War and numerous newspaper and magazine articles. He died in 1947, aged eighty-six.

6. Omar Bundy was a veteran of the Indian wars and the fighting in Cuba, where he was cited for gallantry at El Caney. He fought in the Philippine Insurrection and the Moro Expedition and commanded a regiment on the Mexican border. He was promoted to Major General and left the 1st Division in August 1917, assuming command of the 2nd Division. In July of 1918 he commanded the VI Corps and in September was transferred to the VII Corps. After the war he commanded Camp Lee, Virginia, the Seventh Corps Area at Fort Crook, Nebraska, the Philippine Division, and finally the Fifth Corps Area at Fort Hayes, Ohio, from whence he retired in 1925.

7. George Smith Patton, Jr., is well known for his dashing command of the Armored Corps in North Africa, Seventh Army in Sicily, and the Third Army in Western Europe in World War II. Less well known is his role in World War I as a pioneer with tanks. As the citation for his DSM said, ". . . In the employment of Tank Corps troops in combat he displayed high military attainments, zeal and marked adaptability in a form of warfare comparatively new to the American Army."

8. Hugh Aloysius Drum, son of a regular Army officer killed at the battle of San Juan, had fought in the Philippines, in Mexico and on the Mexican border prior to World War II. He went to France with General Pershing as an original member of the general staff and wound up the war a Brigadier General and Chief of Staff, First Army. He held numerous responsible commands in the U.S. after the war and was General Marshall's principal rival for Chief of Staff of the Army in 1939. He retired a Lieutenant General in 1943, aged sixty-four.

9. Merritte Weber Ireland had been a surgeon in the Santiago campaign in Cuba and the Philippine Insurrection. He was Surgeon General of the AEF and later became Surgeon General of the Army, retiring in 1931 after almost thirteen years in that position, with the rank of Major General.

10. James Addison Logan, Jr., had joined the military as a private with the Pennsylvania Volunteers in the Spanish-American War. He was the Chief of the American Mission with the French Army from September 1914 until July 5, 1917, when he became the Assistant Chief of Staff, G-1 of the GHQ AEF, reaching the rank of Colonel. After the war he was the principal assistant to Herbert Hoover in European relief operations and was adviser to the American Relief Administration in connection with Russian Relief. Resigning from the army in 1922, he was active in international economic affairs and in 1925 entered the banking field with Dillon Read & Co.

11. Theodore Roosevelt, Jr., son of President Theodore Roosevelt, was a writer, explorer, and politician as well as wartime soldier (Lieutenant Colonel in World War I, Brigadier General in World War II). His writings ranged from *Average Americans* (1919) through *All in the Family* (1929) to *Colonial Policies of the United States* (1937). He followed in the footsteps of his distant cousin Franklin D. as Assistant Secretary of the Navy (1921–24) and was leader of the Field Museum expeditions to Asia in 1925 and 1928. He died a Brigadier General on active duty after the Normandy landings, in July 1944.

12. Raymond Poincaré, President of France from 1913 to 1920, was a politician for most of his adult life. He served as Deputy, Senator, Cabinet Officer, and Prime Minister as well as President. Through his oratory, he was instrumental in keeping up French morale during the war. His specialty was economics, and he was respon-

sible for the measures that stabilized the franc during the Great Depression. He died in 1934.

13. Henri Philippe Pétain, a French career soldier, the hero of Verdun, was at this time Commander in Chief of the French Armies. He was made a Marshal in 1918 and after the war commanded in Morocco and was Minister of War. At the outbreak of World War II he was the French Ambassador to Spain, but returned to become the Prime Minister of France in June 1940 and to ask an immediate armistice of the Germans. He remained Prime Minister and Chief of State of "Vichy" France. After the war he was sentenced to death for his actions but President de Gaulle commuted the sentence to life imprisonment. The aged and sad Marshal of France died in 1951.

14. George Brand Duncan, a veteran of Cuba, Puerto Rico, and the Philippine Insurrection commanded the 26th Infantry of the 1st Division in France until promoted to Brigadier General in August 1917. He commanded the 1st Brigade of the division until April 1918 when as a Major General he assumed command of the newly arrived 77th Division and later the 82nd Division. He retired in 1925 as Commander of the Seventh Corps Area at Fort Omaha, Nebraska. He was active in civic affairs in Omaha and later in Lexington, Kentucky, where he died in 1950, at eighty-eight.

15. William Herbert Allaire had served with distinction in the Philippines, commanded the 16th Infantry of the 1st Division, and, promoted to Brigadier General in August 1917, became Provost Marshal General of the AEF. He retired in 1921 and died at the age of seventy-five in 1933.

16. Charles A. Doyen, a distinguished United States Marine, had been commissioned in 1883. He was a veteran of the Philippine Insurrection, where he had commanded a battalion, a regiment, and finally a brigade of Marines. He brought his regiment, the 5th Marines, to France, was promoted to Brigadier General in October 1917, and took command of the 4th Brigade of Marines in the Army's 2nd Division. Ill health forced his return to the U.S., where he died while in command of the Marine Barracks at Quantico, Virginia, in October 1918.

17. Paul Hedrick Clark left his position of Assistant Quartermaster of the 1st Division (a helpful man to have in one's mess) to join the Headquarters of the AEF. He became head of General Pershing's Liaison Mission to the French General Headquarters, and the author of a celebrated series of confidential reports. He was promoted to Colonel and awarded the DSM. Retiring in France in 1922, he led a varied career as a composer of religious music, author, and finally as a rancher near Carlsbad, California, where he died aged sixty-eight in 1946.

III. *The Fall of 1917 (pages 28–44)*

1. Robert Alexander came into the Army as a private in the 4th Infantry in 1886. Having seen service in the Indian Campaign of 1890–91, in the Spanish American War, the Philippine Insurrection, and in Mexico, he served in France for a short while with the 1st Division and then as Commander of the 41st and later the 77th Division. He retired to Tacoma, Washington, as a Major General in 1927.

2. Beaumont Bonaparte Buck, after frontier duty and combat in the Philippine Insurrection, was promoted to Brigadier General in September 1917 and took command

of the 2nd Infantry Brigade of the 1st Division. In August of 1918 he took command of the 3rd Division as a Major General. He retired in 1924, but was recalled to active duty the following year for recruiting duty in San Antonio, Texas. He retired again as a Major General in 1932, and died at the age of ninety in 1950.

3. Georges Clemenceau, the "Tiger," born in 1841, was not unfamiliar with Americans as he had served as a war correspondent with General Grant's Army in 1865. He had been Premier of France from 1906 to 1909, and was soon to take over again for the duration of the war. He retired in 1920 and died in 1929.

4. Noel Marie Joseph Edward de Curières de Castelnau was one of the most distinguished and respected French officers to come out of World War I. He had commanded a group of armies in the center of the French line in 1915, had helped in the defense of Verdun in 1916, and commanded the group of armies in eastern France at the time of the Armistice. Later he was elected to the Chamber of Deputies. He died in 1944, aged eighty-nine.

5. Paul Bernard Malone, a veteran of Cuba and the Philippine Insurrection, at this time was the Assistant Chief of Staff G-5 (Training) for GHQ AEF. He later was to command with distinction the 23rd Infantry of the 2nd Division and the 10th Infantry Brigade of the 5th Division. After the war he commanded the 2nd Infantry Division and the Philippine Division; he retired as a major general commanding the Fourth Army. The author of many books about West Point — the alma mater of his son and two grandsons — he was known throughout the Army for his eloquence. He died in 1960 at eighty-eight.

6. Hanson Edward Ely, having commanded mounted scouts during the Philippine Insurrection, later the 11th Battalion of Philippine Scouts and a battalion of the 7th Infantry at Vera Cruz in 1915, had come to France as a member of a Military Commission to study British and French armies. He was made the first Provost Marshal General of the AEF but soon left this post to become Chief of Staff of the 1st Division and commander of the 28th Infantry which captured Cantigny. He later commanded the 3rd Brigade, 2nd Division, and the 5th Division. He retired in 1931 as Major General, commander of the Second Corps Area, Governors Island, New York.

7. Frank Allen Wilcox had been General J. Franklin Bell's Aide for a time during the Philippine Insurrection and had commanded a battalion in Mexico with the Punitive Expedition. He seemed destined for greater things until his untimely death at the age of forty-nine on Feb. 9, 1918; he was then a Colonel commanding the 16th Infantry.

IV. *The First Raid and the Final Training (pages 45–56)*

1. Archibald Bulloch Roosevelt, born in 1894, a son of Theodore Roosevelt, was a Lieutenant and Captain with the 26th Infantry. After the war he became an investment broker, a member of the New York firm of Roosevelt and Weigold. During World War II he returned to the Army as a Lieutenant Colonel training soldiers at Camp Gordon, Georgia, and later served in the Southwest Pacific.

2. Prior to his service in France, Charles Pelot Summerall had distinguished himself in the Philippine Insurrection and with the China Relief Expedition of 1900. He followed General Hines as Chief of Staff of the Army, retiring as General in 1931

when he became President of the Citadel, the Military College of South Carolina. He died in 1955 at the age of eighty-eight.

3. Much of John Leonard Hines' service before taking command of the 16th Infantry had been with the Quartermaster or Adjutant General's Corps. However, he was no stranger to combat. He had been cited for gallantry in action in Cuba, had fought in the Philippine Insurrection, and was in Mexico with the Punitive Expedition. After several important postwar assignments he succeeded General Pershing as Chief of Staff of the Army on September 14, 1924, a post he held until November 20, 1926. However, he did not retire until 1932 and lived until 1968, a centenarian at his death.

4. Frank Parker, whose attendance at the French Ecole de Guerre was interrupted in 1914 by the war, served as a member of the U.S. Military Mission with the French Army from January 1916 until early 1917; he was promoted to Brigadier General in the 1st Division. After the war he finally graduated from the Ecole de Guerre in 1920. He retired as a Major General commanding the Eighth Corps Area at Fort Sam Houston, Texas. In civil life he was active in the American Legion, and during World War II led the Illinois War Council. He died in Chicago in 1947.

5. Conrad Stanton Babcock had been cited for gallantry in action in the Philippines and, although a Cavalryman, commanded several Infantry regiments during the war, gaining two Silver Star citations and a DSM. He remained in Europe until late 1921, first with the Army of Occupation in Germany and then as Assistant Military Attaché in Paris. He retired as a Colonel in 1937, but in 1940 was advanced on the retired list to Brigadier General. He died in 1950.

v. *The Toul Sector (pages 65–74)*

1. The Annamites were Vietnamese recruited from French Indochina. The Kingdom of Annam was the central, coastal section, however, the French used the term Annamites indiscriminately for all Vietnamese. The Annamites were renowned as tunnellers and diggers, a prowess they displayed again in the Indochina War of the 1960s and 1970s.

2. Marie Eugene Debeney was one of the heroes of the early days of the war. He stubbornly defended the approaches to Verdun in 1916, commanded the Seventh French Army in Alsace and the Armies of the North and North East in 1917, and finally the First French Army. He was Chief of Staff of the French Army 1924–1930, and died in 1943.

3. Sidney Carroll Graves after courageous service with the 1st Division where he won the DSC was reassigned to Siberia with the 17th Infantry. The American Siberian Expedition was commanded by his father, Major General William S. Graves. Major Sidney Graves again showed his gallantry on November 18, 1919, when he rescued six noncombatants entrapped by crossfire in the railroad station at Vladivostok. He was awarded a second DSC for this action. He resigned his commission in 1920 and entered the real estate business in Washington, D.C.

4. John McAuley Palmer after the war had a great influence on American military thought. He played a prominent role in drafting the National Defense Act of 1920 and later worked on special projects for General Pershing from 1921 to 1923. He retired as a Brigadier General in 1926 and in civil life wrote many books, notably, a

biography of General von Steuben in 1937 and *America in Arms,* 1941. General Marshall, who had always remained close to General Palmer, recalled him to active duty from 1941 to 1946, and used him, much as had General Pershing, on special projects. He died in Washington in 1955 at the age of eighty-five.

VI. *The Move to Picardy (pages 75–86)*

1. James William McAndrew, who had previously distinguished himself in combat at El Caney in the Spanish-American War, went on to become Chief of Staff of the AEF. After the war he was Commandant of the Army War College in Washington. He died a Major General in Washington in 1922.
2. Alfred William Bjornstad served in the Spanish-American War with the 13th Minnesota Infantry. A veteran of 34 battles and skirmishes in the Philippines, he was to become Chief of Staff of the III Corps and at the end of the war was back with troops as a Brigadier General commanding the 13th Infantry Brigade of the 7th Division. He retired a Brigadier General in 1928, commanding his wartime unit, the 7th Division.
3. Hjalmer Erickson was born in Norway and entered the Army as a private in the 8th Cavalry. Commissioned during the Spanish-American War he had served in the Quartermaster Corps as well as the infantry. In March 1917 Major Erickson had been sent to the 1st Division to be trained as operations officer so Colonel Marshall could be released for duty with GHQ AEF. Promoted to Colonel, Erickson was assigned in 1918 to command an infantry regiment in the 1st Division. He retired in 1923 but was recalled to active duty and served until 1932.
4. The Château of Fontainebleau, ancient royal residence, has a long association with the military. Napoleon signed his abdication here and for many years it was the location of the French Artillery and Engineer schools. More recently it was the Headquarters of the Allied Forces, Central Europe, until NATO was expelled from France by President de Gaulle.

VII. *Cantigny (pages 87–99)*

1. Colonel Bertram Tracy Clayton, a native of Clayton, Alabama, was a West Point classmate of General Pershing's. He had resigned in 1888 and had been a member of the U.S. Congress from New York 1899–1901. He participated in the Puerto Rican Expedition as a Colonel commanding the New York Volunteer Cavalry. In 1901 he rejoined the Regular Army and served as the Construction Quartermaster at West Point from 1911 to 1914. He was the senior West Point graduate to be killed in action during the war, and Fort Clayton, Canal Zone, is named for him.
2. James Marie Hopper had been born in Paris in 1876 and came to the U.S. at the age of eleven. He had been admitted to the bar in California before taking up writing as a profession. He had been a reporter on San Francisco newspapers, on the staff of *McClure's* Magazine, and was the author of numerous books before becoming a war correspondent for *Collier's* in 1914.

VIII. *Final Weeks in Picardy (pages 100–118)*

1. Frank E. Bamford had entered the service as a private in the 2nd Infantry in 1891. Commissioned in 1893 he was a veteran of the Spanish-American War and the Mexican troubles. Promoted to Brigadier General in August of 1918, he briefly commanded the 2nd Infantry Brigade of the 1st Division before taking command of the 26th Division which he led until the Armistice. He retired in 1921.

2. Ferdinand Foch at the outbreak of war had been in command of the XX Corps which had stopped the Germans driving on the channel port of Calais. After an assignment as Marshal Joffre's planner he again obtained troop command and wound up the war as Supreme Commander of all the Allied Armies. He retired a Marshal of France and died in 1929.

3. It has become a tradition with the American Artillery to offer a national salute in wartime by means of a noontime barrage on the Fourth of July. This was carried out by all units within range of the enemy in World War II, in Korea, and in Vietnam.

4. Chauncey Belknap was discharged as a Major after the war and resumed the practice of law. In 1915–16 he had been legal secretary to Justice Oliver Wendell Holmes of the Supreme Court. A partner in the law firm Patterson, Belknap and Webb in New York City, he has been a director in numerous corporations as well as a Trustee of Princeton University, a member of the Board of Visitors of Harvard Law School, and President of the New York State Bar Association.

5. Fox Conner was a veteran of Cuba and had served with a French Artillery Regiment in 1911 and 1912. Fluent in French, he was of great service to General Pershing as his planner and operations officer, a position he held until August of 1919. General Conner subsequently served in Panama, as Commanding General of the Hawaiian Department, and retired in 1938 as a Major General commanding the First Corps Area in Boston. He died in 1951.

6. Benjamin Caffey, Jr. remained in the Army after the war. In November 1942 he was promoted to Brigadier General and participated in the landings in North Africa that month. He served with the 34th Division, and Headquarters of both Fifth Army and Allied Forces. He retired in 1950.

IX. *Chaumont (pages 119–130)*

1. LeRoy Eltinge had been wounded in the Philippine Insurrection, where he was cited for gallantry. In Mexico he was a Major commanding a unit of the 8th Cavalry in pursuit of Pancho Villa. Upon his arrival in France in July 1917 he was assigned to the Operations Section GHQ AEF. He was made Deputy Chief of Staff in May 1918 and promoted to Brigadier General. He remained with GHQ until June 1919. Reverting to his permanent grade of Major he became Assistant Commandant of the General Service School at Fort Leavenworth in July. He was soon promoted and in 1924 re-attained the grade of Brigadier General. He died in 1931 commanding the 14th Brigade and the 89th Reserve Division at Omaha, Nebraska.

2. Upton Birnie, Jr., spent most of the war in the Operations Section of GHQ. After the war he served in various Field Artillery commands and for four years was on the staff of the Army War College. In 1934 he was made Chief of Field Artillery, retiring as a Major General from this position in 1938. He died in 1957.

3. Walter Schuyler Grant, a 1900 classmate of Upton Birnie's at West Point, had fought in the Philippine Insurrection where he had captured Brigadier General Cabrera, a noted insurrectionist. During the war he was not only Deputy Chief of Staff of the First Army but for a while Chief of Staff of I Corps. After the war he spent much time in schools and in Cavalry commands until in 1935 he was appointed commandant of the War College. He later commanded the Philippine Department and the Third Corps Area. He retired a Major General in 1942 and was immediately recalled to active duty, serving until 1946 on the Secretary of War's Personnel Board. He died in Washington in 1956.

4. Samuel Reid Gleaves, also of the West Point class of 1900, had served with the 1st Cavalry in the Philippines on two occasions and had been an instructor at VMI before service on the Mexican Border. He came to France as operations officer of the 42nd Division and in November 1917 was transferred to the G-3 (Operations) Division of GHQ. After the war he served on the staff of the Chief of Cavalry and the War Department G-3. He was an instructor at the War College at his untimely death in 1926 at the age of forty-seven.

5. Xenophon Herbert Price after the war gained his MS degree from the Massachusetts Institute of Technology and then was assigned as Secretary of the Battle Monuments Commission, charged with commemorating the AEF in Europe and with the care and improvement of the American military cemeteries there. During World War II he was President of the War Department Observer Board in Europe, retiring in 1946.

6. Albert S. Kuegle had been Secretary of the General Staff GHQ for several short periods as well as Secretary of the Operations Section. He served as G-3 GHQ when the GHQ returned to Washington to write their final report. During the interwar years Colonel Kuegle attended service schools and held Infantry commands. He spent World War II mainly in the U.S. and retired in 1948 after 37 years' service.

7. Harold Benjamin Fiske had participated in the capture of Manila from Spain in 1898 and then stayed on for three years to fight the insurgents. He returned to fight in the Philippines the next year, was with General Funston at Vera Cruz and General Pershing on the Mexican border. He went to France with the 1st Division but soon was shifted to the Training Section (G-5) at GHQ. In February 1918 he became the G-5 and remained in that position until 1919. During and after the war General Fiske gained his great reputation as the premier trainer of the Army. He served at the Infantry School and in numerous troop commands. In 1933 he was promoted to Major General and given command of the Panama Department, from whence he retired in 1935. He died in 1960 at San Diego.

8. Stuart Heintzelman, whose grandfather and father had graduated from West Point in 1826 and 1867 respectively, the one rising to Major General in the Civil War and the other dying when Stuart was only four, had himself seen combat in the Philippines and in China before joining the Operations Section (G-3) of GHQ. He soon was shifted to be the G-3 I Corps, Chief of Staff of the IV Corps and finally Chief of Staff of the Second Army as a Brigadier General. After the war he had various assignments including the command of the Twenty-second Infantry Brigade in Hawaii and the Command and General Staff School. He was in command of the Seventh Corps Area at Omaha, Nebraska, when he died, a Major General, on July 6, 1935.

9. Paul Ludwig Hans Anton von Beneckendorff und von Hindenburg had fought in the Seven Weeks War of 1866 and the Franco-Prussian War of 1870. Although he had retired in 1911, he was recalled in 1914 to command in East Prussia and won a

complete victory over the Russians at Tannenberg, one of the classic battles of encirclement. He was promoted to Field Marshal and in 1916 was made Chief of Staff of the German Army, retiring again in 1919. He was elected the second President of the German Weimar Republic in 1925 and re-elected in 1932, defeating Adolf Hitler. However, he was forced to appoint Hitler Chancellor of the Republic in 1933. Upon his death in 1934, Hitler assumed all power in the Reich, combining the positions of President and Chancellor.

10. John A. Lejeune, a native of Louisiana, entered the Marine Corps from Annapolis in 1890. Having served in the Spanish-American War, where he was cited for bravery in Puerto Rico, as well as in the Philippine Insurrection, and at Vera Cruz in 1914, General Lejeune organized the Marines for overseas operations. He succeeded to the command of the 2nd Division in July 1918 and kept it for the rest of the war. In 1920 he was appointed commandant of the Marine Corps. He retired in 1929 and was Superintendent of VMI for the next eight years. He died in 1942. The great Marine Training Camp on the coast of North Carolina is named for him.

11. Preston Brown had graduated from Yale in 1892, served three years as an enlisted man and was commissioned in 1897 in time for the Spanish-American War. In September of 1918 he left the 2nd Division to become Chief of Staff of the IV Corps and then took command of the 3rd Division for the Meuse-Argonne battle. After the war he served in several command positions in the U.S. In 1925 he was promoted to Major General and commanded the First Corps Area, the Panama Canal Department, and in 1934 retired from the command of the Second Army. He died in 1948.

12. Erich Friedrich Wilhelm Ludendorff, born in 1865, led a very checkered career. A great strategist and planner, he had worked closely with von Hindenburg, and his plan of campaign in 1918 almost resulted in Allied defeat. After the war he fled to Sweden but returned to Munich in 1919 where he became involved in several unsavory political ventures, including Hitler's 1923 Beer Hall Putsch. In his later years he was somewhat unbalanced and fanatical in his ideas and actions. He attacked Hindenburg, led crusades against Catholics, Protestants, Jews, and Masons, supported and then deserted Hitler, and finally became a Pacifist. He died in 1937.

x. St. Mihiel (pages 131–147)

1. Hunter Liggett, a veteran of Frontier duty, the Spanish-American War and the Philippine Insurrection, came to France commanding the 41st Division. He soon was assigned to command I Corps and in October 1918 to command First Army. Promoted to Lieutenant General he continued in this command until First Army was disbanded, whereupon he was made commander of the Third Army, the Army of Occupation in Germany. Returning to the U.S. in July 1920, he took command of the Western Department, headquartered at the Presidio of San Francisco, until his retirement in 1921. He died at San Francisco in 1935. His name lives on at the great Army training area, Camp Hunter Liggett, about two hundred miles south of San Francisco.

2. Malin Craig had gone to France as Chief of Staff of General Liggett's 41st Division. He accompanied him as Chief of Staff to I Corps where he was promoted to Brigadier General and remained until the Armistice. He then became Chief of

Staff of the Third Army, where General Liggett rejoined him in May 1919. After the war he served at the Army War College, was Chief of Cavalry and commanded the Panama Canal Department and the Ninth Corps Area. Appointed Chief of Staff of the Army in 1935 succeeding General Douglas MacArthur, he relinquished the position to General George C. Marshall on his retirement in 1939. Recalled to active duty in September 1941, he died in Washington in July of 1945.

3. Robert McCleave had entered the Army through the ranks, being commissioned in 1898. A veteran of the Spanish American War and the Philippine Insurrection, he left First Army in October 1918 to become Chief of Staff of the 3rd Division, a position he held for the remainder of the war. Returning to the U.S., he attended the Army War College and had various staff and line assignments. Promoted to Brigadier General in 1930, he retired in 1933.

4. Monroe Crawford Kerth had served in the Philippines during the Spanish-American War where he was cited for gallantry at Manila. Staying on to fight the Insurgents he was cited twice more and severely wounded in 1899. His wound took more than two years to heal but the outbreak of the war found him an observer with the Rumanian Armies. In May of 1917 he joined the staff of the Military Attaché in Russia as an observer with Russian Armies. In February 1918 he joined the AEF and later became the G-3 of First Army for a short period before becoming Director of the Langres Staff College. After several assignments in the U.S. he became the Professor of Military Science and Tactics at the University of Missouri, retiring therefrom in 1929. He died in 1936.

5. Ernest Joseph Dawley had been commissioned in the Field Artillery in 1910. Serving in France initially with Field Artillery units where he was cited for gallantry, he later joined HQ First Army. Between the wars he held numerous staff posts and Field Artillery commands. In 1940 he took command of the 40th Division and, promoted to Major General, he later commanded the VI Corps. He retired in 1947 and died in 1973.

XI. *Opening of the Meuse-Argonne (pages 148–174)*

1. Willey Howell, a graduate of the University of Arkansas, was commissioned in 1898 from the ranks of the 16th Infantry. A veteran of the Spanish-American War and the Mexican border, he was First Army G-2 from its activation until 1919. He retired as a Colonel in 1928.

2. Alvin Barton Barber graduated fifth in the West Point Class of 1905. Prior to the war he had assisted in the reconstruction of San Francisco after the 1906 earthquake and had participated in the mapping of the Philippines. Initially he went to France with the Railway Commission but he soon joined the General Staff at GHQ until his assignment as G-1 of the Services of Supply in February 1918. In June he was made G-3 I Corps and in August G-1 First Army. In October he went to Second Army as an Assistant G-3. In January, 1919 he joined Herbert Hoover's American Relief Administration and was sent in August to Warsaw as Adviser to the Polish Minister of Railways. He resigned from the Army in 1920 but remained a Technical Adviser in Poland until 1922. In 1923 he was selected as manager of the Transportation and Communications Department of the United States Chamber of Commerce, a position he held for 25 years. He subsequently was a staff director on the National Resources Board and a consultant to the Office of Defense Mobilization. He retired in 1957 and died in 1961.

3. Leon Benjamin Kromer had been in the War with Spain and the Philippine Insurrection as well as serving with his Regiment, the 11th Cavalry, in Mexico during the Punitive Expedition. He came to France with the 82nd Division, but was soon assigned to the I Corps staff and then in October he succeeded Colonel Barber as G-1 First Army. After the war he held various troop, staff and school assignments until 1934 when he was promoted to Major General Chief of Cavalry. He retired in 1938 after 40 years' service and died in 1966 aged ninety.

4. John Lesesne DeWitt had attended Princeton before gaining a Regular Army commission in 1898. A veteran of the Philippine Insurrection and Mexican Border service, he came to France as Quartermaster of the 42nd "Rainbow" Division (so called because soldiers from all 48 states were assigned). In January 1918 he was made G-4 of I Corps and in July G-4 of First Army. After the war most of his service was involved with supply matters, and in 1930 he was appointed Quartermaster General for four years with the rank of Major General. Subsequently he was the commandant of the Army War College and in 1939 took command of Fourth Army and the Western Defense Command. In September 1943 he organized the Army-Navy Staff College, the predecessor to the National War College. In August 1944, when General McNair was killed, he went briefly to France as part of the deception plan to convince the Germans the Allies intended to land in the Pas de Calais area as well as in Normandy. General DeWitt retired a Lieutenant General in 1946 and died in 1962.

5. George H. Cameron had been commissioned in the 7th Cavalry from West Point in 1883. He had served on the Frontier, several times in the Philippines and had been an assistant professor of drawing at West Point as well as in charge of the Training School for Farriers at Fort Riley before attending the Army War College in 1913. General Cameron organized, trained and took to France the 4th Division, leaving it in August 1918 to command the V Corps. In October he was relieved and returned briefly to the command of the 4th Division before returning to take charge of Camp Gordon, Georgia, in November. He was later commandant of the Cavalry School and retired with 41 years' service in 1924. He died in 1944.

6. Horatio Herbert, First Earl Kitchener of Khartoum and of Broome was the celebrated British hero of the Sudan where he annihilated Khalifa's Army at Omdurman and reoccupied Khartoum in 1898. He fought in the Boer War and was Commander in Chief in India 1902–1909. He was engaged in organizing British forces for war from 1914 until his death in 1916.

7. Field Marshal Sir Douglas Haig at this time was the Commander in Chief of the British Expeditionary Forces. He had fought in the Sudan, the Boer War, and in India. In 1919 he was made an Earl and Commander in Chief of the Home Forces in Great Britain. He died in 1928.

8. Willard Dickerman Straight had been in the Chinese Imperial Customs Service 1902–04 and was a Reuters and Associated Press correspondent before he joined the U.S. Consular Service in 1905. A Far Eastern expert and a Consul-General, he gained a Major's commission in 1917 and hastened to join the AEF. He died only 17 days after the Armistice.

xii. *The Crisis of the Battle (pages 175–192)*

1. Joseph Augustus Baer, a veteran of the China Relief Expedition and the Philippine Insurrection, had been cited for gallantry during the Moro Expedition of 1907–1910. During the war he served in the Inspector General's Section of GHQ AEF. After the war he had various school, staff, and troop assignments including duty as Military Attaché to Vienna 1929–33. He retired in 1942 as a Colonel but was recalled to active duty as the Chief of Staff of the 2nd Service Command in New York and promoted to Brigadier General in 1943. He retired permanently in 1944 and died in 1958.

2. James Andrew Shannon was commissioned in the Cavalry with the West Point Class of 1903. He had been in the Battle of Bud Dajo in the Philippines and in the Punitive Expedition. The citation for the DSC which he was awarded post-humously reads in part: "He voluntarily led an officers' patrol to a depth of 3 kilometers within the enemy lines . . . The information thus secured was followed up by an attack the next morning which this officer personally led and wherein he was fatally wounded."

3. The Chief of Artillery in question was Major General Edward F. McGlachlin, Jr., a man not noted for his sense of humor, although a distinguished soldier. He had won the Silver Star citation for gallantry at Bud Dajo in 1906 and had been Commandant of the Field Artillery School of Fire. After the war he was destined to be commandant of the Army War College until his retirement in 1923. He died in 1946.

4. Philip Henry Sheridan, the great Union cavalry commander of the Civil War, had forced General Lee's surrender to General Grant by cutting off the Confederate retreat from Appomattox. He was made a Lieutenant General in 1869, and in 1870–71 accompanied the German armies as an observer. He succeeded General William T. Sherman as commander of the Armies of the United States in 1884, was promoted to General, and died in office in 1888.

5. Count Marie Edmé Patrice Maurice de MacMahon, Marshal of France, after his defeat in 1870 was to assist in putting down the Paris Commune in 1871 and to become the second President of the Third French Republic from 1873 to his retirement in 1879. He died in 1893.

6. Joseph Theodore Dickman had graduated from West Point in 1881. A veteran of frontier duty, the Geronimo Campaign, Cuba, the Philippine Insurrection, and the China Relief Expedition, he had come to France commanding the 3rd Division. In August 1918 he took command of the IV Corps until he was shifted to command I Corps in October. He was named to command the Third Army in Germany on its activation after the Armistice. Returning to the U.S. in 1919, he took command of the Southern Department and Eighth Corps Area at Fort Sam Houston, Texas, until his retirement in 1921. He died in Washington, D.C., in 1927. He contributed a son to the Air Service who was killed in an air crash in 1919, and a grandson who retired a Major General of the Air Force in 1973.

7. Edward Vernon (Eddie) Rickenbacker, who had been an auto-racing champion before the war, had come to France as a member of General Pershing's motor-car staff. Transferred to the Air Service, he became the commanding officer of the 94th Pursuit Squadron, the first American air unit to fight on the Western Front and the U.S. unit credited with the most air victories (69, of which 26 were Rickenbacker's personally). After the war Captain Rickenbacker was a pioneer in

the development of the airline industry, becoming president of Eastern Airlines in 1938. In World War II he undertook numerous special missions, for the Secretary of War. In 1942 when his plane was forced down in the Pacific, he survived for three weeks on a life raft. After the war, he was Chairman of the Board of Eastern Airlines until 1963, in addition to serving on the Board of Directors of many other companies and organizations. One of the most decorated men in World War I, Captain Rickenbacker won the Medal of Honor, ten Distinguished Service Crosses, and numerous foreign awards.

XIII. *The Armistice (pages 193–210)*

1. Parker Hitt had entered the service through the enlisted ranks and was commissioned during the Spanish American War. In 1912 he had transferred to the Signal Corps and was to retire as a Colonel in 1928. Recalled to active duty in 1940, he served until 1944.

2. Carl Boyd had been on duty with the French Cavalry when the war erupted. He remained an observer until early 1917 when he became our Military Attaché in Paris. In August of that year he became Aide to General Pershing until his death on February 12, 1919, aged 40.

3. The battle of the Masurian Lakes was one of the three main battles in von Hindenburg's Tannenberg Campaign, August to September 1914. The overwhelming defeat suffered by the Russians in this campaign was due in large part to the first use of radio intercept in warfare. The Germans knew the location and projected moves of most of the principal Russian units from listening to their uncoded radio transmissions.

4. Stephen Ogden Fuqua had failed to graduate from West Point, but fought in the Spanish-American War as a Captain of Infantry and gained a regular commission in 1901. After the war he went on to become a Major General and Chief of Infantry. He retired in 1938 and died in 1943. His son did graduate from West Point, fought through World War II and Korea, and retired as a Brigadier General.

5. Laurence Halstead, a veteran of the Spanish-American War, the Philippine Insurrection, and the Punitive Expedition, had come to France as Chief of Staff of the 84th Division. He remained the operations officer of First Army until the army was dissolved in April 1919. Returning to the U.S., he performed various duties before he was promoted to Brigadier General, commanding the Pacific sector of the Canal Zone, in 1935. He retired in 1938 and died in 1953.

6. Henry Tureman Allen was one of the more colorful cavalrymen of the period. His career ranged from frontier duty to explorations in Alaska. He had been our Military Attaché in Russia and Germany before he fought in Cuba and the Philippines. He had been civil governor of the island of Leyte in the Philippines, organized and commanded, as a Brigadier General, the Philippine Constabulary, before going in 1904 as an observer with the Japanese Army in Korea. He commanded a regiment with the Punitive Expedition. In World War I he took the 90th Division to France. After the war he commanded in turn the VIII Corps, the IX Corps and the VII Corps prior to taking over command of all Army Forces in Germany. He retired as a Major General in 1923, and was then active as an author,

Director of the Foreign Affairs Council, Vice President and Executive Officer of the U.S. Olympic Games Committee, and as Chairman of the American Committee for the Relief of German Children. He died in 1930.

7. Thomas Benton Catron II remained as Corps G-2 until the corps was inactivated in April 1919. After the war he was with the Tactical Department at West Point and in 1927 became the editor of the *Infantry Journal* for four years. He retired in 1936 but was recalled to active duty for World War II as the Chief of Staff 3rd Service Command. He retired as a Brigadier General in 1946 and died in 1973, aged eighty-four.

8. William Bassett Graham had entered the Spanish-American War as a Sergeant with the 8th Volunteer Ohio Infantry. Commissioned in 1901, he had fought in the Philippine Insurrection before he came to France with the 6th Division. He retired as a Colonel in 1939 but was recalled to active duty in 1942 and 1943.

9. The Adrian barracks referred to were the pre-fabs of their day, and used to house troops or supplies.

10. Joseph D. McKeaney had enlisted in 1896 and after 1900 was a Commissary or Quartermaster Sergeant. Commissioned in 1917 he was just the man to scrounge equipment for the Corps Headquarters. He remained an officer after the war and retired in 1927 a Lieutenant Colonel.

11. Captain Allen was General Allen's son, Henry T., Jr. A graduate of Harvard in 1913, he had been commissioned in 1917. He was cited for gallantry with the 90th Division and remained in the Army after the war, retiring as a Colonel in 1946.

Visit to England

1. James Guthrie Harbord had joined the Army as a private in the 4th Infantry in 1889. Commissioned in the 5th Cavalry in 1891, he had served honorably in Cuba with the 10th Cavalry, with the 11th in the Philippine Insurrection and as Assistant Chief of the Philippine Constabulary 1903–1909 and again 1910–1913. He accompanied General Pershing to France as Chief of Staff AEF. In May 1918 he took command of the Marine Brigade in the 2nd Division and then the Division itself. In July 1918 he was assigned to command the Services of Supply of the AEF. After the Armistice he was designated by President Wilson as Chief of the Military Mission to Armenia. He retired a Major General, Deputy Chief of Staff of the Army in 1922. After retirement he was Chairman of the Board of the Radio Corporation of America. In 1942, he was advanced on the retired list to the rank of Lieutenant General.

2. Captain Frank Pershing, a nephew of General Pershing, had joined him for the visit to England.

3. John George Quekemeyer, a Colonel of Cavalry, had been Chief of the American Mission to the British GHQ in France. He later became an Aide-de-Camp to General Pershing. After the war he was detailed to be Commandant of Cadets at West Point in 1926 but was taken ill and died before he could assume command.

4. F(rancis) Warren Pershing, born in 1909, was the General's only son and the only survivor of the 1915 fire at the Presidio of San Francisco which had killed his mother and three sisters. He had come to France on a short visit in 1919 and accompanied his father to England. He became a stockbroker in New York after graduation from Yale in 1931, and in 1934 formed the firm Pershing and Company, New York City. His second son, Richard Warren Pershing, was killed in Vietnam in 1968.

5. André Walker Brewster, born during the Civil War, was commissioned in 1885. A veteran of frontier duty and the Spanish-American War, he won the Medal of Honor at Tientsin, China, in 1900. In June 1917 he went to France as The Inspector General of GHQ AEF and remained in that position until September 1919. He retired in 1925 as a Major General commanding the First Corps Area in Boston, and died in 1942.

6. John Biddle had won a Silver Star citation in Puerto Rico in the Spanish-American War and had served in the Philippine Insurrection. When the war broke out he was Superintendent of West Point, but soon went to Europe. After various assignments he wound up as a Major General commanding all American forces in the United Kingdom. He retired in 1920 and died in 1930.

Visit to Italy

1. Baguio is a lovely town in the mountains northwest of Manila in the Philippines. It was used as a summer resort by the Americans stationed there before World War II. The Benguet trail was a riding trail nearby famed for its ruggedness.

Index